MATHEMATICS CLASSROOMS
THAT PROMOTE UNDERSTANDING

The Studies in Mathematical Thinking and Learning Series
Alan Schoenfeld, Advisory Editor

MATHEMATICS CLASSROOMS THAT PROMOTE UNDERSTANDING

Edited by

Elizabeth Fennema
Thomas A. Romberg
University of Wisconsin—Madison

LEA LAWRENCE ERLBAUM ASSOCIATES, PUBLISHERS
1999   Mahwah, New Jersey   London

Lawrence Erlbaum Associates, Inc., Publishers
10 Industrial Avenue
Mahwah, New Jersey 07430

Cover design by Kathryn Houghtaling Lacey

Library of Congress Cataloging-in-Publication Data

Mathematics classrooms that promote understanding / edited by
Elizabeth Fennema, Thomas A. Romberg.
     p.   cm. -- (Studies in mathematical thinking and learning
series)
     Includes bibliographical references and index.
     ISBN 0-8058-3027-8 (cloth : alk. paper). -- ISBN 0-8058-3028-6
(pbk. : alk. paper)
     1.   Mathematics--Study and teaching.   I. Fennema, Elizabeth.
II. Romberg, Thomas A.   III. Series: Studies in mathematical
thinking and learning.
QA11.M37537   1999
510.71--dc21   99-17343
                                                    CIP

Books published by Lawrence Erlbaum Associates are printed on acid-free paper,
and their bindings are chosen for strength and durability.

Printed in the United States of America
10   9   8   7   6   5   4   3

To Robert Davis, who throughout his long, prolific career in mathematics education (and most recently as a member of the Advisory Board for the National Center for Research in Mathematical Sciences Education), helped us all know and value mathematical understanding. We will miss his gentle, thoughtful way; his mathematical and philosophical insights; his advice; and his counsel.

Contents

Preface

The concern with teaching for understanding is as old as the 20th century. The intuitive rightness of learning with understanding—as well as the work of mathematics educators such as Colburn, Brownell, and Van Engen, who wrote about it long before the current reform movement—has led to widespread acceptance of the importance of developing students' understanding of mathematics. These and other more contemporary scholars have studied and written about what understanding means as well as how the curriculum should be structured so that students' understanding could be developed. Most instruction in mathematics, however, has not considered this knowledge, and most students have not developed an understanding of mathematics. All this scholarly work from the past has had little impact on instruction.

Why, then, if the work from the past has had little impact, should we return once again to the subject of mathematical understanding? For two major reasons. First, among much of the public including parents, teachers, professional organizations, employers, and various state and federal governments, there is not only support but strong demand for changing schools and instruction to meet the needs of the 21st century. Second, there is an ever-growing body of knowledge about learning and teaching mathematics that we believe can give bold new direction to classroom instruction so that all students learn with understanding.

The research that led to the ideas in this book is based on the work of many scholars in diverse disciplines. Mathematicians and mathematics educators have provided new insight into the nature of mathematics and have worked to identify those processes, concepts, and ideas within the discipline that are critical to successful survival in the 21st century. Psychologists, sociologists, and educational scholars have provided insights into student learning and the process of educational change. Other researchers have demonstrated the merit of cooperating with practicing teachers to gain knowledge about classroom processes.

This book is the direct result of the work of the National Center for Research in Mathematical Sciences Education (NCRMSE).[1] The principal investigators of NCRMSE worked for 5 years with the common goal of providing a research base that would enable the emergence of classrooms in which students could learn mathematics with understanding. Our work is based in that continually increasing body of literature but is also innovative. Most previous work was conducted mainly in isolation from ongoing classrooms and teachers. In contrast, we have worked with teachers and their students. Working as partners with teachers and students has enabled our own knowledge of mathematical understanding and effective instruction to mature and to remain relevant to the real work of mathematics teaching and learning. Engaging in dialogue with teachers about research-based knowledge and together struggling to decide how to implement this knowledge in the classrooms has allowed a number of innovative classrooms to emerge. From these classrooms and from our collaborative partnerships, our understanding of the teaching-learning process that enabled students to learn with understanding has grown.

Concurrently with the evolution of these innovative classrooms, the principal investigators (who are the first authors of the chapters and have worked in different mathematical domains in different grade levels) spent time discussing what we were doing and observing. On the surface, the classrooms of the various projects and the resultant development of the students' understanding seemed unique with little in common. The age and backgrounds of the students varied, as did the expertise of the teacher, the mathematical topics taught, and the classroom organization. However, as our work continued and our understanding of the individual classrooms grew, we realized that our classrooms had many common elements that appeared critical to the development of mathematical understanding. This book reports on and describes those common elements.

The book is divided into three sections. Part I, Setting the Stage, focuses on three major trends: What mathematics should be taught; how we should define and increase students' understanding of that mathematics; and how learning with understanding can be facilitated for *all* students. In the first chapter, Romberg and Kaput discuss current thinking about the content

[1]The preparation of this book and the research reported herein were supported by NCRMSE. NCRMSE was funded by the Office of Educational Research and Improvement (OERI), U.S. Department of Education (grant No. R117G1002) and administered by the Wisconsin Center for Education Research (WCER), School of Education, University of Wisconsin-Madison. However, the contents of this book and the research reported herein do not necessarily represent the position or policies of WCER, OERI, or the U.S. Department of Education.

of the mathematics curriculum, enlarging on the shift away from traditional instruction toward mathematics as a human activity. In chapter 2, Carpenter and Lehrer focus on defining and discussing understanding in terms of connections and on identifying students' mental activities that lead to understanding. They present components of tasks that should be considered in order to increase the opportunities for engagement in these mental activities. In chapter 3, Secada and Berman question the tacit assumption evident in much of the book that the development of understanding is related to individual differences rather than to group differences. They suggest that consideration of groups enriches the dialogue about teaching for understanding.

Part II, Classrooms That Promote Understanding, includes vignettes from diverse classrooms that illustrate classroom discourse, student work, and student engagement in the mathematics described in chapter 1 as well as the mental activities described in chapter 2. These chapters also illustrate how teachers deal with the equity concerns described in chapter 3. Carpenter and colleagues in chapter 4 describe primary classrooms studied by four research programs. In chapter 5, Lehrer et al. present vignettes and discussion of second-grade children learning geometry. In chapter 6, Sowder and Philipp give vignettes of middle-school classrooms from two very different settings. Chapter 7, by Lajoie, takes a closer look at statistics instruction facilitated by technology, and in chapter 8, Kaput suggests a total reorganization of algebra instruction.

Part III addresses Developing Classrooms That Promote Understanding. In chapter 9, Shafer and Romberg discuss the issues involved in assessing student understanding and point to the role played in instructional decision making by teachers' comprehension of each student's knowledge. In chapter 10, Fennema, Sowder, and Carpenter summarize the major ideas presented in the book, describe common points in instruction and curriculum, and address the need for professional development of teachers.

The knowledge we gained of the teaching-learning process reported in this book was a necessary prerequisite for implementing the revisions called for in the current reform movement. The classrooms described in this book show that innovative reform in teaching and learning mathematics is possible. We hope that the book will contribute to building a strong foundation for developing classrooms that enable *all* students to learn critical mathematics with understanding.

ACKNOWLEDGMENTS

The following members of the National Advisory Board of the National Center for Research in Mathematical Sciences Education provided leadership, advice, and encouragement as this book was conceived and written. We are thankful to them.

Robert Davis	Rutgers University
Audrey Friar Jackson	Parkway School District, Crève Coeur, Missouri
Harvey Keynes	University of Minnesota
Jeremy Kilpatrick	University of Georgia
Mary Lindquist	Columbus College
Edward Silver	University of Pittsburgh
Merlin Wittrock	University of California, Los Angeles

We deeply appreciate the help of Fae Dremock, who served as editor. Without her, the book would not have been completed.

SETTING THE STAGE

Chapter 1

Mathematics Worth Teaching, Mathematics Worth Understanding

Thomas A. Romberg
University of Wisconsin–Madison

James J. Kaput
University of Massachusetts–Dartmouth

When authors in this book describe classrooms that promote mathematical understanding, they each attempt to answer the question: What mathematics is it that students are expected to understand? The answers these authors give, however, may surprise some readers because although the titles of the mathematical domains described—number, geometry, quantities, statistics, and algebra—are familiar, the approach to discussing them is not. Rather than providing a list of specific concepts and skills to be mastered as has often been done in the past, each author focuses on a few key ideas in a domain, the interconnections between them, and examples of how students can grasp an understanding of the ideas as a consequence of exploring problem situations. The descriptions of mathematical content in this book are based on the epistemological shift in expectations about school mathematics that has emerged during the past decade; the chapters reflect attempts to redefine content in light of that shift.

The purpose of this chapter is to examine the scope of the mathematical content we expect students to understand after they have participated in the mathematical curricula described. This chapter has been organized under four headings: (a) traditional school mathematics, to clarify what the shift is away from; (b) mathematics as a human activity, to portray the direction the shift is toward; (c) mathematics worth teaching, to provide an overview to the answers provided in the following chapters to the initial question (What is it that students are expected to understand?); and, finally, (d) speculations about school mathematics in the future.

TRADITIONAL SCHOOL MATHEMATICS

Mathematics is perceived by most people as a fixed, static body of knowledge. Its subject matter includes the mechanistic manipulation of a variety of numbers and algebraic symbols and the proving of geometric deductions. This perception has determined the scope of the content to be covered and the pedagogy of the school mathematics curriculum. Specific objectives, which students are to master, have been stated; the teacher's role has been to demonstrate how a manipulation is to be carried out or to explain how a concept is defined; and students have been expected to memorize facts and to practice procedures until they have been mastered.

The arithmetic of whole numbers, fractions, decimals, and percents represents the majority of the first 7 of 8 years of the school mathematics curriculum for all students. For those students who successfully complete the hurdles along the arithmetic path, yearlong courses in algebra and geometry follow. Then, for many college-bound students, what follows is a second-year course of algebra and perhaps a year course of precalculus mathematics. Finally, for a few students, a course in calculus is often available. In each course, the emphasis is on mastering a collection of fixed concepts and skills in a certain order. This layer-cake structure that we have inherited is deeply embedded not only in our curricular structure but in our larger society's expectations regarding schools. This approach to mathematics education reinforces the tendency to design each course primarily to meet the prerequisites of the next course. This layer-cake filtering system is responsible for the unacceptably high attrition from mathematics that plagues our schools.

The traditional three-segment lesson, which has been observed in many classes, involves an initial segment where the previous day's work is corrected. Next, the teacher presents new material, often working one or two new problems followed by a few students working similar problems at the chalkboard. The final segment involves students working on an assignment for the following day.

This mechanistic approach to instruction of basic skills and concepts isolates mathematics from its uses and from other disciplines. The traditional process of symbol manipulation involves only the deployment of a set routine with no room for ingenuity or flair, no place for guesswork or surprise, no chance for discovery; in fact, no need for the human being. Furthermore, the pedagogy of traditional instruction includes a basal text (which is a repository of problem lists), a mass of paper-and-pencil worksheets, and a set of performance tests. There is very little that is interesting to read. Workbook mathematics thus gives students little reason to connect ideas in today's lesson with those of past lessons or with the real world. The tests currently used ask for answers that are judged right or wrong, but the strategies and reasoning used to derive answers are not evaluated. This portrayal of school mathematics—a tedious, uninteresting path to follow, with lots of hurdles to clear—bears little resemblance to what a mathematician or user of mathematics does. What is clear is that students do not do mathematics in traditional school lessons. Instead, they learn a collection of techniques that are useful for certain purposes. Because mastery of techniques is defined as knowledge, the acquisition of those techniques becomes an end in itself, and the student spends his or her time absorbing what other people have done.

Traditional school mathematics has failed to provide students with any sense of the importance of the discipline's historical or cultural importance, nor any sense of its usefulness. Is it any wonder that many students dislike mathematics and fail to learn it? The premise of this book is that traditional teaching and learning of mathematics has not enabled students to learn mathematics with understanding and that our first step must be to redefine mathematics.

MATHEMATICS AS A HUMAN ACTIVITY

School mathematics should be viewed as a human activity that reflects the work of mathematicians—finding out why given techniques work, inventing new techniques, justifying assertions, and so forth. It should also reflect how users of mathematics investigate a problem situation, decide on variables, decide on ways to quantify and relate the variables, carry out calculations, make predictions, and verify the utility of the predictions. Underlying this perspective of human activity is our use of Thurston's (1990) metaphor of a tree to describe the discipline of mathematics:

> Mathematics isn't a palm tree, with a single long straight trunk covered with scratchy formulas. It's a banyan tree, with many interconnected trunks and branches—a banyan tree that has grown to the size of a forest, inviting us to climb and explore. (p. 7)

For school mathematics, this vision emphasizes human actions, "climbing and exploring." Thurston's image of mathematics as the everspreading banyan tree reflects the notion that mathematics is a plural noun in that there are several intertwined trunks or branches (strands or domains). Furthermore, this image extends to the tree's ever-widening root system, drawing in the wide range of activities, interests, linguistic capability, kinesthetic sense, and informal knowledge that students bring to us. It is this broadly inclusive metaphor of mathematics, and the exploration of problems as a way of learning mathematics, that underlies all the subject matter examples of this book.

The discipline of mathematics involves a vast assemblage of ideas in several related content domains and is defined by the community of mathematicians, mathematics educators, and users of mathematics (Hersh, 1997). The content domains have been derived via a continually evolving, culturally shared science of patterns and languages, which is extended and applied through systematic forms of reasoning and argument. Mathematics is both an *object* of understanding and a *means* of understanding. These patterns and languages are an essential way of understanding the worlds we experience—physical, social, and even mathematical. Mathematics is ever alive—as alive as any branch of science today—and is neither static nor fixed in time, but changing. Because mathematics evolves, so also must the school curriculum—the educational organization and sequencing of that content.

The emerging redefinition of school mathematics is based on an epistemological shift in perspective regarding what is important to students to know and understand and is reflected in curriculum documents from several countries (e.g., Australia, Japan, the United Kingdom), as well as from the United States. The problem being faced is that there has been a conflict between school mathematics as it has been organized and taught and the emerging perspective about mathematics. To provide even a sketch of a content outline or sequence for K through 12 mathematics that reflects this epistemological shift is well beyond the scope of this chapter and this book. Instead, our aim is to provide a background to the choices about what mathematics to teach (for understanding) from the many choices that are or will become available. Note that in contrast to the traditional classroom, doing mathematics from this perspective cannot be viewed as a mechanical performance or an activity that individuals engage in solely by following predetermined rules.

Curriculum activities that reflect this perspective are those that involve students in problem solving and that encourage mathematization. Such tasks include situations that are subject to measure and quantification, that embody quantifiable change and variation, that involve specifiable uncertainty, that involve our place in space and the spatial features of the world we inhabit and construct, and that involve symbolic algorithms and more-abstract structures. In addition, they encourage the use of mathematical languages for expressing, communicating, reasoning, computing, abstracting, generalizing, and formalizing. These systems of signs and symbols extend the limited powers of the human mind in many directions, and they make possible a long-term (cross-generational) cultural growth of the subject matter. Finally, such situations embody systematic forms of reasoning and argument to help establish the certainty, generality, consistency, and reliability of the individual's mathematical assertions.

If mathematics is to serve students' needs to make sense of experience arising outside of mathematics instruction and mathematics itself, including making sense in the various sciences, it must be firmly rooted in and connected to that experience. And its systems of signs and symbols must be learned and experienced as genuine, functioning languages—for expressing, communicating, reasoning, computing, abstracting, generalizing, and formalizing—that the student experiences as serving his or her real needs. Similarly, the systematic logical forms of reasoning and argument must be learned through their satisfying personally and socially experienced needs for certainty and reliability—for establishing, for the student, what is true and what is not true.

In summary, there are several ways of viewing the discipline and choices to be made about which aspects of mathematics are to be included in the school curriculum, but the patterns, signs, symbols, and rules from certain branches of contemporary mathematics should be learned by all students and ideas from other branches known by some students. Furthermore, students should not only know the concepts and procedures for some parts of mathematics but also understand how mathematics is created and used.

This view of mathematics is, above all, integrative: It sees everything as part of a larger whole, with each part sharing reciprocal relationships with other parts. It stresses the acquisition of understanding by all (including the traditionally underprivileged), to the highest extent of their capability, rather than the selection and promotion of an elite. It is a philosophy that simultaneously stresses erudition and common sense, integration through application, and innovation through creativity. Most important, it stresses the creation of knowledge. Against this broad and ambitious view of mathematics, traditional school mathematics appears thin, lifeless, and isolated.

If students follow our approach to mathematical content, we believe that they will learn to formulate problems and develop and apply strategies to find solutions in a range of contexts. By exploring problems, they will learn to verify and interpret results and generalize solutions. In so doing, they will learn to apply mathematical modeling and become confident in their ability to address real-world problem situations. If they reason through their problem situations, students will develop the habit of making and evaluating conjectures and of constructing, following, and judging valid arguments. In the process, they will deduce and induce; apply spatial, proportional, algebraic, and graphical reasoning; construct proofs; and formulate counterexamples. In this sense, problem solving should be the basis of the mathematics curriculum.

MATHEMATICS WORTH TEACHING

Because students are more likely to learn mathematics in the context of problem situations, the work of the National Center for Research in Mathematic Sciences Education (NCRMSE) Principal Investigators focused on curricular ideas organized in a vertical strand structure of mathematics. There are two aspects to this work. The first involved specifying the scope of the mathematics in each strand that students are expected to know and understand, and the second involved outlining the characteristics and sequence of instructional activities that would engage students in learning mathematics with understanding. Our initial step in specifying the content was to identify the content domains (or strands) that society expects all students to learn with understanding. The domains we examined were number, quantities, algebra, geometry, and statistics. The domains were selected because of their generality and ability to subsume more specialized components of the discipline.

The second step involved identifying the big ideas in each domain that are worthy of extended time and effort. These big ideas are important for students to find, discover, use, or even invent for themselves. For example, the initial related concepts of addition and subtraction of whole numbers (a substrand of the whole-number strand) involve:

- symbolic statements that characterize the domain (e.g., $a + b = c$ and $a - b = c$, where a, b, and c are natural numbers);
- the implied task (or tasks) to be carried out (for addition and subtraction, this may involve describing the situations where two of the three numbers [a, b, and c] in the statements are known and the third is unknown);
- rules that can be followed to represent, transform, and carry out procedures to complete the task (e.g., "Find the unknown number using one or more of such procedures as counting; basic facts; symbolic transformations, such as $a + [\ ] = c \leftrightarrow c - a = [\ ]$; and place value [e.g., $345 = 3\ (100) + 4\ (10) + 5\ (1)$]);
- computational algorithms for larger numbers (e.g., adding 34 and 28 involves finding the sums of $30 + 20$, $4 + 8$; regrouping 12 into $10 + 2$, and finding the sum of $30 + 20 + 10 + 2$);
- the set of situations that have been used to make the concepts, the relationships between concepts, and the rules meaningful (e.g., join-separate, part-part-whole, compare, equalize).

Note that the set of situations that give meaning to the concepts and rules are considered equally as important as learning to follow the procedural rules. In fact, it is assumed that they are the means by which the procedural rules are understood. The structure of each strand also acknowledges that the big and powerful ideas and connections between them require years to develop and are understood in a variety of forms. Thus, the big ideas are stressed for all students throughout the school years rather than at the end for an elite minority.

From this example, it should be clear each strand comprises several closely related substrands. For example, the whole-number strand includes assigning numbers to sets or objects by counting or measuring, understanding place value, adding and subtracting, multiplying and dividing, and exploring the properties of such numbers (e.g., evenness and primeness). The big ideas in each substrand must be identified as was outlined earlier for addition and subtraction. Such detailed specifications describe the scope of the mathematical topics and ideas students should be expected to know. Understanding these ideas, however, involves relating a key idea to other ideas, explaining and justifying relationships, and so forth. Furthermore, the key ideas in different strands are closely interrelated. For example, measuring lengths, areas, volumes, angles, distances, and so on are important aspects of geometry.

Thus, to sequence instruction based on the tenets of mathematics as a human activity implies that tasks cannot be organized in a particular sequence to cover each detail, as is done in traditional curricula. Instead, instructional units or tasks that focus on investigation of problem situations need to be created. From such situations, the key ideas in each strand can be acquired or constructed and related to other ideas in other strands or substrands, and the uses of these ideas in other disciplines identified. The criteria for the selection of such tasks involve answering the following five questions:

Do the Tasks Lead Anywhere? To answer this question involves extending the map of the domain by beginning with the prior knowledge that students have and then developing instructional tasks that allow students to proceed gradually from their informal knowledge of the ideas in the domain to more formal notions. Note, however, that mapping domains is not an easy task because it involves forming a network of multiple possible paths and is not partitioned into discrete segments. It should also be noted that there is no one correct sequence of concepts and activities in any domain.

Again an important aspect of this step is that learning with understanding in any domain takes time. Proceeding from informal ideas to a more formal understanding of a domain may take several years, with periodic review and extension of prior notions. To accomplish this, instructional tasks need to be designed, organized with other activities, and tentatively sequenced, so that students have an opportunity to investigate increasingly complex problem situations within (and often across) domains. For example, for students to learn how to add and subtract with understanding, we might start with a variety of problem situations involving one-digit numbers where students could either model or count to find the answers. Later, students could solve problems in similar situations involving multidigit numbers where modeling and counting are inefficient, which would enable them to invent and learn to use computational algorithms. In addition, tasks should not focus only on the ideas in a single strand or substrand, but rather break through the artificial barriers between mathematical topics.

The selection of tasks is not an easy task. Although there is no doubt that many interesting tasks exist or can be created, "Do they lead anywhere?" is a serious question. Romberg (1992) stated that:

> Too often a problem is judged to be relevant through the eyes of adults, not children. Also, this perception is undoubtedly a Western, middle-class, static vision. Concrete situations, by themselves, do not guarantee that students will see relevance to their worlds, they may not be relevant for *all* students nor prepare them to deal with a changing, dynamic world. (p. 778)

For example, Hatano and Inagaki (1998) described an instructional episode with first-grade children in a Japanese classroom. The students familiar with join-separate problems were presented with the comparison problem, "There are 12 boys and 8 girls. How many more boys than girls are there?" Most children answered correctly that there were four more boys, but one child insisted that subtraction could not be used because it was impossible to subtract girls from boys. Furthermore, none of the students who had answered correctly could offer a persuasive argument against this assertion. It was only after the students physically modeled the situation that they realized that finding the difference involved subtracting the 8 boys who could hold hands with girls from the 12 boys (the total number of boys).

Do the Tasks Lead to Model Building? One way of making situations meaningful is to expect students to represent phenomena by means of a system of theoretically specified objects and relations (i.e., build a model such as boys and girls holding hands). Meaningful inquiry, involving cycles of model construction, model evaluation, and model revision, is central to the professional practice in mathematics but is largely missing from school instruction. Modeling practices are diverse, ranging from the construction of physical models to the development of abstract symbol systems.

In fact, any instructional unit should begin with an empirical situation, engaging to students, that presents a problem for which an answer is sought. However, the use of such words as *problem, answer,* and *engaging* can be misleading. Because real situations rarely appear well defined, the identification of a problem amenable to mathematical treatment is often difficult and involves many skills not related to mathematics. Nevertheless, the situation needs to be worthy of investigation (engaging). Finding a solution involves determining the essential or significant features of the situation, translating these features into a mathematical model, validating the model, and interpreting the results, usually in multiple cycles. Note that the task of problem solving is never complete when a mathematical answer is obtained. The mathematical results must be reinterpreted in terms of the initial problem situation. Furthermore, modeling emphasizes a need for forms of mathematics that are typically underrepresented in the standard curriculum, such as spatial visualization and geometry, discrete structures, and measures of uncertainty. In particular, incorporating the practice of modeling in instruction allows for the further exploration and identification of important big ideas in a domain.

Do the Tasks Lead to Inquiry and Justification? The identification process in mathematical modeling involves an attempt to sort out the essential or significant features of the situation. This simplification or idealization is a crucial stage because the general problem is often exceedingly complex, involving many processes. Some features will appear significant; many, irrelevant. Simplification is obtained when, by ignoring insignificant features, an originally complex problem is idealized to one that is mathematically tractable. Note that the history of the discipline is filled with instances of mathematicians inventing a way of representing an important feature of a problem (e.g., Descartes' invention of a way of describing the location of a fly on his bedroom ceiling [a point on a plane surface]). Although students cannot be expected to reinvent all mathematics, they should be expected to invent routines, formulas, or expressions as a consequence of their investigations. Furthermore, as they create such assertions they should be expected to justify them in some form. Some form of validation is usually carried out throughout the formulation of a model (i.e., the formulas or other mathematical relations set up in the model are continually checked with the initial situation). Also, the mathematics used in the model must be self-consistent and obey all the usual laws of mathematical logic.

With appropriate guidance from teachers, a student's informal models can evolve into models for increasingly abstract mathematical reasoning. The development of ways of symbolizing problem situations and the transition from informal to formal semiotics (called progressive formalization) are important aspects of these instructional assumptions.

As part of each activity, students should develop an appreciation for the evidential grounds for a claim and learn to evaluate those grounds by having opportunities to participate in genuine mathematical inquiry in school. By genuine inquiry, we mean the process of raising and evaluating questions grounded in experience, proposing and developing alternative explanations, marshaling evidence from various sources, representing and presenting that information to a larger community, and debating the persuasive power of that information with respect to various claims. In mathematics, for example, students are routinely taught computational algorithms but rarely are they asked to invent their own strategies for solving problems and to discuss why those strategies work. The information presented by authors in the next section demonstrates that students can invent sophisticated procedures for solving problems, operating with numbers, and reasoning about space and geometry. Beyond its contribution to students' identities as effective learners in a discipline, genuine inquiry also provides them with practice in and eventual understanding of the criteria for evidence and explanation patterns characteristic of mathematics.

Do the Tasks Involve Flexible Use of Technologies? As instructional tasks are created, we must add increased flexible use of new technologies to support the learning environments. Rather than just providing paper-and-pencil tasks for students to do independently at desks, we must provide tasks and materials that allow students to explore a domain, often solving problems as a group. The technology may also include video recordings, calculators, and computers as student tools. Evaluation involves judgments by students and teachers of the coherence of presentations, the reasoning given, and so on. Note that simulations and computer-based models have proven to be the most powerful resources for the advancement and application of mathematics and science since the origins of mathematical modeling in the Renaissance. As suggested later in this chapter, the move from static models (built in inert media) to dynamic models and the associated visualization and analytic tools (built in interactive media) is profoundly changing not only the nature of mathematics but the nature of inquiry in the discipline itself.

Are the Tasks Relevant to Students? To be relevant, an instructional activity should intrinsically motivate students to seek information so they can make sense of a problem situation, find satisfactory explanations for the validity of a given rule, and be able to justify the success of a procedure. Thus, the tasks should include expecting students to generate inferences, to check their plausibility, and to coordinate pieces of old and new information to build an enriched and coherent model or representation of the problem situation. The depth of knowledge of a student in any domain comes from structured experiences that promote personal ownership of the ideas in that domain. Unfortunately, what motivates a student may vary from individual to individual. What is clear is that the tasks should build upon what students know, produce cognitive incongruity, create some curiosity to resolve the incongruity, and so forth. But at the same time, a task cannot be too challenging (produce too much cognitive conflict), causing students to dismiss the activity as impossible or meaningless.

SPECULATIONS ABOUT SCHOOL MATHEMATICS
IN THE FUTURE

During the past quarter century, Thurston's everspreading banyan tree has been given very powerful fertilizer. On that tree of mathematics, new branches have emerged and grown rapidly; many old branches have been revitalized; and some branches have withered. As Valentine, a boisterous young mathematical biologist in Stoppard's (1993) play *Arcadia*, noted: "The future is disorder. A door like this has cracked open five or six times since we got up on our hind legs. It's the best possible time to be alive, when almost everything you thought you knew is wrong" (p. 48).

Although this is a bit of theatrical hyperbole, he was pointing to something profoundly important in the evolution of science and mathematics that will grow with increasing force in the next century: the iterative mathematics now possible in the computational medium and the nonlinear science that it makes possible. Later this chapter, we examine aspects of this evolution not to provide an introduction to this explosively growing way of approaching mathematics and science but to orient the reader first to the fact that mathematics continues to change even more rapidly than ever before and, second, to the directions in which this change is occurring.

But first we examine the depth of the change from past schooling practices to the practices concretely illustrated by the authors in the following chapters. Previously, students studied number for number's sake, or algebra for algebra's sake, and later applied what they had learned to solve problems and perhaps even to engage in serious mathematical modeling. We suggest the reverse: that number, algebra, and most other core school mathematics should arise in the service of making sense of individual experience. Furthermore, as the content chapters illustrate very powerfully, students are capable of a significant amount of mathematics at an early age. Because mathematics is a living, dynamic discipline, further changes in school mathematics are inevitable.

We now illustrate the direction of future work briefly examining nonlinear dynamic systems. Since the explosion in nonlinear mathematics and science in the 1970s, nonlinear dynamic systems have transformed the sciences—physical, social, biological, neuropsychological—and much of analytic mathematics. Classical mathematics and science are now seen to provide only a very narrow, idealized view of phenomena compared to the new nonlinear models. Consider, for example, classical models of the motion of a pendulum. They were accurate only if the pendulum was assumed to be a point-mass suspended by a weightless, frictionless string, that, most importantly, swung through only a very small angle about the vertical from a stationary support. Imagine that you are holding a string from which a pencil is hanging. You are swinging the pencil by moving you hand from side to side. This situation violates all of these conditions but can be modeled as a nonlinear dynamic system. Moreover, the mathematics that results includes much of the traditional mathematics as special, simplified cases.

Computer technology plays twin roles in this explosion of new mathematics and science by providing iterative numerical solutions to nonlinear difference and differential equations that are not solvable analytically (i.e., they do not have solutions as formulas) and graphical depictions of the states of the systems being modeled. The resulting models stretch our notions of randomness and determinism. For example, things can be both deterministically defined—indeed, quite simply defined—yet have chaotic and unpredictable longer-term behavior. We are also learning how complex systems of all sorts—the brain, economies, fluid flows, epidemics, biological ecological systems, chemical reactions, and so on—can be self-organizing.

The consequences of these developments are, first, that most dynamic situations in the world are now recognized to be nonlinear, not linear; and, second, that the simplest of nonlinear systems can embody an extraordinary amount of complexity. Closed-form algebraic solutions are rare, and most solutions are iterative, numeric, and graphic. This fact has profound implications for our ability to use mathematics to predict the behavior of nonlinear dynamic systems. For example, no matter how accurate our data or how powerful our computers, it is difficult to improve weather-forecasting accuracy beyond 4 days. To get a 5-day accuracy matching today's 4-day accuracy rate (about 80%) is a large and expensive undertaking that involves getting much more data about the atmosphere around the world and even more powerful computers than the fastest available supercomputers now used to model the atmosphere. Similar constraints apply wherever we turn because, as we are learning, most phenomena in the world are the result of nonlinearly interacting systems.

As already noted, the second factor associated with technology's role in this kind of mathematics is its graphical ability to display states of the system being modeled. These graphical images reveal astounding visual complexity and beauty that contain mixes of regularities and chaotic phenomena. They are usually in two dimensions and usually in color (which acts as a third dimension to display variation). The kinds of analyses that take place in such contexts are highly visual: Patterns and shapes play an important role whereas the ability to manipulate complicated symbol strings plays a reduced role. In a deep sense, the beauty of mathematics becomes available in a new way, and our ways of working with the mathematics are deeply changed (see Stewart, 1990). A whole new set of ideas becomes important in such contexts. For example, although once regarded as relevant only to elite students, topological ideas (e.g., issues of closeness and separability of points, boundaries of regions, open and closed sets, orbits, accumulation points, limits) and point-set topology (once treated as an abstract specialty) have come alive again. (They were invented a century ago to help make sense of dynamical systems studied more abstractly than they are today.)

These examples concern the mathematics of growth and change, which includes the ideas of traditional calculus as a subset. Long-held assumptions about who can learn what mathematics, and in what order, are being directly challenged by a variety of efforts currently underway. For example, the SimCalc Project (Kaput & Roschelle, in press) is building a mix of technologies and curricula intended to democratize access to the basic ideas underlying calculus beginning in the middle-school grades and even earlier; the Math in Context Core Plus Curriculum high school materials (Coxford et al., 1997) include iterative mathematics as a 4-year strand; the continuing work of Devaney and colleagues (see Devaney, 1998) shows that the ideas of chaos, fractals, and nonlinear mathematics are not only learnable by students as early as middle school but serve as enticing gateways to other mathematics such as linear algebra historically reserved for a small segment of much older students. These examples are but the tip of a newly emerging iceberg. Dynamic geometry illustrates another class of examples in another mathematical strand. The geometry involved is not Euclidean geometry but a new kind of mathematics. And the kinds of thinking and understanding that it requires are subtly different in important ways from that required in traditional geometry. Similarly, although computational techniques in statistics and probability have long been essential, many new forms of statistics have appeared in recent years, evolving, particularly, from resampling techniques. These new forms, sometimes referred to as bootstrapping techniques, depend directly on the computer medium and greatly extend the amount of information that can be extracted from even small sets of data. Indeed, the phenomenon of new mathematics growing in this fertile new computational medium is increasingly common. Old branches of mathematics are growing rapidly as well, and new ones are sprouting. No longer can we assume that the content of school mathematics worth understanding is fixed. The new mathematics, and newly available old mathematics, are becoming a vital part of the intellectual needs of all of our students. They are not merely the intellectual province of a few knowledge elite.

CONCLUSION

The study of mathematics by all students is important, but society's perception of the scope of content that students are expected to understand is changing, as is the field of mathematics itself. These changes make it imperative that any answer to the question "What mathematics is worth teaching?" be periodically considered. No longer can we assume that mathematics is a fixed body of concepts and skills to be mastered.

Nevertheless, regardless of the specfic content, the aims of mathematics teaching can be described, in practical terms, as teaching students to use mathematics to build and communicate ideas, to use it as a powerful analytic and problem-solving tool, and to be fascinated by the patterns it embodies and exposes. In this chapter, we have asked the reader to think of mathematics as an ever-expanding banyan tree that invites students to climb and explore. We have emphasized that instructional tasks should be relevant and should invite exploration that leads to further exploration, model building, inquiry, justification, and flexible use of technology. Equally important is the learning of attitudes and habits; the sense of mathematics as a creative process requiring imagination, initiative, and flexibility; and the habits of working systematically, whether independently or cooperatively. Finally, and most important, the learning of mathematics should be an experience from which students derive enjoyment and earn confidence.

REFERENCES

Coxford, A., et al. (1997). *Core plus mathematics project. Contemporary mathematics in context.* Chicago: Everyday Learning.

Devaney, R. L. (1998). Chaos in the classroom. In R. Lehrer & D. Chazan (Eds.), *Designing learning environments for developing understanding of geometry and space* (pp. 91–104). Mahwah, NJ: Lawrence Erlbaum Associates.

Hatano, G., & Inagaki, K. (1998). Cultural contexts of schooling revisited: A review of the learning gap from a cultural psychology perspective. In S. Paris & H. Wellman (Eds.), *Global prospects for education: Development culture and schooling* (pp. 79–104). Washington, DC: American Psychological Association.

Hersh, R. (1997). *What is mathematics, really?* New York: Oxford University Press.

Kaput, J., & Roschelle, J. (in press). SimCalc: Accelerating students' engagement with the mathematics of change and variation. In M. Jacobson & R. Kozma (Eds.), *Learning the sciences of the 21st century: Research, design, and implementation of advanced technology learning environments.* Mahwah, NJ: Lawrence Erlbaum Associates.

Mathematical Sciences Education Board. (1990). *Reshaping school mathematics.* Washington, DC: National Academy Press.

Romberg, T. A. (1992). Problematic features of the school mathematics curriculum. In P. Jackson (Ed.), *Handbook on research on curriculum* (pp. 749–788). New York: Macmillan.

Stewart, I. (1990). Change. In L. Steen (Ed.), *On the shoulders of giants: New approaches to numeracy* (pp. 183–217). Washington, DC: National Academy Press.

Stoppard, T. (1993). *Arcadia.* London: Faber & Faber.

Thurston, W. P. (1990, January). Letters from the editors. *Quantum,* 6–7.

FOR FURTHER READING

Cobb, P. (1994, September). *Theories of mathematical learning and constructivism: A personal view.* Paper presented at the Symposium on Trends and Perspectives in Mathematics Education, Institute for Mathematics, University of Klagenfurt, Austria.

Ekeland, I. (1988). *Mathematics and the unexpected.* Chicago: University of Chicago Press.

Freudenthal, H. (1983). *Didactical phenomenology of mathematical structures.* Dordrecht, The Netherlands: Reidel.

Gray, J. (1989). *Ideas of space: Euclidean, Non-Euclidean, and relativistic.* Oxford, England: Clarendon.

Romberg, T. A. (1983). A common curriculum for mathematics. In G. Fenstermacher & J. Goodlad (Eds.), *Individual differences and the common curriculum* (pp. 121–159). Chicago: National Society for the Study of Education.

Steen, L. (1981). *Mathematics tomorrow.* New York: Springer-Verlag.

Steen, L. (Ed.). (1990). *On the shoulders of giants: New approaches to numeracy.* Washington, DC: National Academy Press.

Stewart, I. (1989). *Does God play dice?* Oxford, England: Basil Blackwell.

Weller, M. (1991). *Marketing the curriculum: Core versus non-core subjects in one junior high school.* Unpublished doctoral dissertation, University of Wisconsin–Madison.

Chapter 2

Teaching and Learning Mathematics With Understanding[1]

Thomas P. Carpenter
Richard Lehrer
University of Wisconsin–Madison

In order to prepare mathematically literate citizens for the 21st century, classrooms need to be restructured so mathematics can be learned with understanding. Teaching for understanding is not a new goal of instruction: School reform efforts since the turn of the 20th century have focused on ways to create learning environments so that students learn with understanding. In earlier reform movements, notions of understanding were often derived from ways that mathematicians understood and taught mathematics. What is different now is the availability of an emerging research base about teaching and learning that can be used to decide what it means to learn with understanding and to teach for understanding. This research base describes how students themselves construct meaning for mathematical concepts and processes and how classrooms support that kind of learning.

WHY UNDERSTANDING?

Perhaps the most important feature of learning with understanding is that such learning is generative. When students acquire knowledge with understanding, they can apply that knowledge to learn new topics and solve new and unfamiliar problems. When students do not understand, they perceive each topic as an isolated skill. They cannot apply their skills to solve problems not explicitly covered by instruction, nor extend their learning to new topics. In this day of rapidly changing technologies, we cannot anticipate all the skills that students will need over their lifetimes or the problems they will encounter. We need to prepare students to learn new skills and knowledge and to adapt their knowledge to solve new problems. Unless students learn with understanding, whatever knowledge they acquire is likely to be of little use to them outside the school.

WHAT IS UNDERSTANDING?

Understanding is not an all-or-none phenomenon. Virtually all complex ideas or processes can be understood at a number of levels and in quite different ways. Therefore, it is more appropriate to think of understanding as emerging or developing rather than presuming that someone either does or does not understand a given topic, idea, or process. As a consequence, we characterize understanding in terms of mental activity that contributes to the development of understanding rather than as a static attribute of an individual's knowledge.

HOW UNDERSTANDING IS DEVELOPED

We propose five forms of mental activity from which mathematical understanding emerges: (a) constructing relationships, (b) extending and applying mathematical knowledge, (c) reflecting about experiences, (d) articulating what one knows, and (e) making mathematical knowledge one's own. Although these various forms of mental activity are highly interrelated, for the sake of clarity we discuss each one separately.

Constructing Relationships

Things take meaning from the ways they are related to other things. People construct meaning for a new idea or process by relating it to ideas or processes that they already understand. Children begin to construct mathematical relations long before coming to school, and these early forms of knowledge can be used as a base to further expand their understanding of mathematics. Formal mathematical concepts, operations, and symbols, which form the basis of the school mathematics curriculum, can be given meaning by relating them to these earlier intuitions and ideas. For example, children as young as kindergarten and first grade intuitively solve a variety of problems involving joining, separating, or comparing quantities by acting out the problems with collections of objects. Extensions of these early forms of problem-solving strategies can be used as a basis to develop the mathematical concepts of addition, subtraction, multiplication, and division (see chapter 4, Carpenter et al., this volume).

Unless instruction helps children build on their informal knowledge and relate the mathematics they learn in school to it, they are likely to develop two separate systems of mathematical knowledge: one they use in school and one they use outside of school. For example, children often are not bothered by the fact that they get one answer when they calculate with paper and pencil and another when they figure out the same problem using counters or some other material. They do not see that the answers they get with procedures they learn in school should be the same as the answers they get when they solve problems in ways that make sense to them.

Extending and Applying Mathematical Knowledge

It is not sufficient, however, to think of the development of understanding simply as the appending of new concepts and processes to existing knowledge. Over the long run, developing understanding involves more than simply connecting new knowledge to prior knowledge; it also involves the creation of rich, integrated knowledge structures. This structuring of knowledge is one of the features that makes learning with understanding generative. When knowledge is highly structured, new knowledge can be related to and incorporated into existing networks of knowledge rather than connected on an element-by-element basis. When students see a number of critical relationships among concepts and processes, they are more likely to recognize how their existing knowledge might be related to new situations. Structured knowledge is less susceptible to forgetting. When knowledge is highly structured, there are multiple paths to retrieving it, whereas isolated bits of information are more difficult to remember.

Although developing structure is a hallmark of learning with understanding, the nature of that structure is also critical because not all relationships are mathematically fruitful. Learning with understanding involves developing relationships that reflect important mathematical principles. The examples in the chapters that follow illustrate how addition and subtraction of multidigit numbers is related to basic concepts of place value, fractions are related to the concept of division, knowledge of graphing is extended to more general forms of data representation and interpretation, and informal ideas about space can be developed into the mathematical structures of geometry.

One of the defining characteristics of learning with understanding is that knowledge is learned in ways that clarify how it can be used. It often has been assumed, however, that basic concepts and skills need to be learned before applications are introduced. This is a faulty assumption: Children use their intuitively acquired knowledge to solve problems long before they have been taught basic skills.

We have come to understand that applications provide a context for developing skills, so, in teaching for understanding, skills are linked to their application from the beginning. For example, in the projects described in Carpenter et al. (chapter 4, this volume), children start out solving problems involving joining, separating, and comparing—before they have learned about addition and subtraction. The operations of addition and subtraction are presented as ways of representing these problem situations. In the classroom episode described in Lehrer, Jacobson, Kemeny, and Strom (chapter 5, this volume), children's natural language about shape and form eventually are transformed into mathematical propositions and definitions.

Reflecting About Experiences

Reflection involves the conscious examination of one's own actions and thoughts. Routine application of skills requires little reflection: One just follows a set of familiar procedures. Reflection, however, plays an important role in solving unfamiliar problems. Problem solving often involves consciously examining the relation between one's existing knowledge and the conditions of a problem situation. Students stand a better chance of acquiring this ability if reflection is a part of the knowledge-acquisition process.

To be reflective in their learning means that students consciously examine the knowledge they are acquiring and, in particular, the way it is related both to what they already know and to whatever other knowledge they are acquiring. But learning does not only occur with the addition of new concepts or skills: It also comes about through the reorganization of what one already knows. Reflecting about what one knows and how one knows can lead to this sort of reorganization.

Our notion of the emerging nature of understanding is seen in students' developing ability to reflect on their knowledge. Initially students have limited ability to reflect on their thinking. One characteristic of students' developing understanding is that they become increasingly able to reflect on their thinking.

Articulating What One Knows

The ability to communicate or articulate one's ideas is an important goal of education, and it also is a benchmark of understanding. Articulation involves the communication of one's knowledge, either verbally, in writing, or through some other means like pictures, diagrams, or models. Articulation requires reflection in that it involves lifting out the critical ideas of an activity so that the essence of the activity can be communicated. In the process, the activity becomes an object of thought. In other words, in order to articulate our ideas, we must reflect on them in order to identify and describe critical elements. Articulation requires reflection, and, in fact, articulation can be thought of as a public form of reflection.

As with reflection, students initially have difficulty articulating their ideas about an unfamiliar topic or task, but by struggling to articulate their ideas, especially with means like mathematical symbols or models, students develop the ability to reflect on and articulate their thinking.

Making Mathematical Knowledge One's Own

Understanding involves the construction of knowledge by individuals through their own activities so that they develop a personal investment in building knowledge. They cannot merely perceive their knowledge simply as something that someone else has told them or explained to them; they need to adopt a stance that knowledge is evolving and provisional. They will not view knowledge in this way, however, if they see it as someone else's knowledge, which they simply assimilate through listening, watching, and practicing.

This does not mean that students cannot learn by listening to teachers or other students, but they have to adapt what they hear to their own ends, not simply accept the reasoning because it is clearly articulated by an authority figure. Neither does this mean that understanding is entirely private. The development of students' personal involvement in learning with understanding is tied to classroom practices in which communication and negotiation of meanings are important facets.

In this more general sense, students author their own learning. They develop their own stances about different forms and practices of mathematics. For example, some students are fascinated by number, others by space, still others by questions of chance and uncertainty. Students who understand mathematics often define interests that guide their activity. Ideally, learning is guided by personal histories of aptitude and interest, not simply by curricular sequences.

An overarching goal of instruction is that students develop a predisposition to understand and that they strive to understand because understanding becomes important to them. This means that students themselves become reflective about the activities they engage in while learning or solving problems. They develop relationships that may give meaning to a new idea, and they critically examine their existing knowledge by looking for new and more productive relationships. They come to view learning as problem solving in which the goal is to extend their knowledge.

IS UNDERSTANDING THE SAME FOR EVERYONE?

In proposing the five forms of mental activity from which mathematical understanding emerges, we are not suggesting that all students learn in exactly the same way or that understanding always looks the same in all individuals. What we are proposing is that the development of understanding involves these forms of mental activity in some form. For an idea to be understood, it must be related to other ideas, but there are many ways that ideas might be related. We are not suggesting that relations must be formed in the same way or through the same activities, only that understanding depends on ideas being organized in some productive way that makes them accessible for solving problems. The ability to extend and apply knowledge is a hallmark of understanding, but this does not imply that all people extend and apply their knowledge in the same way. By the same token, reflection and articulation can take on a variety of forms, but we cannot conceive of understanding developing without some sort of reflection and articulation. Personal histories of developing understanding will vary. Such variation is often an important catalyst for conceptual change as students reconcile their own views with those of others.

CRITICAL DIMENSIONS OF CLASSROOMS THAT PROMOTE UNDERSTANDING

What does all this mean for instruction? Essentially, for learning with understanding to occur on a widespread basis, classrooms need to provide students with opportunities to (a) develop appropriate relationships, (b) extend and apply their mathematical knowledge, (c) reflect about their own mathematical experiences, (d) articulate what they know, and (e) make mathematical knowledge their own. In order to organize a classroom that enables students to engage in these activities (discussed previously), there are at least three dimensions of instruction that need to be considered: (a) tasks or activities that students engage in and the problems that they solve; (b) tools that represent mathematical ideas and problem situations; and (c) normative practices, which are the standards regulating mathematical activity, agreed on by the students and teacher.

Tasks

Mathematics lessons frequently are planned and described in terms of the tasks students engage in. Tasks can range from simple drill-and-practice exercises to complex problem-solving tasks set in rich contexts. Almost any task can promote understanding. It is not the tasks themselves that determine whether students learn with understanding: The most challenging tasks can be taught so that students simply follow routines, and the most basic computational skills can be taught to foster understanding of fundamental mathematical concepts. For understanding to develop on a widespread basis, tasks must be engaged in for the purpose of fostering understanding, not simply for the purpose of completing the task. (For an example of how learning to use multidigit numbers within the context of computational activities becomes a task in which students' understanding of place value grows, see Carpenter et al., chapter 4, this volume.)

Tools

Tools are used to represent mathematical ideas and problem situations. They include such things as paper and pencil, manipulative materials, calculators and computers, and symbols. Problems are solved by manipulating these tools in ways that follow certain rules or principles (see Lajoie, chapter 7, this volume, on tools for data representation and visualization). Computational algorithms, for example, involve the manipulation of symbols to perform various arithmetic calculations. These same operations can be performed by representing the numbers with counters or base-10 blocks and combining, grouping, or partitioning the counters or blocks in appropriate ways. Connections with representational forms that have intuitive meaning for students can greatly help students give meaning to symbolic procedures. In Carpenter et al. and Sowder and Philipp (chapters 4 and 6, this volume), examples involving adding and subtracting whole numbers and dividing fractions illustrate how such connections can be developed.

Standard mathematical representations and procedures involve symbols and operations on those symbols that have been adopted over centuries and have been constructed for the purposes of efficiency and accuracy. The connections between symbols and symbolic procedures and the underlying mathematical concepts that they represent are not always apparent. As a consequence, practicing formal procedures involving abstract symbols does little to help students connect the symbols or procedures to anything that would give them meaning. One of the ways to resolve this dilemma is for students to link the critical steps in procedures with abstract symbols to representations that give them meaning (see Kaput, chapter 8, this volume).

Representations may be introduced by the teacher or constructed by students. Lehrer et al. (chapter 5, this volume) describe classroom episodes in which students invented representations for quantities, forms, measures, and large-scale space. Each form of representation provided opportunities for developing new mathematical knowledge. As noted in Romberg and Kaput (chapter 1, this volume), the syntactically guided manipulation of formal representations is an important goal of instruction and, if we want students to understand the representations they use, we should encourage them to reflect explicitly on the characteristics of those representations useful for understanding and communicating about mathematical ideas and for solving problems.

Normative Practices (Norms)

The norms in a particular class determine how students and the teacher are expected to act or respond to a particular situation. Normative practices form the basis for the way tasks and tools are used for learning, and they govern the nature of the arguments that students and teachers use to justify mathematical conjectures and conclusions. These norms can be manifest through overt expectations or through more subtle messages that permeate the classroom environments.

Although the selection of appropriate tasks and tools can facilitate the development of understanding, the normative practices of a class determine whether they will be used for that purpose. In classrooms that promote understanding, the norms indicate that tasks are viewed as problems to be solved, not exercises to be completed using specific procedures. Learning is viewed as problem solving rather than drill and practice. Students apply existing knowledge to generate new knowledge rather than assimilate facts and procedures. Tools are not used in a specified way to get answers: They are perceived as a means to solve problems with understanding and as a way to communicate problem-solving strategies. The classrooms are discourse communities in which all students discuss alternative strategies or different ways of viewing important mathematical ideas such as what is a triangle (see Lehrer et al. and Sowder and Philipp, chapters 5 and 6, this volume). Students expect that the teacher and their peers will want explanations as to why their conjectures and conclusions make sense and why a procedure they have used is valid for the given problem. In this way, mathematics becomes a language for thought rather than merely a collection of ways to get answers.

Structuring and Applying Knowledge

For students to learn with understanding, they must have opportunities to relate what they are learning to their existing knowledge in ways that support the extension and application of that knowledge. In classrooms where students learn with understanding, there are a number of ways that instruction can provide them the opportunities to structure their knowledge. For example, students may be asked specifically to identify relevant relationships. Students may be expected to specify explicit links between symbolic procedures and manipulations of physical materials, as in the Conceptually Based Instruction classes described in Carpenter et al. (chapter 4, this volume). The relationships may also be drawn in less direct ways, as when students compare and contrast alternative strategies that they have generated to solve a problem, as in the Cognitively Guided Instruction classes described in the same chapter.

It is critical that providing opportunities for students to develop structured knowledge is a major and continuing focus of instruction. Students cannot be expected to develop critical knowledge structures by practicing procedures. Watching a demonstration, listening to an explanation of how things are related, or even engaging in a few teacher-directed hands-on tasks is not enough. Students need time to develop knowledge structures, and instruction should offer students extended opportunities to develop relationships through the tasks that they engage in.

The selection and sequencing of tasks and tools is critical. They should not be selected exclusively on mathematical structure. We must take into account children's thinking, the knowledge they bring to a situation, and the way their thinking typically develops. A tacit assumption underlying much of the traditional mathematics curriculum has been that problem solving involves the application of skills, and, consequently, skills must be learned before students can profitably engage in problem solving. The examples in the chapters that follow document that this is not the case. In these examples, problem solving and the learning of basic concepts and skills are integrated; in fact, problems and applications provide the context for learning fundamental mathematical concepts and skills.

As noted earlier, there is an extensive body of research documenting that children acquire a great deal of intuitive or informal knowledge of mathematics and begin developing problem-solving abilities outside of school. The formal concepts and skills of the mathematics curriculum need to be related to these informal concepts and problem-solving skills, or students will not see how the mathematics they learn in school applies to solving problems in the world. Furthermore, this informal knowledge can provide a solid foundation for giving meaning to the abstract mathematical symbols, concepts, and skills that students learn in school.

Tasks and tools need to be selected such that mathematics instruction builds on children's informal mathematical knowledge and that problems and applications, and the related mathematical concepts and skills, are connected from the beginning.

Reflection and Articulation

One of the primary ways that learning with understanding occurs is through reflection. Initially, students generally use concrete tools as implements to solve a given task. As students reflect on the use of the tools, the manipulations of the physical materials become abstracted. Eventually students no longer have to actually manipulate the physical tools themselves; they can think directly about more-abstract symbolic representations of the tools (see Carpenter et al. and Lehrer et al., chapters 4 and 5, this volume). The process is recursive. The more-abstract representations become themselves objects of reflection, leading to an awareness of the underlying mathematical concepts that the tools, and the symbolic abstractions of the tools, embody. As the concepts and principles embodied in a given tool become objects of reflection, higher-level mathematical principles emerge, and so on. For example, students start out solving addition and subtraction problems by modeling the joining and separating action using counters. By reflecting on their procedures and their emerging knowledge of groupings of 10, they come to use more efficient procedures that involve the use of some sort of 10-structured material like base-10 blocks. As students describe and reflect about the solutions using materials grouped by 10, they become increasingly less dependent on the base-10 materials themselves; they start to use abstract representations of the base-10 materials (see Carpenter et al., chapter 4, this volume). As students compare different abstract strategies and reflect on these differences, they begin to see that certain procedures have advantages over others, and they begin to see explicitly how properties like commutativity and associativity are involved in their procedures.

Encouraging Reflection. The question is: How do we encourage this type of reflection? Providing explicit guidelines for encouraging reflection is difficult, but a critical factor is that teachers recognize and value reflection. When that is the case, teachers establish classroom norms that support reflection. A specific norm that plays a critical role in supporting reflection in the descriptions of classrooms that follow is the expectation that students articulate their thinking. Asking students why their solutions work, why a given solution is like another solution, how they decided to solve the problem as they did, and the like, not only helps to develop students' ability to articulate their thinking, it encourages them to reflect.

At this point, we should distinguish between two types of reflection, both of which are important: (a) reflection by students about what they are doing and why, as tasks are being carried out; and (b) reflection about tasks and their solutions after the tasks have been completed. Discussion of alternative strategies that students have used to solve a given problem involves reflection about a task after it has been completed. The probing questions that a teacher might ask at this point address this type of reflection.

Discussing alternative strategies, however, addresses more than the issue of reflection on completed tasks. When students know that they are expected to explain their responses, they are more likely to reflect on a task as they are carrying it out. Reflection on the task while carrying it out can also be encouraged directly by asking students to articulate what they are doing during the process of solving a problem. One possibility is for teachers to talk to students as they are solving a problem, asking the students to explain assumptions and why they are pursuing the strategy that they have chosen. Questions like "What are you doing?; Why are you doing that?" and "How will that help you to solve the problem?" encourage reflection. Being asked such questions on a regular basis helps students internalize them, so that they will ask themselves the same questions as they think about a given task.

Another way to encourage reflection on tasks in progress is to have students work in small cooperative groups. When students are actually solving a problem together, they must articulate their assumptions, conjectures, and plans to one another. For this kind of reflection and articulation to occur, however, classroom norms must establish that these kinds of interactions are what cooperative group work is all about.

A Basis for Articulation. For articulation to be meaningful to all the participants in a class, there must be a common basis for communication. The selection of appropriate tools can fill this role, but teachers must ensure that everyone has a consistent interpretation of the tools and their use. Manipulative materials can provide common referents for discussion, but students do not always impart the same meanings to manipulations of physical materials that knowledgeable adults do. It is important that discussions include opportunities for students to articulate how they are thinking about and using tools.

Notations, (e.g., those developed for representing quantity, two-dimensional graphs, etc.) can provide a common basis for discussion, and they can help students to clarify their thinking. Notations thus play a dual role, first, as a window (for teachers and others) into the evolution of student thinking and, second, as a tool for thought. Notations are records that communicate about thinking. Appropriate notational systems allow students to articulate their thinking in very precise ways, and the precision demanded by the notational system can make students sharpen their thinking so that it can be articulated.

Classroom Norms

One norm that underlies teaching for understanding is that students apply existing knowledge in the generation of new knowledge. Learning is not perceived by either the teacher or students as assimilation and practice. Learning is viewed as problem solving, and students are expected to actively work to relate new concepts and procedures to their existing knowledge.

A specific class norm that supports this conception of learning is that students regularly discuss alternative strategies (which they have generated to solve a given problem) with the teacher, with other students, and within the context of whole-class discussion. It is not enough to have an answer to a problem; students are expected to be able to articulate the strategy they used to solve the problem and explain why it works. This means discussing how the solution is related to the parameters of the problem and how the procedures used in the solution are related to underlying mathematical concepts or some external representation that has established meaning.

In discussing alternative strategies, students not only explain their own solutions and their own thinking, but they also discuss how strategies used by different students are alike and different. In other words, they consider the connections between alternative solutions. This is one of the important ways in which relationships are made explicit. As students report and discuss solutions representing different levels of abstraction and understanding, they have the opportunity to link more-abstract strategies with more-basic strategies. For example, when some students solve a problem using manipulative materials and other students solve the problem with symbolic representations, the discussion of the relationship between the two strategies draws attention to connections that give the abstract symbolic procedures meaning (see the class interaction at the beginning of Carpenter et al., chapter 4, this volume).

Making Knowledge One's Own

As with reflection and articulation, classroom norms play a central role in helping students develop a personal sense of ownership of their knowledge. Again, specifying guidelines is difficult, but it is critical that teachers place a high value on the individual student's involvement and autonomy. All students should have opportunity to discuss their ideas, and each student's ideas should be taken seriously by everyone else in the class. The overriding goal of the classroom should be the development of understanding.

Reflection is inherently personal, and encouraging reflection is critical in helping students develop a sense of ownership of their knowledge. Students need to be given some control over the tasks they engage in and the tools they use to solve them so that they believe they have control over their own learning.

TEACHERS AND UNDERSTANDING

Inherent in much of the previous discussion is the assumption that understanding is a goal not only for students but also for teachers. Understanding plays a critical role in the solution of any complex problem, and teaching certainly involves solving complex problems. Our conception of teacher understanding is based on the same principles as our conception of student understanding.

We focus on two components of teachers' understanding and the relations between them: (a) understanding of mathematics and (b) understanding students' thinking. In order to provide instruction of the kind envisioned in this book, teachers need to understand the mathematics they are teaching, and they need to understand their own students' thinking. The mathematics to be taught and the tasks and tools to be used might be specified by an instructional program, but without requisite understanding of mathematics and students, teachers will be relegated to the routine presentation of (someone else's) ideas neither written nor adapted explicitly for their own students. In short, their teaching will be dominated by curriculum scripts, and they will not be able to establish the classroom norms necessary for learning with understanding to occur. They will not be able to engage students in productive discussion of alternative strategies because they will not understand the students' responses; neither will they be able readily to recognize student understanding when it occurs.

Understanding mathematics for instruction involves more than understanding mathematics taught in university mathematics content courses. It entails understanding how mathematics is reflected in the goals of instruction and in different instructional practices. Knowledge of mathematics must also be linked to knowledge of students' thinking, so that teachers have conceptions of typical trajectories of student learning and can use this knowledge to recognize landmarks of understanding in individuals.

Teachers need to reflect on their practices and on ways to structure their classroom environment so that it supports students' learning with understanding. They need to recognize that their own knowledge of mathematics and of students' thinking, as well as any student's understanding, is not static.

Teachers must also take responsibility for their own continuing learning about mathematics and students. Class norms and instructional practices should be designed to further not only students' learning with understanding, but also teachers' knowledge of mathematics and of students' thinking. Tasks and tools should be selected to provide a window on students' thinking, not just so that the teacher can provide more appropriate instruction for specific students, but also so the teacher can construct better models for understanding students' thinking in general.

CONCLUSION

For students and teachers, the development of understanding is an ongoing and continuous process and one that should pervade everything that happens in mathematics classrooms. For many years there has been a debate on whether an individual should learn skills with understanding from the outset or whether he or she should acquire a certain level of skill mastery first and then develop an understanding of why skills work the way they do. A mounting body of evidence supports the importance of learning with understanding from the beginning. When students learn skills without understanding, the rote application of the skills often interferes with students' subsequent attempts to develop understanding. When students learn skills in relation to developing an understanding, however, not only does understanding develop, but mastery of skills is also facilitated.

If we have learned one thing through our studies, it is that the development of understanding takes time and requires effort by both teachers and students. Learning with understanding will occur on a widespread basis only when it becomes the ongoing focus of instruction, when students are given time to develop relationships and learn to use their knowledge, when students reflect about their own thinking and articulate their own ideas, and when students make mathematical knowledge their own.

We do not have precise prescriptions for how classrooms should be organized to accomplish these goals. In this chapter we have provided some issues and components to consider when thinking about instruction, but ultimately responsibility for learning with understanding rests with the teachers and students themselves. Teachers must come to understand what it means for their students to learn with understanding and must appreciate and value learning with understanding. Like their teachers, students must come to value understanding and make understanding the goal of their learning. That is the ultimate goal of instruction.

In the chapters that follow, we provide examples of instruction that provides opportunity for the development of understanding as we have characterized it. There are a number of similarities among the examples, but we are not suggesting that understanding will occur only in classes similar to the ones described. We do, however, argue that for learning with understanding to occur, instruction needs to provide students the opportunity to develop productive relationships, extend and apply their knowledge, reflect about their experiences, articulate what they know, and make knowledge their own.

NOTES

1. Authors contributed equally to the writing of this chapter.

FOR FURTHER READING

Anderson, J. (1990). *Cognitive psychology and its implications.* Cambridge, MA: Harvard University Press.

Hiebert, J., Carpenter, T. P., Fennema, E., Fuson, K., Human, P., Murray, H., Olivier, A., Wearne, D. (1997). *Making sense: Teaching and learning mathematics with understanding.* Portsmouth, NH: Heinemann.

Kaput, J. (1992). Technology and mathematics education. In D. Grouws (Ed.), *Handbook of research on mathematics teaching and learning* (pp. 515–556). New York: Macmillan.

Lehrer, R., & Chazan, D. (1998). *Designing learning environments for developing understanding of geometry and space.* Mahwah, NJ: Lawrence Erlbaum Associates.

Schoenfeld, A. (1995). *Mathematical problem solving.* New York: Academic Press.

Schon, D. (1987). *Educating the reflective practitioner.* San Francisco: Jossey-Bass.

Wertsch, L. (1991). *Voices of the mind.* Cambridge, MA: Harvard University Press.

Yakel, E., & Cobb, P. (1996) Sociomathematical norms, argumentation, and autonomy in mathematics. *Journal of Research in Mathematics Education, 27,* 458–477.

Chapter 3

Equity as a Value-Added Dimension in Teaching for Understanding in School Mathematics[1]

Walter G. Secada
Patricia Williams Berman
University of Wisconsin–Madison

Our purpose in this chapter is to suggest how educators who are interested in teaching for student understanding of mathematics can enrich their efforts by incorporating concerns for equity in their curriculum, program development, classroom processes, assessment, or research efforts. By equity we mean the consideration of teaching for understanding based on the question: Does an emphasis on developing student understanding result in greater or less fairness? What is inequitable is unfair; what is equitable promotes fairness.

INCORPORATING EQUITY IN TEACHING
FOR UNDERSTANDING

Some might argue that concerns about equity are beyond the scope of teaching mathematics for understanding and that it seems almost absurd to ask whether teaching mathematics for understanding promotes fairness. Proponents of this view might ask:

How could working with individual students, as illustrated in other chapters of this book, be unfair? If we develop *each* student's mathematical abilities and understandings, will not that student be better off than if we do not do so? Is it not unfair to withhold an innovation, such as teaching for understanding, because we are concerned about its fairness or unfairness?

Our response is very simple. If educators fail to *purposefully* try to incorporate an equity perspective within the teaching of mathematics for understanding, then there is a very real danger that this new and evolving form of teaching mathematics will, in fact, exacerbate group-based differences and treat students unfairly. Students whose social and demographic backgrounds may position them to profit more from teaching for understanding may end up getting the lion's share of the benefits at the expense of students who are not in a similar position. For instance, evolving models of teaching for understanding may be more effective with children from upper-social-class families than with children from lower-social-class families, or these models may depend on full proficiency in English as a prerequisite for student success. Both these possibilities would render equitable teaching for understanding more difficult in mathematics classes with diverse student populations. When educators incorporate equity concerns from the start, they are more aware of the potential traps that capture unintended outcomes and can thus make provisions to avoid those traps.

There are at least three locations where an equity perspective should be considered: in how teaching for understanding is framed, how it is evaluated, and how it is implemented on a large scale. In this chapter, we take a closer look at each of those three locations from the standpoint of how equity concerns might give salience to problems and issues that would otherwise be missed. We show how an equity perspective can do two things at each location: (a) it can alert educators to how this innovation *could* exacerbate sociodemographic-group-based achievement differences and (b) it could suggest ways by which purposeful actions might help alleviate such differences.

FRAMING TEACHING FOR UNDERSTANDING FROM AN EQUITY PERSPECTIVE

Teaching for understanding has been characterized, in this book, by a group of inter-related ideas: (a) a definition of understanding as the connections among mathematical ideas and those between mathematical ideas and the (real world and other) settings in which they apply, (b) the mental activities through which understanding develops, and (c) the tasks, tools, and norms (involving students and teachers) that support those mental activities by students. Although this group of ideas is thought to apply to all students, how the ideas are applied requires sensitivity to issues of equity. For instance, understanding may be composed of connections among ideas, but the contexts for establishing understanding and for connecting ideas to one another should not all be familiar only to middle-class students, White students, and males. Contexts need variety to match the diversity of students in today's schools.

An equity perspective encourages educators to scrutinize these ideas for any assumptions that might lead to bias in their application. One very potent example of how an educational practice can be framed by ideas that are biased (and hence that lead to inequities) can be seen in the educational doctrine of separate but equal that undergirds the practice of *de jure* segregation. That is, school districts argued that they could keep two separate educational systems—one for White students and the other for African-American students. This doctrine and the assumptions about people on which it rests are inherently biased against a specific sociodemographic group and, hence, are inequitable.

On a more positive note, an equity perspective can encourage educators to look for ways of incorporating what is known about students of diverse social backgrounds in the formulation of these ideas. The following discussion is intended to show how such an equity perspective might be applied to teaching for understanding's underlying ideas.

The Mental Activity of Extending Mathematics Into a Real-World Domain

One mental activity by which understanding can be developed involves the extension of mathematics into different domains. Such efforts are thought to create relationships between mathematics and those domains and also, in certain circumstances, to increase student interest in mathematics. However, people hold deep convictions about the domains into which one should extend different kinds of mathematical activity. Consider a very common primary-grade activity that could be used to develop student understanding: the school store. In this setting, children engage in mercantile exchanges through which they are expected to develop understanding about money, addition, subtraction, multistep problems, and some initial ideas about multiplication. The school store can help students learn to organize information, for instance, by keeping inventory lists and computing profit-and-loss margins against expenses.

Yet consider an alternative setting that is seldom found in primary grades: a social service agency with a sliding fee scale based on ability to pay for services such as tutoring, baby-sitting, or child care. In this setting, students could also engage in mercantile exchanges while learning to add and subtract. Students would encounter multistep problems, organize information, and depending on the service, think about profit-and-loss margins. In such a setting, however, students also encounter issues of social class, an often verboten topic in the U.S. schooling system.

Although the school store has been a traditionally accepted context for the extension of mathematics and can be found in use in many schools throughout the United States, the context of the social service agency seems an exotic, if not a dangerously political, extension of mathematics. Viewed from the standpoint of the development of mathematical understanding, there is no *a priori* reason to choose one over the other. Both contexts provide realistic settings for children to develop their mathematical knowledge and skills. Some children would be more familiar with one context over the other, but both contexts would help children to enrich their beliefs about the contexts in which mathematics can be found.

Educators without an equity perspective shy away from the social service agency. Given an equity perspective, however, educators embrace such considerations as (a) With which context would lower-social-class children have more familiarity than their upper-class peers? (b) Which context could begin to equalize the playing field for learning mathematics? (c) Whose interests are served by presenting the school store as a natural setting in which to do mathematics while removing a social service agency from consideration for such a purpose?

Classroom Norms

Classrooms in which students learn mathematics with understanding are characterized by a variety of observable activities, described elsewhere in this book. Students in these classrooms learn to articulate their thinking, they share and compare a variety of approaches to solving the same problem, they often argue among themselves concerning the basis for their conjectures, and they generally learn to create their own understanding.

Articulation of Thinking. One classroom norm with potential consequences for equity is the expectation that students articulate their thinking verbally and in writing. In comparison to more conventional classroom practices, which tend to focus on a student's final answer rather than the thinking that produced that answer, learning activities in classrooms that promote student understanding allow much less mental privacy and require communication skills.

The potential social consequences of this are multiple. When students articulate their thinking, differences in their thinking are made visible and open to scrutiny. Such a practice runs the risk of underscoring and amplifying existing differences among students, both socially and academically, because solutions and arguments are subjected to judgment by peers. The norm of public sharing may place children who are learning English as a second language and–or children who have been socialized into deferring to others at a distinct disadvantage. At the same time, this practice carries the potential of establishing classroom norms in which differences in thought are the rule rather than the exception and in which those differences are to be respected. Teachers who work from an equity perspective are alert to the promise of teaching for understanding and to potential traps when the public sharing of the individual student's thoughts is the classroom norm and, because of that awareness, they try to develop solutions to those traps.

Variety of Solution Strategies. A second classroom norm with a potential impact on equity is the acceptance of a variety of solution strategies for the same problem. In encouraging multiple solution paths, teachers again confront the risk of underscoring individual and–or group-based differences. At the same time, this practice, when managed with sensitivity, encourages widespread participation; expresses appreciation for diversity in thought; establishes value for these differences among students; allows the approval of the solution to come from the mathematics itself rather than from the teacher; and features the substance, content, and logic of a procedure or a task rather than its performer. When the classroom culture encourages the acceptance and scrutiny of a variety of strategies, mathematical authority resides not in personal characteristics but in the quality of the individual's work. This resonates with Dr. Martin Luther King's dictum that individuals be judged not by the color of their skin (or their gender, or some other personal characteristic), but by the content of their character (or, in this case, by the content of their mathematical reasoning).

Individual Construction of Knowledge. In the classrooms that are advocated in this book, students are expected to assume responsibility for learning, and mathematical authority is shared among students and between students and the teacher. On the one hand, this practice is a challenge for equity because students possess diverse capabilities and dispositions, many of which may be group-based. On the other hand, not only permitting but expecting each student to share in this responsibility for learning can provide opportunities for equity.

However, when the norms for classroom behavior, as illustrated in this book, are substantially different from the expectations for behavior at home, care must be taken. Although the nature of a student's thought processes, the content of her or his reasoning, and the social and intellectual quality of the mathematical arguments are highly valued in classrooms that promote student understanding, parents who hold traditional values—many of whom are minorities and from lower-social-class backgrounds—are likely to be shocked and to look askance when such practices are brought home.

In informal conversations with educators who are trying to develop classrooms that promote student understanding of mathematics and science in urban settings, the senior author has heard enough stories of children being severely and physically punished for behaving "disrespectfully" to adults in their communities (i.e., for questioning adults' assertions and the

authority underlying children's obedience and acquiescence to adult direc-
tives), that we believe we may be placing some—not all—children in an
untenable position of having to negotiate between two worlds of competing
adult values. The risks are dual. First, the child's emotional and physical
well-being may be jeopardized. Second, educators may inadvertently create
a new set of stereotypes about the appropriateness of teaching for understanding in classrooms that include certain groups of children. As educators
with an equity perspective become aware of these dangers, they can seek to
create alternatives.

A Final Note. We must bear in mind that we can only describe classrooms by the overt activities that take place within them and by observing
the manner in which each individual student participates in these learning
activities. Because understanding is necessarily related to cognitive processes rather than concrete, outward demonstrations of proficiency, educators can only infer an individual student's understanding. We cannot assume
that classroom practices that utilize these activities guarantee automatic
and equitable understanding across groups. As a result, teachers need to
exercise caution in making inferences regarding students' understanding,
particularly where socialization patterns or cultural norms contradict classroom norms of behavior.

EQUITY ISSUES IN EVALUATING INNOVATIVE
PROGRAMS OF TEACHING FOR UNDERSTANDING

Any innovation in mathematics education, no matter how appealing on its
face, should be scrutinized as to whether it increases, leaves intact, or
decreases social-group differences in mathematics achievement. At the very
least, innovations should do no harm; that is, if an innovation cannot help
to close group-based differences in mathematics achievement, then at least
it should not widen them. An unfortunate feature of many innovations is
that those who are positioned to take advantage of innovations also reap a
disproportionate amount of the benefits. For instance, the initial evaluations
of *Sesame Street* found that poor children—those children for whom the
program had originally been developed—profited from watching the program: Their initial reading performance was better than that of poor
children who did not watch the program. However, a reanalysis of the
original evaluation data found that middle-class children gained even more
from watching *Sesame Street* than did their lower-class peers. Contrary to the
show's original promise, *Sesame Street* helped to worsen the gap between poor
and middle-class children before they had even entered school.

More recently, Fennema, Carpenter, and their colleagues found differences between female and male students enrolled in Cognitively Guided

Instruction (CGI) primary-grade classes in their use of advanced problem-solving strategies when solving whole-number-arithmetic word problems (Fennema et al., 1998). CGI is one of the best known instructional programs focused on the development of student understanding in mathematics. Children in CGI classes do better on solving mathematics problems than do children who are not in CGI classes. What is more, children in CGI do no worse than—and in some cases, they do better than—non-CGI children on basic computational skills. The CGI findings are important and parallel to those concerning *Sesame Street* two decades ago: Students in the CGI program do better than children not in the program, yet the program may exacerbate gender differences. Findings such as these raise the possibility that similar results might be found for other forms of sociodemographic diversity.

Evaluations of other programs have shown mixed results. An evaluation of the QUASAR project compared students by race–ethnicity and language proficiency. The mathematics performance gap between Black and White students at the beginning of Grade 6 did not increase over time and was slightly narrowed by the end of Grade 8. The gap at the beginning of Grade 6 between students receiving Spanish-language bilingual instruction (i.e., limited-English-proficient students) and those receiving regular English-language instruction (i.e., English-proficient students) was essentially closed by the end of Grade 8 (Lane & Silver, in press). Primary-grade students in the *Children's Math Worlds* project (Fuson et al., 1997) followed a well-structured mathematics curriculum that was taught multilingually by teachers who focused their efforts on the development of student understanding. The results on standardized tests showed that "90% of the CMW children were at grade level on computation and 65% were at grade level on word problem solving" (Fuson et al., 1997, p. 1). On many complex word problems, these children scored as well as, and in some cases better than, older American children taught traditionally, Taiwanese children, and Japanese children.

CGI, QUASAR, and *Children's Math Worlds* are all programs designed to teach mathematics with understanding. Although students enrolled in these programs learn more than students who are not enrolled in the programs, the mixed results in regard to the closing of gaps in student achievement based on gender, race, ethnicity, and social class should alert educators to the need to more carefully monitor how similar programs are developed.

THE LARGE-SCALE IMPLEMENTATION OF TEACHING FOR UNDERSTANDING

A third location for scrutinizing whether teaching for understanding in mathematics will promote fairness lies in how this particular innovation is implemented on a wide scale. An educational innovation may have appeal-

ing characteristics in principle and while it is under development; yet when
it is implemented on a wide scale, it fails to live up to its original promise
due to slippage between its original intents and how it is implemented.
For instance, ability grouping and tracking, in theory, are supposed to
help teachers manage the variability in student ability that they confront,
to help students work with others who are similar in mathematical development, and to help put students on paths that match their futures to
their aspirations. Although tracking, according to its proponents, is supposed to work one way in theory, its large-scale implementation has not
worked that way. Students in the lower tracks experience the negative
consequences of differential class size, differential curricula, differential
resources, and differential levels of teacher experience and qualifications,
resulting in the wholesale disregard of large numbers of students. Whether
tracking helps students in the top tracks more than if they were in un-
tracked situations remains an open question, but for students enrolled in
low tracks, the practice of tracking has been a disaster. The equity question
at the juncture of large-scale implementation is not whether tracking lives
up to its promise—although that might be an important question. The
equity question is whether tracking, as it is currently constituted in schools
(not in some idealized form), is fair to students based on their social-group
membership. Because lower tracks typically enroll a disproportionate number of ethnic and racial minorities and children from lower-social-class
backgrounds, tracking's worst consequences fall on poor students and minorities, and as a result, tracking exacerbates demographic group-based
achievement differences. In other words, the large-scale implementation
of tracking is unfair, regardless of how it is supposed to work in theory.

Another danger in the large-scale implementation of an innovation is
that it gets reserved for some groups of children but not for others. For
example, Maria Montessori developed her methods to educate children
living in Milan's slums. Due to the costs of running Montessori schools
and to widely held beliefs about what constitutes adequate social services
for this nation's poor children, we seldom see poor children enrolled in
current-day Montessori schools. In its large-scale implementation, access
to a Montessori education is limited to the children of the wealthy, thereby
exacerbating preexisting social-group achievement differences.

It is a bit early to ask about the large-scale implementation of teaching
mathematics for understanding because the ideas and practices of this
approach are still under development. Yet it is not too early to raise some
cautions. In the large scale, for instance, it is possible (if not probable) that
teaching for understanding will be reserved only for students in high-ability
groups or tracks. In fact some teachers have stated that CGI should be reserved
for highly capable students (E. Fennema, personal communication, May
1997). That teaching for understanding may be implemented first in districts

that have the resources needed to provide professional development for teachers, or teaching for understanding may be implemented improperly (if at all) in districts without the resources to support teachers' professional development. In other words, it is possible that teaching for understanding will be implemented first in this nation's wealthier and suburban schools, and improperly—if at all—in its urban and poor, rural schools. Some support for our concern can be found in a study of the school-level reform of mathematics (Secada & Adajian, 1997). Over 70% of the schools that self-nominated as places that were seriously trying to reform their mathematics programs described themselves as suburban.

In the current economic and political climate, schools may find it easier to implement teaching for understanding approaches for students who attend school consistently, who are not homeless, or whose life situations do not place them at risk. All these possibilities would result in an exacerbation of achievement differences based on students' social-group membership. All such implementations would be inequitable.

Likewise, it is possible for the curricular goals that are associated with the teaching for understanding movement to remain limited for certain groups of children whereas other children, experience understanding-based instruction in challenging curricula that employ a wealth of resources and cover a range of new and interesting topics. In such cases, teaching for understanding would work synergistically with differential curriculum opportunities to increase the unequal provision of educational opportunity.

But these are cautions. Educators working from an equity perspective could challenge the practices that would reserve teaching for understanding (and its associated benefits) for a select group of students. They could insist, for instance, that these kinds of programs first be implemented in those areas where children have been traditionally ill-served by the regular mathematics program. Similarly, equity advocates could work with program developers to modify teaching for understanding so that it is implemented in contexts under which these approaches had not already been developed or tested.

CONCLUSION

It would be most unfortunate if our comments were taken to mean that we do not support the development and widespread distribution of approaches to teaching mathematics for student understanding. We endorse such an effort wholeheartedly. Beyond the empirical evidence that teaching for understanding shows much promise for teaching children of diverse sociodemographic backgrounds, we believe that treating children as if they can and should understand what they are being taught conveys a fundamental respect for them as individuals.

Our intent was to show how an equity perspective adds nuance and raises cautions about an overenthusiastic rush toward judgment and toward widespread implementation. We hope to alert our colleagues and other educators about the pitfalls of implementing any educational innovation, even one as promising as teaching for understanding appears to be, when concerns for equity are missing. We also hope to suggest some ways by which, having alerted educators to problems and issues, an equity perspective might help educators to design safeguards and to use this innovation to promote the achievement of equity.

Through its focus on the individual student, teaching for understanding helps educators to design some very powerful instructional methods. Through its focus on the student as a member of a particular sociodemographic group and on the fair treatment of students, equity helps educators to design and implement those methods without doing accidental harm. In the long run, an equity perspective also can help school mathematics become part of the solution to the larger questions of why we educate children in schools in the first place, that is, to help them live and work together as productive adult members of a diverse society.

NOTES

1. The work reported herein was supported by the National Center for Improving Student Learning and Achievement in Mathematics and Science (NCISLA), which is administered by the Wisconsin Center for Education Research (WCER), School of Education, University of Wisconsin–Madison and funded by the Educational Research and Development Centers Program, PR/Award number R305A60007, as administered by the Office of Educational Research and Improvement (OERI), U.S. Department of Education. However, the contents do not necessarily represent the position or policies of NCISLA, WCER, or OERI's National Institute on Student Achievement, Curriculum, and Assessment, U.S. Department of Education.

REFERENCES

Fennema, E., Carpenter, T. P., Jacobs, V. R., Franke, M. L., & Levi, L. (1998). A longitudinal study of gender differences in young children's mathematical thinking. *Educational Researcher, 27*(5), 4–11.

Fuson, K. C., De La Cruz, Y., Lo Cicero, A. M., Smith, S. S., Hudson, K., & Ron, P. (1997). *Towards a mathematics equity pedagogy: Creating ladders to understanding and skill for children and teachers.* Manuscript submitted for publication.

Lane, S., & Silver, E. A. (in press). Fairness and equity in measuring student learning using a mathematics performance assessment: Results from the QUASAR project. In M. T. Nettles (Ed.), *Equity and excellence in educational testing and assessment* (Volume II). Dordrecht, The Netherlands: Kluwer.

Secada, W. G., & Adajian, L. B. (1997). Mathematics teachers' change in the context of their professional communities. In E. Fennema & B. S. Nelson (Eds.), *Mathematics teachers in transition* (pp. 193–219). Mahwah, NJ: Lawrence Erlbaum Associates.

Part II

ROOMS THAT PROMOTE UNDERSTANDING

Chapter 4

Learning Basic Number Concepts and Skills as Problem Solving

Thomas P. Carpenter
Elizabeth Fennema
University of Wisconsin–Madison

Karen Fuson
Northwestern University

James Hiebert
University of Delaware

Piet Human
Hanlie Murray
Alwyn Olivier
University of Stellenbosch

Diana Wearne
University of Delaware

Learning computational skills and developing understanding of mathematics have frequently been seen as competing objectives, but a growing body of research is finding it neither necessary nor productive to choose between skills and understanding: They are both important. In order to learn skills well, to retain them, and to be able to apply them to solve problems, skills must be learned with understanding. By the same token, learning critical skills can support the development of understanding. For example, learning what has traditionally been considered routine computational skills offers an ideal site for developing understanding of fundamental number concepts.

In this chapter, we describe four programs to illustrate how learning to add and subtract can support the concurrent development of skills and understanding. Each of the four programs has been tested extensively in primary classrooms. In all four programs, the learning of multidigit concepts and skills is perceived as a problem-solving activity rather than as the acquisition of established rules and procedures. Teachers do not demonstrate procedures or expect all children to use a particular algorithm. Children spend a great deal of time working out their own problem-solving solutions, which involve fundamental number concepts. Alternate strategies are shared and discussed with classmates and teachers. The construction and discussion of strategies provide a basis for students to engage in the types of mental activities necessary for the development of understanding. As children in these programs develop understanding, their ability to apply skills develops concurrently.

In all four programs, children spend the majority of their time engaged in problem solving. The teacher plays an active role in establishing class-room norms, selecting tasks, making appropriate tools available, coordinating the discussion of strategies, joining the students in asking questions about strategies, and occasionally sharing an alternative strategy. The intent is to create classroom norms where the construction of strategies becomes central and where teachers support students' efforts to solve problems. Teachers serve as a resource and guide by not intervening too much or too deeply. Teachers provide input to classroom discussion, but they also convey to the students that they themselves can figure out strategies and do not need to appeal to the authority of the teacher to find out whether a procedure is correct or acceptable.

In classrooms from each program, mathematical tasks generally are set in a problem context drawing on experiences that the class has shared—a field trip, a science project, a book they have read, and the like. During a typical class period, the scenario for the day is presented along with the first problem. Students work individually or in small groups to solve the problem, using a variety of tools available in the classroom. After the problem is solved, students share their strategies. Strategies are then discussed by encouraging students to ask questions if they do not understand, to comment on the strategies, and to compare them to others they have used or shared. Explicit attention is paid to the similarities between strategies using physical tools and those using written symbols. After the discussion, a second problem is posed, and the lesson continues in this way.

AN EXAMPLE OF A FIRST-GRADE CLASS

Although the following vignette is adapted from a series of tasks in one teacher's classroom, the events, class discussion, and pedagogy are typical of what is played out daily in classrooms from all four programs. Some features of the example are specific to instruction in two of the projects, but except for some minor details the episode might have taken place in any one of them. (The names used in the dialogue are pseudonyms.)

Ms. K's first-grade class was preparing for a field trip to a restaurant owned by the parents of one of the children in the class. They were comparing prices of items on the menu. Ms. K read the following problem several times and wrote the numbers on the overhead projector:

At Bucky's Burger Barn a hamburger costs $3.65, and a steak sandwich costs $4.92. How much more does a steak sandwich cost than a hamburger?

The children set to work on the problem at their desks. A number of tools, which children could use to solve problems, were stored in one corner of the room, and some children went to get tools they needed. The tools included counters of various kinds, plastic coins, and base-10 blocks. The base-10 blocks included 1-cm cubes, ten-bars (10-cm long with each cm marked), and 10 × 10 cm squares (with each cm marked). As the children were solving the problem, Ms. K talked with individual children about their solutions:

Ms. K: Kurt, can you tell me what you are doing?

Kurt: I'm trying to find out how much more four ninety-two is than three sixty-five.

Ms. K: OK, how are you going to do that?

Kurt: Umm. I'd make three sixty-five.

Ms. K: OK, go ahead.

[Kurt uses base-10 blocks to make 365. He puts out 3 hundred-flats, 6 ten-bars, and 5 unit cubes; see Fig. 4.1.]

Ms. K: Then what would you do?

[Kurt uses the base-10 blocks to make 492, putting out 4 hundred-flats, 9 ten-bars, and 2 single units.]

Ms. K: OK, what are you going to do next?

[Kurt doesn't respond.]

Ms. K: What are you trying to find?

Kurt: How much bigger four ninety-two is than three sixty-five.

Ms. K: Can what you did here [indicating the two sets of base-10 blocks Kurt has put out] help you?

Kurt: Ummm. I want to find out how much more there is here [pointing first to the set of 492] than here. [He points to the set of 365, then proceeds to match the two sets, pairing off the hundreds, tens, and ones. When there are not enough ones in the 492 group to go with the 5 ones in the 365 group, he trades a ten for 10 ones.] There's one twenty-seven more. That's $1.27.

This episode lasted about five minutes. During the entire time, Ms. K listened to Kurt describe how he was solving the problem. She provided

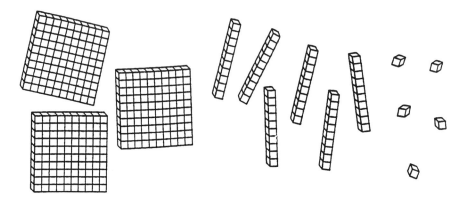

FIG. 4.1. Representing 365 with base-10 blocks.

support to get him going and to call his attention to what he was doing, but the solution was his. This type of interaction is typical. Ms. K listened as individual children explained their solutions to the problem. For children like Kurt, Ms. K provided support as it was needed, in Kurt's case to get going and to solve the problem, but she seldom showed them how to solve a problem.

Other children had solved the problem by themselves, and at this point, Ms. K gave them the opportunity to describe their strategies:

Ms. K.: Can you tell me what you did, Becky?

Becky: Well, I know that 5 more than 65 would be 70, and then it would be 20 more to 90, and then 2 more would be 92. So that's 5 and 20 and 2, and that's 27. Then I knew that I needed a dollar more to make it $4. So it's $1.27. [Becky has written in her math journal "65 + 5 + 20 + 2 = 92. 5 + 20 + 2 = 27. The extra dollar from the 4 makes it $1.27."]

Ms. K: That's good, Becky. Can you solve it another way?

[Becky goes to work on a second solution.]

While most of the children worked individually to solve the problem, Ms. K talked to six students about their solutions. She asked each child to explain his or her strategy for solving the problem and waited patiently as each student explained his or her solution. She also saw how a number of students were solving the problem by observing how they manipulated the blocks or by reading the solutions they wrote in their math journals.

After about 15 minutes of individual work on the problem, Ms. K asked individual students to share their responses with the entire class:

Kisha:	[Puts 2 translucent plastic quarters, 4 dimes, and 2 pennies on the overhead projector] That's the 92 cents. [She takes away the two quarters.] That's 50. [She takes away one dime]. That's 60. [She takes away one of the dimes and starts to replace it with 10 pennies.]
Ms. K:	Can you tell us what you are doing now?
Kisha:	I can't take away the 5, so I need more pennies.
Ms. K:	Why can you do that?
Kisha:	Because a dime is the same as 10 pennies.
Ms. K:	I see; you are trading a dime for 10 pennies so you can take way 5 pennies.
Kisha:	Yeah. [She continues to count out 10 pennies, and then removes 5 pennies from the group of 12 pennies. She counts the pennies.] It's 27.
Ms. K:	So the steak sandwich costs 27 cents more than the hamburger?
Kisha:	[After a moment's pause] No! A dollar and 27.
Ms. K:	OK. Where did the dollar come from?
Kisha:	I knew that $4 was one more than $3.
Ms. K:	Can someone tell me how Kisha's solution is like Kurt's? [Kurt shared his solution right before Kisha.] Vicki?
Vicki:	Kisha used the coins, and Kurt used the blocks.
Ms. K:	OK, they used different materials. Did they use the same strategy?
Vicki:	No. Kurt made both the four ninety-two and the three sixty-five. Kisha just made the 92.
Ms. K:	Why did they get the same answer?
Josh:	Kurt lined up the 92 and the 65, and he took away the ones that lined up together. Kisha just took away the 65 without making another group.
Ms. K:	Did someone solve it a different way? Kevin?
Kevin:	Well, I know that 90 take away 60 gives me 30. Then I took away 5 more, and that made 25. Then I had to put back the 2 from the 92, so it's 27, I mean $1.27. [As he talks, he writes on the overhead projector "$90 - 60 - 5 + 2 = 27$."]
Ms. K:	Can someone tell me why he put "+" 2?
Jackie:	Because the 2 is with the 92. He started out with 90, so he's got to put the 2 back. He's taking away the 65, so the 60 and the 5, they're both minuses.
Ms. K:	Can someone tell me how Kevin's solution is like Kisha's?

[A discussion ensues on how Kevin's solution is like Kisha's. During the discussion, one student points out that when Kevin subtracts 60 from 90, that is exactly what Kisha does with the coins.]

After five students reported their solutions and the similarities and differences were discussed, Ms. K presented another problem, and the entire scenario was repeated. During the entire mathematics class, the students solved only three problems. For the previous problem, Ms. K heard nine students explain their answers: the six she talked with at their desks and the three who presented during the group discussion (whom she had not talked with). During the day, she listened to over half the class individually explain their solutions. Over a 2-day period, every student had the opportunity to explain a solution to her, and she talked with some students almost every day.

Rather than moving quickly from student to student during seatwork, Ms. K spent a substantial amount of time with each student she talked with. This communicated to the students that their ideas were important. They knew they would have to explain their solutions, so they knew that they needed to understand them.

In this vignette, several features of each of the four instructional programs are seen. Mathematics is centered on problem solving. Children solve problems by drawing relationships with knowledge they already have, reflect on what they have done, and articulate their thinking. The mathematics becomes their own because they construct the solutions. The children have appropriate tasks to engage in and tools that facilitate their problem solving.

THE FOUR PROGRAMS

In the following description of the four programs, we discuss how this lesson fits into each program. Although a wide variety of mathematics topics are covered in each program, in this chapter we focus on the development of understanding and skills related to place-value concepts and adding and subtracting multidigit numbers.

Cognitively Guided Instruction (CGI)

The CGI project is directed by Thomas Carpenter and Elizabeth Fennema at the University of Wisconsin–Madison and Megan Franke at University of California at Los Angeles. CGI is not a program of instruction in a traditional sense. There are no explicit, recommended tasks. CGI operates from a perspective that teachers' understanding of children's mathematical thinking is a critical factor in helping children learn mathematics with understanding. The goal of the CGI Professional Development project is to help teachers better understand children's thinking so that they can help children relate what they are learning to what they already know. The teachers decide how to use that knowledge. Although there is no specified program of instruction, most CGI classrooms share certain common features.

In CGI classes, procedures for adding and subtracting two- and three-digit numbers develop as natural extensions of the procedures that children use to solve problems involving small numbers. When children enter school, most of them are able to solve a variety of basic word problems by modeling the action or relationships described in the problems. Initially, they model the problems by using some kind of counters to represent the quantities, action, and relationships in the problems. Over time, these physical modeling strategies are abstracted and abbreviated as children naturally begin to use counting strategies and number facts. Essentially the same pattern occurs for children's solutions of problems with larger numbers. Children's symbolic procedures evolve out of direct-modeling strategies with physical materials that incorporate groupings of ten (see, again, Fig. 4.1 for examples of base-10 blocks).

In CGI classrooms, word problems provide the basis for almost all instruction that involves both single and multidigit numbers. In the early grades, teachers begin by giving children a variety of word problems that can be solved by modeling and counting using single unit counters. Teachers do not demonstrate ways to solve problems, but a great deal of time is spent discussing alternative strategies that children have devised for solving each problem. The discussions serve as models for other children, and they provide an opportunity for children to reflect on their own solutions. Initially, children solve problems involving multidigit numbers by modeling the problems with single unit counters. These solutions do not require any real conceptions of place value beyond the ability to count.

There is very little specific instruction devoted to place-value concepts per se. Essentially, children learn place-value concepts as they explore the use of base-10 blocks and other base-10 materials to solve word problems and as they listen to other children explain their solutions. Appropriate tools, connected base-10 blocks or stacking cubes stored in rods of 10 cubes, may be made available as early as the first or second week of school in the first or second grade. The teachers make the base-10 tools available, but they do not demonstrate how to use them to represent numbers or solve problems. Children initially use the tools in quite inefficient ways, which do not make use of the groupings of ten. For example, they often count the individual units in each ten-bar as they use them to solve problems. The ten-bar simply serves as convenient collections of unit counters that do not get mixed up. With teacher encouragement, some children come to recognize that each ten-bar is made up of 10 units and that they do not have to count all the individual units in a ten-bar. They share their strategies for counting units of ten to solve problems, and gradually other children adopt these more efficient strategies. Soon most children are constructing two-digit quantities by making collections of tens and ones.

Over time, children become increasingly flexible and efficient in the use of base-10 materials. As their use of the tools becomes more automatic, they come to depend less on the manipulations of the physical tools, and they are able to abstract their solutions with physical tools so that they can add and subtract multidigit numbers without them.

Throughout the year, different children in a CGI class operate at many different levels with respect to place-value knowledge. One important consequence is that there is no prevalent strategy that all children use at a particular point in time. Children have the latitude to use a strategy that makes sense to them at the time. A consequence of the variety of strategies in use at any given time is that children have the opportunity to learn more advanced strategies by interacting with other students who are using them. Thus, children continuously shift among representations both in their own solutions of different problems and in their discussions of different strategies for the same problems with classmates. The continuing discussion of multiple representations and moving back and forth among representational types help children to see the connections among different representations.

Conceptually Based Instruction (CBI)

CBI, directed by James Hiebert and Diana Wearne at the University of Delaware, shares many common features with CGI, and much of the foregoing discussion could apply to either project. Like CGI, CBI focuses on building relationships by having children reflect on similarities and differences highlighted by the different representations. External representations (physical materials, pictures, words, symbols) are used as tools for solving problems, demonstrating and recording children's strategies for solving problems, and communicating their strategies. Once a particular tool like base-10 blocks is introduced, it is used consistently to allow students to practice using it and to become familiar with the uses and connections it affords. Class discussions focus on how the tools can be used and on how they are similar and different. A primary goal is to help students become comfortable with different forms of representation and build relationships among those forms.

Each form of representation affords and constrains strategies in particular ways. The base-10 blocks, for example, support regrouping strategies, especially in subtraction contexts that students perceive to require a take-away action. Discussions of connections between written and physical strategies in this context help to illuminate how regrouping is used in subtraction—a student must trade a ten for 10 ones or put a ten with the ones in order to take away more ones than are initially present.

Classroom lessons are organized around the solving of several problems, usually drawn from a common theme or scenario. The problems are constructed so students can solve them with strategies already in their repertoire or with new, more efficient strategies. This feature is intended as a support for connecting new knowledge with prior knowledge.

Physical tools and verbal stories are used as the initial representations for quantities and actions on quantities. Pictures of the tools that have been manipulated by the students are then used for convenience and for focusing class discussions. Finally, written symbols are introduced as efficient tools for recording children's problem-solving strategies that have been explored and discussed using the other representations. Once a particular form of representation is introduced, it is used continually and interchangeably with previous forms.

During the first few days, only base-10 blocks are used to solve problems. The reasons for this are (a) to encourage all students to become familiar with the features of the base-10 blocks, (b) to develop class discussions in a context in which all students can participate (i.e., referents for the discussion are relatively unambiguous, and all students are equally familiar with them), and (c) to provide a referential base that students can later use to support their inventions and–or explanations (i.e., base-10 blocks can serve as a ready referent for students when they explain or defend their strategies). After students have some experience with the blocks, written symbols are used, and students develop more sophisticated strategies using blocks and written symbols simultaneously. Each child has a full set of blocks, and they are always available. By the end of first grade, almost all students are familiar with the tool-like power of the blocks. At the least, blocks can be used as a default option and–or can be used to check the outcome of a newly invented mental or written strategy for adding or subtracting two-digit numbers. By the end of second grade, most students use written symbols to solve two- and three-digit problems, but they continue to use blocks to check their answers or to help them invent strategies for new kinds of problems.

Supporting Ten-Structured Thinking (STST)

The STST project is directed by Karen Fuson at Northwestern University. Instruction in STST classes provides the most explicit guidance and support for making connections between representations of the four projects. As with the other three projects, multidigit procedures are constructed by the children themselves, either individually or collectively, so that the learning of multidigit procedures is viewed as problem solving rather than as the acquisition of established procedures. What distinguishes the STST project from the other three projects is that (a) connections are much more explicitly drawn between representational forms in order to give meaning to multidigit numbers and operations on them and (b) children are provided specific conceptual supports to provide meaning to problem-solving strategies and to problem situations.

When children or the teacher discusses adding and subtracting two- and three-digit numbers, he or she consistently specifies relations between number words, numerals, and quantities. Initially, children are expected to demonstrate explicit connections between symbolic procedures for adding and subtracting and operations on base-10 blocks or other materials that show ones, tens, and hundreds. Thus, when children describe a procedure that they have invented, they are expected to be able to justify each step in the procedure by showing how it corresponds to a legitimate manipulation of physical tools. For example, in an STST classroom, Kevin's solution might have been explained something like this (recall that he is subtracting 65 from 92):

Kevin: Well, I know that 90 take away 60 gives me 30. Then I took away 5 more, and that made 25. Then I had to put back the 2 from the 92, so it's 27.

Teacher: Can you show us that with the blocks, Kevin?

Kevin: Well, I am taking 65 from 92, so first I have to have the 92 [puts out 9 ten-bars and 2 unit cubes]. So first I took away the 60 from the 90 [removes 6 ten-bars]. So that leaves 30 there [points to the 3 ten-bars], and I need to take 5 from that [trades one of the ten-bars for 10 unit cubes and takes 5 of them away]. That gives me 25 there [pointing to the 2 ten-bars and the 5 unit cubes] and with these 2 [pushing the 2 unit cubes from the original 92 over to the other ten-bars], that's 27.

What is important to note here is that each step in the initial solution is matched directly with a manipulation of the blocks. They are carried out at the same time, and each step is explained by indicating how it is carried out with the base-10 blocks. This illustrates how children describe and justify their solution in words as they relate their written solutions to the corresponding physical representation. Having to describe how their operations on written symbols correspond to manipulations of the multidigit quantities makes it less likely that children simply imitate the solutions of other children and more likely that they understand the solutions that they generate.

Problem-Centered Mathematics Project (PCMP)

The PCMP is directed by Piet Human, Alwyn Olivier, and Hanlie Murray of the University of Stellenbosch in South Africa. Instruction in PCMP classes is aimed at helping children construct and use increasingly abstract units of number. Initially, for young children, a number like 27 means only 27 single objects. It is a number in a counting sequence, like 5 or 9, and there is no understanding of the number in terms of place-value concepts. The goal is to help children see that the number can take on a number of meanings. In addition to 27 ones, it also means 20 and one 7, or 25 and one 2, and so on. The basic approach in PCMP classes is to help children construct these increasingly sophisticated concepts of different units, including ten, and to build these concepts on children's counting-based meanings by encouraging increasingly abstract counting strategies and child-generated computational algorithms.

In PCMP classrooms, number-concept development goes hand in hand with children's construction of computational algorithms, and little distinction is made between the two. Children use problem-solving methods appropriate for their level of knowledge. For example, some children might add 28 + 15 by modeling the problem with counters and counting by ones; others, with more sophisticated concepts of number, might decompose the numbers so that tens and ones can be added separately (e.g., 20 plus 10 is 30, and 8 more is 38, and 2 more is 40, and then the 3 that is left from the 5 makes 43).

Children do not use structured tools like base-10 blocks, which embody base-10 groupings. Instead, they use loose counters, collect them into groups of ten, and count (e.g., 10, 20, 30, 31, 32, 33, 34). Children have two sets of numeral cards: multiples of ten and ones. To represent the numeral 34, for example, they take the 30 card and the 4 card and place the 4 over the zero of 30. At this stage, the representation of two-digit numerals is handled as the juxtaposition of two numbers: a tens number and a ones number.

Computational procedures build directly on children's number concepts and their knowledge of properties of number operations rather than on connections to operations with manipulative materials. Any computational procedure involves transforming the given task to one or more easier tasks that children already know how to do. The process of changing the task to equivalent but easier subtasks involves three distinguishable sets of subtasks: (a) transformation of the number, (b) transformation of the given computational task, and (c) the carrying out of the computation. For example, the addition of 24 + 38 involves the transformation of the numbers: 24 = 20 + 4 and 38 = 30 + 8. The computational task (20 + 4) + (30 + 8) is transformed to the equivalent task [(20 + 30) + 4] + 8. The resulting computations involve tasks that are familiar and may be based on recall of known number combinations together with knowledge of number concepts: 20 + 30 = 50; 50 + 4 = 54; 54 + 8 = 62.

The standard vertical addition algorithm depends on these very transformations, but the transformations are hidden. In using a standard vertical algorithm, children often lose sight of the fact that they are actually adding 20 and 30; they think of the addition in terms of columns of numbers: 5 + 8 and 2 + 3. In PCMP classes, the procedures are carried out at the conceptual level; children actually think of the addition as 20 + 30, not 2 + 3. Children never are expected to use standard computational algorithms.

The instructional approach emphasizes the role of negotiation, interaction, and communication between teacher and students and among students in the evolution of their cognitive processes. Problems are set to students in small groups. Students are expected to demonstrate and explain their methods, both verbally and in writing, with the teacher providing needed support with respect to notation and terminology. Children also are encouraged to discuss, compare, and reflect on different strategies, trying to make sense of other students' explanations, thereby learning from each other. Thus, children develop more sophisticated concepts of number by reflecting on their own strategies for solving problems and discussing them with other children and with the teacher.

Teachers spend a great deal of time listening to pupils, accepting their explanations and justifications in a nonevaluative manner, with the purpose of understanding and interpreting children's available cognitive structures. This enables the teacher to provide appropriate learning experiences that facilitate the child's development.

COMMONALITIES AND DIFFERENCES IN DEVELOPING UNDERSTANDING

The five interrelated forms of mental activity from which mathematical understanding emerges are clearly present in all four programs. Although providing opportunity for constructing relationships is a defining feature of instruction in each of the programs, each emphasizes somewhat different relationships and goes about helping children construct relationships in different ways. The programs are more similar in the ways that they deal with the other four dimensions.

Constructing Relationships

In all four programs, the vast majority of classroom time is spent engaged in tasks in which connections between or within representational forms are made explicit, usually by the children themselves. They discuss multiple strategies involving multiple representations; they use symbolic procedures in which connections to basic number concepts and properties of operations are explicitly drawn. They are not presented with procedures to follow, and they are not expected to engage in manipulations of symbols without understanding what they are doing. In the Problem-Centered Mathematics Project, standard vertical algorithms are never introduced, and the other three programs defer the use of traditional vertical algorithms for addition and subtraction until children have demonstrated some basic understanding of multidigit numbers and procedures. In all four programs, time is spent ensuring that children's knowledge is connected rather than practicing skills.

A key feature of all four programs that ensures that children connect new concepts and procedures to their existing knowledge base is that all learning, including (in particular) the learning of multidigit procedures, is taken as a problem-solving activity. Children are not provided with algorithms to learn: They construct them. Because children construct their own procedures, there is no reason to imitate a procedure that they do not understand. Because they are the ones who decide what steps to follow, children recognize the reason for each step in a procedure. In other words, because children construct and explain their own procedures, they are able to connect the steps in the procedures to their purposes.

Although the four programs all provide extensive opportunity for students to connect emerging number concepts and procedures to previously learned concepts and procedures, there are fundamental differences between the programs in the nature of the connections and in the ways those connections are formed. One of the fundamental differences is in the roles played by connections between and within representational forms. These differences are manifested in the children's use of tools. The Problem-Centered Mathematics Project does not employ structured base-10 tools like base-10 blocks. In the other three programs, structured base-10 tools play a prominent role.

Within the three programs in which structured base-10 tools are used, there are critical differences in the ways in which tools are used. In the Supporting Ten-Structured Thinking project, specific attention is drawn to the connections between operations on base-10 blocks and operations on symbols. Each step in the symbolic procedure is linked to the corresponding operation on the base-10 blocks. In Conceptually Based Instruction, step-by-step mapping enters the class discussion as one way of justifying a particular procedure. Step-by-step mapping, however, is not required;

for some students, procedures with blocks and written symbols do not develop simultaneously. Procedures with blocks are developed first, and procedures with written symbols are then developed by reflecting on the blocks procedures. In Cognitively Guided Instruction, manipulations with blocks generally are not linked step-by-step to manipulations with symbols. Symbolic procedures emerge as more efficient variants of procedures with blocks. Connections between blocks and symbols are constructed as children abstract the operations on the blocks in creating their own invented symbol procedures.

Having children explain how they have solved problems with the blocks may play a significant role in extending the physical modeling strategies with base-10 blocks to more-abstract symbolic procedures. When children talk about combining tens, trading tens for ones, and the like, their verbal descriptions of operations with physical materials come to sound very much like the invented symbolic procedures that replace them.

The diversity among the four programs also is reflected in the order in which connections are constructed. In the Conceptually Based Instruction project, children spend a substantial amount of time on the grouping tasks designed to develop multidigit concepts before they are given problems involving addition and subtraction of multidigit numbers. In the other three projects, the learning of multidigit concepts is more integrated with multidigit addition and subtraction from the start.

Extending and Applying Mathematical Knowledge

Children in the classes of all four projects learn to extend and apply their mathematical knowledge because that is how all knowledge is generated. Learning new procedures is taken as a problem-solving task in which children construct new procedures by extending their knowledge of basic number concepts and procedures. All tasks are posed in problem contexts. As a consequence, children do not learn computational procedures that they later may apply to solve problems; they learn procedures in the context of, and for the sake of, solving problems.

Reflection and Articulation

Reflection plays a major role in the development of children's mathematical thinking in all of the projects. It is through reflecting on manipulations of physical materials or elementary counting strategies that children develop more mature symbolic procedures for adding and subtracting. One of the primary motivations for children to reflect is the class norm that they consistently articulate their solution processes. By regularly explaining how they solve problems and negotiating how solutions are alike and different, children become more reflective and more articulate in explaining their thinking.

One of the critical factors in establishing a problem-solving environment in the classes is that children are asked to describe and explain the strategies they use to solve any given problem. Children talk about how they have solved a problem to the teacher, to other children, and to the whole class. This discussion of alternative strategies not only provides an opportunity for children to reflect on and articulate their thinking, it also provides opportunity to construct relationships among different strategies by juxtaposing alternative strategies and discussing commonalities and differences among them. It provides an opportunity for children to discuss how their strategies can be applied to different problems in different ways, and it communicates to children that their own strategies are valued. Thus, the discussion of alternative strategies not only serves the goal of providing opportunity for students to articulate their thinking, it provides a basis for developing the other four forms of mental activity from which mathematical understanding emerge.

Ownership

Students in all four programs are personally involved in constructing their own solutions to problems. Teachers seldom provide students demonstrations of procedures for them to imitate. Class norms are established such that each student has opportunity to explain his or her way of solving problems, and each student's ideas are listened to and valued. In constructing their own procedures for solving problems, students take responsibility for their own learning: They realize that mathematics can make sense, and that they can make sense of it.

CONCLUSIONS

Providing students with opportunities to develop critical connections is a hallmark of all four programs, although they go about it in quite different ways. In spite of the differences in the connections that the programs emphasize and the ways they go about helping students form the connections, in all four programs it is possible to identify how connections are formed between symbolic procedures and the more elementary representations and procedures that students already understand. In every case, forging these connections is consistently the focus of instruction.

There are major differences among the four programs in the tasks and tools used to form connections, but in every case a primary goal of instruction is that tasks and tools are used to help students form critical connections.

The programs are more alike in the classroom norms established for helping students to extend knowledge, reflect about mathematical experiences, articulate what they know, and develop a sense of ownership.

All of this is made possible by the fact that the teachers understand children's thinking so that they are able to help children extend their knowledge by connecting new knowledge to it. The teachers know how specific mathematical ideas develop in children, and they consistently listen to their own students explain how they solve problems in order to figure out what their students know and which tasks may help them extend and elaborate their knowledge. By listening to each child's ideas, the teachers provide a model that helps to establish a class norm that everyone's thinking is respected. This encourages the students to value their own thinking and to reflect on it. If there is any one thing that a teacher can do to make his or her classroom most like the classrooms described in this chapter, it is to ask students to explain their thinking and to listen to the students for the purpose of *understanding* their thinking.

FOR FURTHER READING

Hiebert, J., Carpenter, T. P., Fennema, E., Fuson, K., Human, P., Murray, H., Olivier, A., & Wearne, D. (1997). *Making sense: Teaching and learning mathematics with understanding.* Portsmouth, NH: Heinemann.

Cognitively Guided Instruction

Carpenter, T. P., Fennema, E., & Franke, M. L. (1996). Cognitively Guided Instruction: A knowledge base for reform in primary mathematics instruction. *The Elementary School Journal, 97,* 3–20.
Fennema, E., Carpenter, T. P., Franke, M. L., Levi, L. W., Jacobs, V., & Empson, S. B. (1996). A longitudinal study of learning to use children's thinking in mathematics instruction. *Journal for Research in Mathematics Education, 27,* 403–434.

Conceptually Based Instruction

Hiebert, J., & Wearne, D. (1993). Instructional tasks, classroom discourse, and student learning in second grade. *American Educational Research Journal, 30,* 393–425.
Hiebert, J., & Wearne, D. (1996). Instruction, understanding, and skill in multidigit addition and subtraction. *Cognition and Instruction, 14,* 251–283.

Supporting Ten-Structured Thinking

Fuson, K. C., & Smith, S. T. (1995). Complexities in learning two-digit subtraction: A case study of tutored learning. *Mathematical Cognition, 1,* 165–213.
Fuson, K. C., Smith, S. T., & Lo Cicero, A. M. (in press). Supporting Latino first graders' ten-structured thinking in urban classrooms. *Journal for Research in Mathematics Education.*

Problem-Centered Mathematics Project

Murray, H., Olivier, A., & Human, P. (1992). The development of young students' division strategies. In W. Geeslin & K. Graham (Eds.), *Proceedings of the Sixteenth International Conference for the Psychology of Mathematics Education: Vol. 2* (pp. 152–159). (ERIC Document Reproduction Service No. SE 055 811)

Olivier, A., Murray, H., & Human, P. (1990). Building on young children's informal arithmetical knowledge. In G. Booker, P. Cobb, & T. N. de Mendicuti (Eds.), *Proceedings of the Fourteenth International Conference for the Psychology of Mathematics Education: Vol. 3* (pp. 297–304). (ERIC Document Reproduction Service No. SE 057 623)

Chapter 5

Building on Children's Intuitions to Develop Mathematical Understanding of Space

Richard Lehrer
Cathy Jacobson
Vera Kemeny
Dolores Strom
University of Wisconsin–Madison

Children come to school with a rich and varied set of informal experiences of space. Looking at shape and form in the world, children build intuitions about perspective, symmetry, and similarity. Walking in their neighborhoods, children reason about distance, direction, and their composition (e.g., routes). Drawing what they see, children represent and use elements of space for play and for communication. Building structures with blocks, toothpicks, or Tinkertoys, children experience firsthand how shape and form play roles in function (e.g., round objects roll; most others do not) and structure (e.g., some structures bear loads; others do not). Everyday experiences like these, and the informal knowledge children develop over time by participating in them, constitute a springboard for developing children's mathematical understanding of space: a children's geometry. For example, senses of position and direction derived from walking can be elaborated mathematically in a variety of ways—as coordinate systems, as compass directions, as maps, and as dynamic Logo models.[1] Each of these mathematical forms of thought has antecedents in children's experiences as well (e.g., coordinate systems in city blocks, maps in children's drawings), and, collectively, these experiences constitute a good grounding for making mathematical sense of the spatial world.

Spatial experience, however, provides only the grounds for subsequent mathematical development. Our research suggests that mathematical reasoning about space develops slowly, if at all, in everyday contexts or in traditional forms of mathematical instruction in the early grades. Because mathematical reasoning about space does not evolve spontaneously and because this form of reasoning is typically underserved in the elementary school, we collaborated with a small group of primary-grade teachers to design classrooms that would promote understanding of the mathematics of space and geometry. Together, we sought to characterize trajectories of learning when students had opportunities to reason about space for prolonged periods of time. Teachers either invented or appropriated problems and tasks whose solutions would help children understand one or more big ideas about space and geometry. For example, children designed quilts to learn about transformations and symmetry (see Kaput, chapter 8, this volume) or drew top, side, and front views of model buildings to develop understanding of perspective and 3-dimensional structure. Teachers orchestrated classroom conversations in which children articulated and justified their solutions and understandings.

We built on children's experiences in four related areas: (a) large-scale space, especially wayfinding, leading to the mathematics of position, direction, and scale; (b) drawing, leading to the mathematics of maps and related means for visualizing and modeling space; (c) perceptions and physical experiences with shape and form, leading to the mathematics of dimension, classification, transformation; and (d) early number, leading to the mathematics of measure of length, area, and volume. To illustrate our approach, we describe episodes drawn from primary-grade classrooms that illustrate how mathematical understanding, with the skilled guidance of teachers, emerged from children's informal knowledge.

FROM FINDING OUR WAY TO MAPPING

How can walking lead to mathematical understanding? Jennie Clement, a second-grade teacher, addressed this question by creating a simple task. After taping an X on the floor of their classroom, children, working in pairs, were asked to write directions that enabled their peers, starting from a variety of positions and orientations in the classroom, to find the X. Children initially thought that this task would be simple, but as they attempted to articulate directions, they quickly discovered otherwise. For example, directions like "walk and then turn" led classmates to points other than the X. Also, the children who measured length with their footsteps soon realized that their classmates did not necessarily have feet of the same length.

From these humble beginnings, Ms. Clement worked throughout the year to expand the scope of wayfinding to forge relationships with other mathematical ideas. This was accomplished by introducing children to mathematical tools like the navigational (magnetic) compass and by developing forms of mathematical representation like the footstrip (an imprint of a student's foot laid end to end). The navigational compass afforded a new frame of reference for thinking about direction: Direction was no longer only relative to the walker but could be absolute, governed by the Earth's magnetic field. The footstrip lifted feet from acts of walking, so that children could reason about feet as measures of distance rather than simply the means of traversing that distance. (Children's ideas about length measure are described in the last section of this chapter, so we do not pursue the progression from feet-for-walking to feet-for-measuring here.)

Other tasks and tools enlarged children's ideas about position, direction, and distance. For example, children represented routes in large-scale spaces, like their neighborhoods or the school's playground, with Logo, a computer tool that helped promote further reflection about distance and direction. That introduced the idea of scale: How is the distance traveled by a turtle on a computer screen related to the distance traveled during a person's walk? Children read a story (reflecting the frequent use of children's literature as a bridge to mathematics in Ms. Clement's classroom), drew a map of an imaginary town inspired by what they had read, and then wrote directions for a snowplow involving compass direction and a unit of length (the length of a side of a Unifix cube) measure (see Fig. 5.1).

Such forms of activity also helped children develop a deeper under-standing of maps as models of space. This development is exemplified by a third grader's maps of the school's playground at the beginning and end of his efforts. Ryan's initial map of his school's playground is depicted in Fig. 5.2a. Note that the map is very much like a drawing. A favorite play structure dominates the space. After participating in classroom tasks similar to those described previously, Ryan revised his map. Revision served as a

FIG. 5.1. Map of an imaginary town, with directions for the route of a snowplow (second grade).

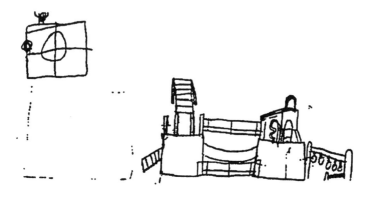

(a)

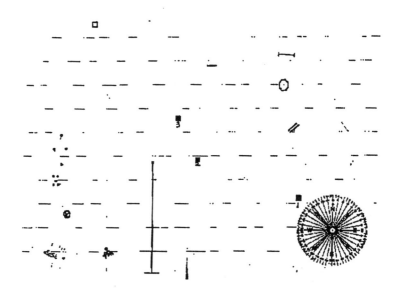

(b)

FIG. 5.2. Ryan's maps of the school playground (third grade). (a) Initial map focusing on the pictorial representation of the play structure. (b) Final, revised map, reflecting understanding of distance, direction, and scale.

ready point for reflection and articulation of his ideas about distance, direction, angle, scale, and origin (i.e., Should the map be constructed piecemeal, from one point to another, or should everything be drawn in reference to some central point?). Ryan's solution to these issues is displayed in Fig. 5.2b. Note that the revised map (the fourth in a series) is much less like a drawing and includes conventions for measuring distance, direction, and scale. The revised map also suggests an emerging understanding of how ideas like distance and direction can be put to use to develop a (polar) coordinate system to represent a large-scale space.

Summary

Experiences of walking and drawing served as the starting points for developing mathematical descriptions of position, direction and distance. Finding their way from one location to another, children learned to measure distance and direction and to describe routes as sequences of these measures. Rerepresenting routes by animating the motion of Logo's turtle helped children articulate and reflect on their emerging understandings of distance, direction, and measure. These understandings were put to use constructing maps of spaces like classrooms and playgrounds. Mapping space facilitated the development of understanding of (polar) coordinate systems (e.g., Ryan's revised map) and, thus, the development of new views of the spaces in everyday experience.

FROM DRAWING TO DIAGRAMS

Nearly every attempt to develop understanding about space involves spontaneous invention and use of inscriptions (writings). Children's initial inscriptions are usually guided by their rich history of drawing and by their efforts to represent literally what they see. In classrooms that promote understanding, drawings (although often interesting in their own right) can be transformed into representations (i.e., diagrams and related notational systems) that select and amplify mathematically interesting elements of space. For example, recall the decisions about selection and means of representation evident in the transition from Ryan's first to final maps of the playground evident in Fig. 5.2. The map changed in more than appearance. Eventually, it served as a means of making the playground into an object that Ryan could carry about and consider in its own right. Inscribing the space as a map created a world in which it became meaningful to consider previously perceived but unexamined ideas about location, distance, direction, scale, and the means for symbolizing them.

Developing understanding often means creating inscriptions of space, like those developed by Ryan, that enhance mathematically important information and discard mathematically irrelevant features. For example, Fig. 5.3 displays transitions in Melissa's net (a 2-dimensional depiction that folds to form the 3-dimensional shape) of a cereal box. Note the interaction between what this first-grader saw and what she inscribed. Mathematically important qualities of the shape, like the number of faces or the congruence of faces, became increasingly salient as Melissa tried to understand why initial nets, when folded, failed to form the cereal box. Less mathematically relevant features, like the brand name of the cereal, dropped from consideration.

Working with inscriptions, not just with objects in the world, plays an important role in developing understanding. Consider, for example, the nets of a cube created by another first-grade student, Crystal, whose work is displayed in Fig. 5.4. By carefully considering why some of these nets worked yet others did not, Crystal and her classmates began to understand how edges in solids are formed and how solids can be described as combinations of faces (sides), vertices (corners), and edges.

Although the use of inscriptions like nets have a serious purpose, their implementation in the classroom is often whimsical. Children in Angie Putz's first-grade class designed nets for a major class construction project: making solids to represent Whoville (Dr. Seuss). Sean, a first-grade boy, developed the net displayed in Fig. 5.5 for his Super Soccer Tee, a building in Whoville. The net was constructed with Polydrons (rightmost portion of the figure), useful tools for generating and testing different representations of 3-dimensional structure. Although the context was one of fantasy and play, the resulting solid is one of the five Platonic solids.

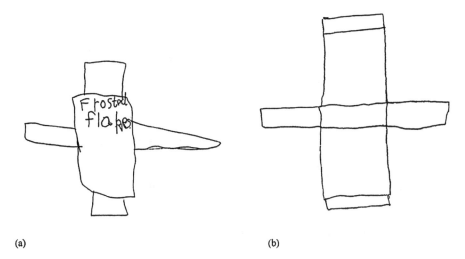

(a)   (b)

FIG. 5.3. Melissa's (a) initial and (b) revised representations of a cereal box (first grade).

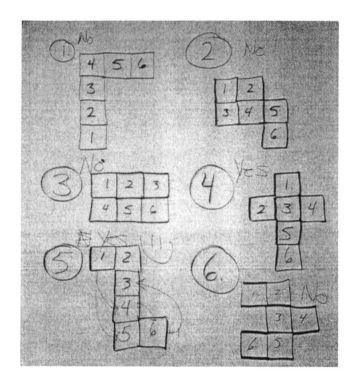

FIG. 5.4. Crystal's nets of a cube (first grade).

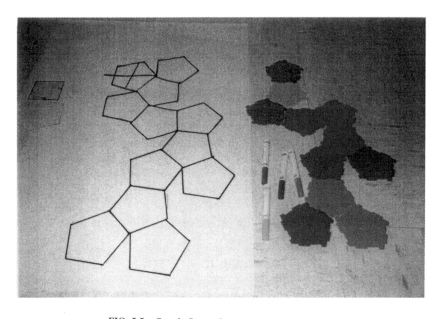

FIG. 5.5. Sean's Super Soccer Tee (first grade).

Spatial inscriptions play an important role in other contexts as well. In Ms. Clement's second-grade classroom, children read a story depicting different places to live (urban, rural). When asked about their preferred place to live, most children elected the wide country, perhaps reflecting the somewhat rural character of their Midwestern school. Ms. Clement placed two titles on the tag board (Tall City, Wide Country) in the front of the classroom, and children indicated their preferences by placing a learning link (a metallic paper clip) under the appropriate title. The result was a literal implementation of a bar graph. However, when children in this class were asked to use this information to make a graph, a variety of forms of inscription emerged. Some children drew a picture of the physical array and added numbers for ease of counting. However, the correspondence between the numbers displayed and the count of objects was not always one to one. Other children considered the possibility that the count of preferences could be represented nonliterally by rectangular partitions, although again the correspondence between quantity and partitions was not always clear (see Fig. 5.6a, b). Some children even suggested that the orientation of the axes need not reflect the original implementation with learning links but could be changed (see Fig. 5.6c). These children constructed bar charts that appeared more conventional but the rationale for use of rectangles of identical dimension was not immediately apparent. By asking children to create their own graphs, Ms. Clement was able to see how they were thinking about the use of space and number to communicate information. Yet earlier use of prefabricated graphs had given little hint of the range and diversity of children's thought about graphical notations.

Summary

Mathematical inscriptions seem to flow easily from children's drawings and other efforts to render the world visible. Because inscribing space is a means for lifting out, selecting, and preserving mathematically important ideas, children's inscriptions of space and form provide opportunity to develop understanding. Rather than working solely in the real world, students reason in and explore the worlds described by their initial and revised inscriptions. By developing relationships between objects in the world and rendering those relationships in mathematical inscriptions, children integrate mathematics with experience and enhance their understandings of both.

FROM PERCEPTION TO CONCEPTION OF FORM

Shapes are visual patterns, evident in both the natural (e.g., snowflakes and honeycombs) and the designed (e.g., buildings and boats) worlds. Understanding the mathematics of shape involves understanding ideas like

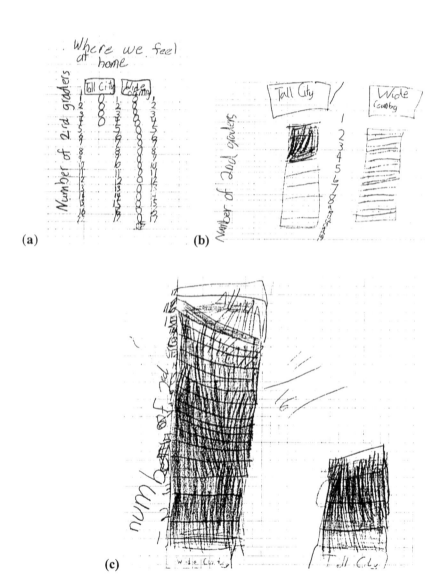

FIG. 5.6. Student solutions to representing classmates' preferences for places to live (second grade). (a) Picture-like representation. (b) The use of rectangular partitions to represent amount. (c) Reorientation of the axes so that quantity corresponds to height.

similarity, symmetry, and scale, and involves mathematical activities like identification, classification, and transformation. Many of these ideas are first understood informally through perception of shape and form. For example, infants perceive distinctions related to contour and symmetry, and young children anticipate mathematical similarity during pretend play with miniature objects or by building scale models. In the classrooms, teachers with whom we collaborated built on this informal knowledge to develop a mathematics of shape and form.

Teachers invoked children's informal knowledge in many different ways. Some teachers employed perspective drawing, whereas others engaged children in design problems ranging from packages to quilts. Classification problems involving polygons like triangles and quadrilaterals or those involving 3-dimensional solids were frequently employed by teachers to promote children's explorations of properties of shape and form. Here we illustrate one such exploration of shape and form in the second grade. We focus on initial classroom conversations about classifying triangles and the ways these conversations provided grounds for seeing triangles in a new light: as mathematical objects rather than as objects in the world.

The purpose of talking about triangles in this second-grade classroom went far beyond simply teaching children how to recognize them. In fact, most children had been introduced to shapes like squares, rectangles, and triangles well before the second grade and showed no difficulty in telling them apart, in much the same way that they could differentiate a chair from a table or an automobile from a plane. The purpose of the classroom conversation summarized here was to introduce children to the rudiments of taking an informal, everyday shape and changing it into a more formal, mathematical one.

Reframing Everyday Definitions

When the second-grade teacher, Carmen Curtis, posed the task, "What does a shape need to be a triangle?" the children in her classroom easily came up with three sides and three corners. This simple everyday definition started turning into a mathematical definition in two ways. First, Ms. Curtis started a running list of rules for triangles by writing the agreed-on rules (3 sides, 3 corners) on the blackboard. Her actions served as a way of reframing the task. Instead of an exercise in memorization and recall, children were involved in the creation of a definition. Private ideas, identified with children's names, occupied the side board. Consensual ideas, not identified with any particular child but accepted because of adequate justification (or taken as obvious), were displayed in the rule list on the front board. This use of the boards marked a transition from personal, informal knowledge to less personal and more formal (because justified) knowledge.

The second means of transforming intuitions about triangles into mathematics was to provide a context wherein children would come to question
their intuitive knowledge. Every child thought that triangles would be easy
to categorize and were surprised to find that classmates did not readily
agree with the classifications he or she proposed. Ms. Curtis made children's disagreements more readily apparent by presenting them with potential candidates to be included in or excluded from the class of triangles
(see Fig. 5.7). She knew that the triangles the children were most likely
to have encountered earlier were equilateral or isosceles triangles, so she
included these types of triangles among the candidates. Her candidates
for triangles, however, also included nonprototypical or unusual triangles,
as well as nontriangles (by Euclidean convention) featuring curved lines
or curved corners. She also presented a triangle oriented in an unusual
position; that is, pointing downward. This set of items provided opportunity
for a conversation through which the children were made aware that mathe-

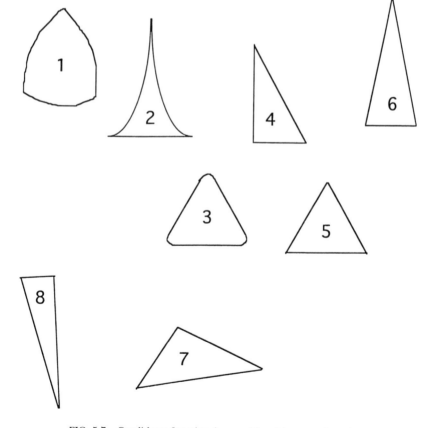

FIG. 5.7. Candidates for triangles considered by second graders.

matical definitions have to provide unambiguous criteria for deciding if an object fits or not.

Reconsidering Resemblance

The children's first inclination was to select prototypical (equilateral triangles or isosceles triangles with sides no longer than more than twice the length of the base) in the common pointing upwards orientation (having the base parallel to the lower edge of the paper and the opposite vertex above the base). This selection was based on unstated, implicit views held by students about the relative lengths of the sides and orientation of prototypical triangles. Ms. Curtis made these implicit views more explicit by asking if each should be part of the definition. Note how children were made to reflect on their implicit views:

Ms. Curtis:	Could that possibly be a rule for triangles? All the sides of a triangle have to be the same length.
Children:	No, yes, no . . .
Beth:	Only the diagonal sides.
Ms. Curtis:	You think the diagonal sides have to be the same length?
Beth:	Yeah.
Ms. Curtis:	So do two sides of a triangle have to match? Have equal length?
Beth:	The ones on the side.
Ms. Curtis:	Beth thinks maybe they do. OK. So this is a question. So far our questions are: Can the sides be curved? [Ms. Curtis writes the questions in capitals on the blackboard as she summarizes the preceding conversation.] Beth thinks they can't. She is saying we should make that part of our rule that they can't be curved. Another question we are coming up with [writes on the board in capitals]: Do two sides have to be equal? And the sides that have to be equal, Beth is saying, are [writes on the board in capitals]: the diagonal ones.

As the children reflected on their ideas about triangles, they moved beyond reasoning based on resemblance to already known prototypes to reasoning about properties that characterize a class of objects. Ms. Curtis then went on to promote efficient and unambiguous use of language:

Ms. Curtis:	Beth, can you come up to one of these triangles and show us what you mean when you say the diagonal sides? [Beth

	goes to the board and points at shape 5, an equilateral triangle.]
Ms. Curtis:	OK, touch the sides you are calling the diagonal sides. [Beth touches the two slanted sides.]
Ms. Curtis:	OK, then what are you calling the other side?
Beth:	This one? That is the bottom.
Ms. Curtis:	Our rules for triangles say that a triangle needs three sides. So, I would say, side, side, side [marking each of the sides].
Beth:	But this is the bottom of the triangle [pointing at the bottom of the triangle].
Ms. Curtis:	But why is it the bottom? Why does it get a special name? Why can't it be side, side, side?
Beth:	These two are the sides [pointing at the two slanted sides] because this one is laying flat [pointing at the bottom] but these ones are going up [gestures, showing how the sides slant].

Beth focused on mathematically irrelevant (for purposes of the ongoing definition) surface features like diagonal and bottom. Ms. Curtis attempted to help her (and the class) move in the direction of listing properties conventionally relevant for defining the figure as a triangle. Ms. Curtis proposed that because the sides of the equilateral triangle were congruent, the sides each played the same role so there was no reason to differentiate two of them by separate names (i.e., diagonal, bottom). Ms. Curtis assumed that this common name, side, would focus children's attention on the sides of the figures rather than on their orientation.

Beth, however, was not ready to abandon referencing the sides of a triangle with respect to its orientation. Ms. Curtis decided to focus attention on an isosceles triangle (shape 6), where at least one pair of sides could be differentiated without recourse to orientation:

Ms. Curtis:	What about number 6? [an isosceles triangle, with sides being considerably longer than the bottom]
Beth:	This one isn't a triangle. Because these things [pointing at the long sides] are going way up high, and they have to be kind of smaller.
Ms. Curtis:	So, triangles can't go way up high?
Beth:	They can.
Ms. Curtis:	They can? Then why can't [shape] 6 be a triangle?
Beth:	It can.
Ms. Curtis:	It can? I thought you said it was not a triangle.

[Beth appears perplexed.]

Ms. Curtis:	OK, so [shape] 6 is one you are not really sure about?
Beth:	Yes.
Ms. Curtis:	And one thing you are not sure about is that it goes way up high. Is there anything else about [shape] 6 that makes you not quite sure it is a triangle?
Beth:	No.
Ms. Curtis:	No, that's the only thing you think—that it maybe goes too high?

At this point the conversation seemed to have arrived at an impasse. Beth held a clear point of view (that of prototype-based classification) and did not find the evidence compelling enough to change. Ms. Curtis invited the class into the conversation, perhaps hoping other students would offer competing, and perhaps more conventional, views. What she got was another prototype-based answer:

Ms. Curtis:	[turning to the class] Can anyone help Beth with this idea? She is wondering: Can triangles go way up high? Or do they have to be like number 5? What would you tell her, Allie?
Allie:	That number 6 is too thin.
Ms. Curtis:	Too thin? Oh, so triangles can't go way up too high, and they can't get too thin?
Beth:	Triangles have to be a little fatter up to the side.
Ms. Curtis:	A little fatter up to the side? Well, [shape] 6 is fatter here [pointing close to the bottom] than here [pointing close to the opposite vertex].

This part of the conversation concluded with Ms. Curtis drawing two shorter sides inside shape 6 to form a more-familiar isosceles triangle. Engaging Beth, Ms. Curtis asked if the modifications had transformed shape 6 into a triangle. Beth readily agreed. Later in the discussion, the issue of orientation resurfaced. One student, Jackson, indicated that he was willing to accept shapes as triangles, but only if they looked the same, regardless of the side placed on the bottom (a requirement of rotational symmetry about the vertices). This constraint meant that Jackson would only accept equilateral triangles as triangles:

Jackson:	[A triangle] has to be able to go on every side [indicating turning motion with his hand], so how it is with number 5? It is supposed to be able to go on every side.

Ms. Curtis: So that any side can be the bottom?

Jackson: Yes, on [shapes] 6 and 8, not any side can be the bottom. Just one side can be the bottom. So if you turn it this way [shows a quarter turn] then it is not a triangle.

Ms. Curtis: Why?

Jackson: Because you can't turn it any way, because it only has *one specifical bottom* [student's emphasis].

Ms. Curtis: Then there has to be a rule of what can be the bottom of a triangle and what can't?

Jackson: All sides can be the bottom.

Ms. Curtis: All sides can be the bottom. So, this could be a bottom for [shape] 6, this could be a bottom for 6, and this could be a bottom for 6. [Ms. Curtis chalks over each side of the original shape 6, the long-sided isosceles triangle.]

Children: Yes. . . . No. . . . Yes. . . . No.

Later Ms. Curtis asked Jackson to show which sides of (the original) shape 6 could and could not be a bottom. He pointed at the noncongruent side as the only one that could be the bottom. His reasoning was that this triangle had one short and two "super long" sides. This discussion led to the posing of a third question about triangles: "Can a triangle have sides that are all different?"

Note how Ms. Curtis helped Jackson articulate and reflect on the consequences of his assertions. She helped Jackson establish a mathematical voice by restating his point of view (making it more explicit) and by offering it to the class for further discussion. Her instruction was guided by the awareness of the important conceptual leap that the children had to make from prototype- and appearance-based reasoning about shapes to reasoning based on classes defined by a set of properties. She was convinced that her instructional time was well spent by letting the children explore the demarcation line between these two conceptual phases (prototypes and properties). She refused to make the step toward property-based reasoning for them. Letting children explore their individual conceptions made the surfacing of unconventional ideas about classifying triangles unavoidable. However, Ms. Curtis put these to good use by letting children express their ideas about special sides (e.g., "specific bottoms") and canonical orientations so that their implications for classification could be drawn out and examined. So, while children were exploring properties of triangles, they were also learning about their consequences. Moreover, children were placed in the role of generating and testing the utility of a mathematical definition. Another consequence of her focus on the children's conceptual development was that Ms. Curtis did not feel the need for the day-by-day closure of a particular subject matter. In this case, she was comfortable with leaving many of the issues about triangles unresolved and going on to another task the following day, when students generated triangles with strips of construction paper.

Constructing Triangles

The construction task was inspired by the children's talk about the defining properties of a triangle. Ms. Curtis hoped that children would put their emerging ideas about properties to use in a way that would be visible both to the constructor and to his or her classmates. Students selected paper strips of different lengths to construct a triangle. Some chose paper strips equal in length; others selected strips of different length. They rotated the constructed triangles to various orientations and talked about whether these changes in orientation affected the characterization of these shapes as triangles. Class conversation veered from students' perceptions of these manipulable objects (the constructed triangles) to what they had earlier listed as properties of triangles (three sides and three corners).

One child, Sadie, constructed a triangle with two strips of equal length: She first formed a right angle and then attached a third strip of paper that was so long that it had to bend and curve to close the figure. She proclaimed that her construction was a triangle. Ms. Curtis and her class-mates attempted to dissuade her: "Have you ever seen a triangle like that?" She replied: "No, but it doesn't matter. Look [gesturing to the board], it has three corners [gesturing to each vertex] and three sides [gesturing to each strip of paper]." Although her construction violated conventional Euclidean definition, it demonstrated an appreciation of viewing figures through the lens of properties rather than as prototypes, and it represented the first steps toward a powerful form of mathematical argument (axiom-based reasoning).

Nevertheless, as children reflected on what they had learned, they were still divided on the central issue: What's a triangle? Most were willing to concede that rotations did not seem to change anything, so orientation was no longer considered. Features of triangles that they had talked about were invariant to turning. However, issues of the length of sides and whether or not all sides must be straight remained points of contention. Most of the remaining issues were, in fact, points of convention, but in our view, the important achievement was that children had participated in conversations that would allow them to develop understanding of the virtues of property-based classifications of shape. The trajectory of the classroom conversation provided a means for transforming children's natural language about shapes to a mathematical language of property and assumption.

Throughout the remainder of the school year, children in this classroom had many further opportunities to reflect about triangles. They used triangles in tasks such as drawing nets, building quilts, and constructing solids from Polydron™ pieces. Spirited discussions arose about what properties of triangles were responsible for compositions of triangles resulting in squares, rectangles, and other quadrilaterals. Conversations about the properties of triangles were sprinkled liberally throughout these tasks, and by the end of the year the children were comfortable using properties to distinguish between triangles and other polygons, as well as to differentiate among kinds of triangles.

Summary

When these children first began thinking about familiar shapes, triangles, they treated them like objects in the world. Triangles were equilateral triangles aligned horizontally on a page or other surface, and the likelihood that a shape would be classified as a triangle was related to its correspondence to this prototypic image. Children were surprised, however, to discover that they did not all classify the same shapes as triangles. Contested claims about real triangles were adjudicated by recourse to rules. Rules converted descriptors expressed in natural language (e.g., three corners) into properties that constituted a mathematical definition. Ms. Curtis encouraged children to generate potential rules (properties) and then explore the consequences of these properties for classifying the forms displayed in Fig. 5.7. In addition to developing and exploring properties of triangles, children began to understand definition as a way of making mathematical objects. Recall, for example, Sadie's insistence that her paper-strip construction was a triangle because it was consistent with the class definition (the collection of rules), even if her classmates (and her teacher) found her construction unappealing. Collectively, these classroom episodes suggest a work in progress, not an accomplished exposition of a definition of triangle. Nevertheless, children had the opportunity to consider shapes as bearers of properties and definitions as ways of thinking about the essence of what they perceived in a manner that could be shared by all.

FROM COUNTS TO MEASURES

Measure integrates the mathematics of quantity with the mathematics of space and so provides a ready means of developing increased understanding of geometry and space. The classroom example here illustrates the progressive nature of understanding and the ways teaching about measure coordinates spatial and numeric sense-making. Ms. Curtis was guided by her knowledge of the ways children think about measure and built on children's notions of counting, as well as their expectations about measuring tools like rulers, as she designed a spiral of tasks intended to clarify important ideas about length measure through the development of understanding rather than through the mastery of skills alone.

When designing tasks that promoted young children's understanding of length measure, Ms. Curtis found it helpful to consider the conceptual landmarks about measure that are embedded in the design of a tool like a ruler. Rulers are designed with units of length arranged sequentially and labeled numerically such that distance between the zero point (the origin of the measure) and some other point on the ruler is easily read off as a cumulative quantity of standard units of distance (e.g., 10 cm). Unfortunately, much of the mathematical work involved in designing the ruler is transparent to users. In other words, users of rulers are expected to understand a series of design decisions about length: The units on the ruler are identical and conventional, partitions of units are marked for continuous measure (e.g., 3⅜ cm.), and the number read off is an interval of distance, which is arrived at by iterating units. The latter suggests that the origin of measure is arbitrary (e.g., 0 or 10 can each serve as the origin: The distance between 0 and 10 is the same as that between 10 and 20). Collectively, these taken-for-granted understandings constitute an informal theory of length measure.

Young children, however, often do not understand these assumptions. They (e.g., first and second graders) often engage in practices that we refer to as ruler fetish. For example, if no ruler is available, first-grade children often simply draw something that looks like one, label the ruler arbitrarily with numbers, and then, as they measure, read off one of these numbers as a valid measure. Given a ruler with inches on one side and centimeters on the other, second-grade children often solve the problem of finding the length of an object longer than the ruler by combining inches and centimeters. Some of the same tendencies, although masked by greater proficiency using rulers, are also demonstrated by older students (e.g., third, fourth, and fifth graders) whenever less-conventional problems are posed (e.g., starting the measure of length at a number other than zero). Observations like these have convinced us of the importance of helping children understand length measure, not just gain simple proficiency using rulers to find length.

What Is Measure?

Ms. Curtis began the first lesson soliciting children's tacit knowledge about measure: "What is measure?" Children's responses were highly variable, ranging from measuring the power of a nuclear generator to finding the height of a person. After establishing that many different aspects of the world could be measured, Ms. Curtis pressed students to think about conceptions of measure. Most children simply noted that they had used rulers but were uncertain about what they might do without them. Ms. Curtis began to convert children's informal knowledge to mathematical knowledge by soliciting children's ideas about the meaning of measure:

> Ms. Curtis: Forget inch. Forget yard. Forget ruler . . . Those are tools. But are they what measurement is? What does it mean to measure? What are the *rules* for measuring?
>
> Abby: Use numbers.
>
> Nicole: Keep track of numbers.

Although students knew that measurement had something to do with numbers, they were uncertain about what role the numbers played. Using a bookshelf as a prop, Ms. Curtis focused attention on "what we know" by asking children how they might measure the length of the bookshelf if they used their feet. She demonstrated by walking along the bookshelf with variable paces, counting: "1 [a longer pace], 2 [a shorter pace], 3 [a longer pace] . . ." Introducing a body-centered sense of length measurement—pacing—bridged action in the world to measurement of that action (see also the previous section on wayfinding). By violating tacitly held ideas about uniform units of measure, Ms. Curtis set the stage for children to generate more explicit expressions of measuring length.

Children immediately objected to her pacing. One child, Jack, suggested that the paces were "Uneven, so you can't just count them. They're long, short." Galena concurred. Ms. Curtis noted that she did the same thing again and again, so perhaps her procedure was useful. Daniel said: "No. Inches are all the same size. Use your feet." He got up and paced foot-to-foot the length of the bookshelf, explaining that his procedure worked because "both feet are the same size. It's not as if one foot is this long [gesturing with hands to indicate approximately 3 feet] and the other is shorter [gesturing with hands to indicate approximately 1 foot]." After listening to Daniel and experimenting with foot-to-foot pacing, the class decided to augment their rules for measure: "You do the same size, over and over again."

Although children were unanimous in their agreement about the need for identical units (same size), Ms. Curtis recognized that the nature of the iteration of units (over and over again) had not been carefully examined. Although children appeared to be accumulating a quantity of units (footsteps) to measure the length of the bookshelf, the procedure of placing one foot directly after the other made the idea of tiling (filling the distance with units) transparent. Because the concatenation of units, not their total number, measures a distance, units must tile the object being measured. To make this aspect of length measure more problematic, Ms. Curtis switched to using science books (handily retrieved from the bookshelf) as a unit of measure and filled the distance with these texts, albeit incompletely: She deliberately left gaps or cracks between textbooks, and the lengths of these gaps were not uniform. In previous years, we had noted that many children who use units of length (e.g., Unifix cubes, sticks, etc.) often do not consider the cracks between them when measuring. This suggests that some children think of number as a marker of the unit used (e.g., the seventh unit) but not as an indicator of the quantity of units needed to tile the distance traversed.

Ms. Curtis, referring to the rules for measurement counted the number of textbooks, noting that she was "keeping real careful track" (meaning that she was establishing one-to-one correspondence between each number and each textbook, as in "the seventh textbook") and that "each one [textbook] is the same size." Some children were convinced that the measure, 11 science books long, was indeed valid, but as Ms. Curtis had hoped, most were not. Daniel again was particularly vehement, insisting that the science books "need to touch" because otherwise it would be impossible to tell "how much is here [gesturing toward one of the gaps]." After further exploration, two students who were initially convinced that 11 textbooks was a valid measure found Daniel's argument compelling. However, they also noted another problem raised by tiling with the textbooks: "There are not enough science books!" The two children who noticed this were stymied.

Another child, Anna, suggested:

> You keep the 11 [referring to the 11 textbooks, now pushed together and aligned at one end of the bookshelf]. Then you keep track of that 11 in your mind and mark it [demonstrating with her finger]. Then you get the textbooks from the beginning and use them, starting here [gesturing toward the end of 11th textbook]. But it's not one. It's 12, then 13 . . .

Anna's understanding of iteration helped the other two children see that units, even if fixed in a ruler or aligned on the classroom floor, are mobile and exchangeable. Iterating units in this case meant that the same science book that was used once in filling a linear distance could be used any number of times, a conceptual leap that originally eluded the two boys measuring with the textbooks.

Once the children's sense of over and over again had expanded, another problem arose: "What do we do with the little space that's left?" (The distance could not be covered in integer units of science texts.) Children decided that they would have to account for part of the science textbook, but the class ended without resolving this issue.

Personal Units: Parts and Wholes

During the next lesson, Ms. Curtis provided each child with several strips of colored paper, each of the same length. Each child's units were called by her or his name, and children used these units to measure the length of a variety of objects in the classroom. During this activity, children revisited ideas of iteration, identical units, and tiling, but because these were now part of the consensual rules for measuring, most of the time was devoted to the problem of measuring with parts of units. This problem arose because Ms. Curtis made sure that not every object could be measured in integers of personal units.

The problem of measuring with parts of units created other opportunities to learn. Children had to decide how to partition each unit and how to represent each partition. Most children split a strip into two to create halves, then again, to create quarters, and then, eighths. Repeated splitting elaborated their sense of fractions. For example, Andy noted: "$\frac{1}{4}$ is $\frac{1}{2}$ [folding original strip in half] of $\frac{1}{2}$." Andy then repeated the action, folding the two halves in half, then unfolding to show four equal partitions and gesturing at one fourth.

Although partitioning units helped students measure lengths less than one unit, it also raised another conceptual hurdle, that of the zero point, or origin, of the measure scale. Many children who measured an object $2\frac{1}{2}$ units long often reported the result as $3\frac{1}{2}$. Their reasoning was that the 3 marked the third unit of measure, and they also recognized that they were using $\frac{1}{2}$ of the whole unit. So they summarized both of these ideas as the number, $3\frac{1}{2}$. Questions that focused children's attention on the relationship between the starting point of measure and the endpoint, rather than on either point alone, helped children reconsider the number of units as a quantity indicating the distance of the interval, rather than as a count relating to the ordinal position of the unit.

Personal Tape Measure: Inscribing Units

Up to this point, children had used physical instantiations of a variety of units (their feet, science books, strips of paper) to measure the length of objects in their classroom. To further refine their understanding of core conceptual issues, such as iteration, unit, origin, and part–whole relations, Ms. Curtis had children construct personal tape measures, using their personal units of measure and marking the tapes in whatever way they found most useful. This task helped children develop inscriptions for measuring length, an instructional task that focused attention on the rules of measurement and the implications of those rules for constructing a measuring tool. Many children glued their personal units to a strip of machine tape, using partitions of some of the units to distinguish halves, fourths, and (for some children) eighths. Constructing these tape measures helped children see "what the marks are good for" on standard rulers. Other children simply used their units as measuring tools to indicate lengths on the strips of paper, skipping the intermediate step of gluing the units to the tape. For these children, the act of measuring became symbolic: The accumulation of these marks replaced the physical act of iterating literal units. The process of creating a tape measure engaged children in the design of the very tool that they initially had found transparent, thus providing them an opportunity to understand the functions of this tool.

Design of the tape measures set the stage for additional considerations, like the value of standard units. Ms. Curtis raised the issue of how the class might reconcile their different, yet valid, measures of the same object or what might happen if, using personal units, they ordered windows from the local lumberyard, which relied on feet and inches. Children seemed to appreciate the role of standard units from this functional perspective. As Nancy put it, a carpenter could use "Carmens" (the personal unit of Ms. Curtis) to cut the lumber, if Ms. Curtis provided the carpenter her tape measure. Nancy went on to note: "But then the carpenter might have to order the glass for the window from somebody else, and what will that person think of "48 Carmens wide"? Amid much laughter, children decided that perhaps it would be best if people all agreed on a standard unit of length, no matter how arbitrary such decisions might be.

Relative Lengths

In a culminating task about length measure, children saw a photo of the skeletons of two fossilized fish, one of which had consumed the other. Ms. Curtis told the children the length of the larger fish was 14 feet, then asked them to find the (approximate) length of the smaller one. This task focused on length measure to find the relationship between two objects, rather than simply measuring each. Moreover, the task required children to represent the relationship between the lengths of the fish in the photo and their respective lengths in the real world.

Sara began the estimation by "using my eyes," guessing that if both fish could be uncurled and compared side by side, the smaller fish would be about 5 feet long. Another child tested Sara's idea by using her fingers to mark the beginning and ending points of the smaller fish and then estimated the number of times the smaller fish "fit into" the larger fish. Finding that this multiple was greater than three, she proposed that the smaller fish could not be 3 feet because "five and five and five is 15 and that's more than 14." This strategy of using the smaller fish as a unit of measure for the length of the larger fish and finding the scalar multiple was adopted throughout the lesson by the children. For Ms. Curtis, the lesson provided children with opportunities to engage in mental math, making conjectures about the possible length of the smaller fish and then finding a way to reason about scalar multiples to test their conjectures.

For example, in response to a rejection of a proposal of 2 feet (Nancy noted that "It can't be two because that would mean that seven of this one, the smaller fish, could fit into the big one"), Ms. Curtis asked: "What would be true if the fish was four feet?" Hands immediately shot into the air. Kristin proposed partitioning the smaller fish into one fourth ("a half of a half"). Then, she proposed that "if the smaller fish really is 4 feet, 14 of the $\frac{1}{4}$s should fit the larger fish." Using her fingers to maintain a constant interval, she demonstrated her procedure to the class. Her classmates agreed with her logic but doubted that the unit created with her fingers was uniform ("Your fingers keep on moving!"). Another classmate, Jack, proposed that if the smaller fish were 4 feet, "then there should be exactly three smaller fish in the larger one." Using his fingers, verified by similar procedures enacted by classmates, he found that there were more than three smaller fish in the larger one. Thus, the class concluded that the length of the smaller fish had to be more than four feet but less than five. These and related conjectures all took children's ideas about length measure far from their origins in walking and laying books end to end. They demonstrate that by the end of the spiral of lessons, the children's understanding of length measure had undergone a significant transformation: What had previously been understood physically through enacting was now understood symbolically as well, so that children could work with their developed symbols and inscriptions to reason about length measure.

Summary

The sequence of tasks invented by Ms. Curtis helped children progressively elaborate and mathematize their informal knowledge about length and its measure and provided students forums for the invention of systems of notation. Working from children's general conceptions of measure, Ms. Curtis guided children toward making explicit the core concepts previously embedded in their activities. Her tasks highlighted different aspects of measure, like unit or iteration, and provided opportunities for children to coordinate their emerging understandings of measure into a mathematical model. In the last task (involving the relative lengths of the fossil fish), the mathematical model was used as a cognitive tool for comparing lengths of photographed objects.

Through these tasks, understandings first rooted in activity and perception were lifted out and mathematized primarily through the inscription of units (e.g., the construction of the tape measure) and the explicit representation of rules for measuring. In Ms. Curtis' classroom, children, rather than simply becoming proficient with rulers, developed theories of length measure that featured important mathematical ideas, like iteration of identical units, zero point (origin), and partitions of units.

Collectively, these children's engagement with problems in length measure illustrates understandings that started with children's intuitions and built successively on the history of activity and of inscriptions invented as they solved problems. The tasks developed by Ms. Curtis provided sufficient structure and constraint for coordinating students' experiences in the world with mathematical representations of these experiences. Guided by her knowledge of likely trajectories of student thinking, she also reacted productively to further opportunities to develop understanding as they arose during classroom activity, even when these opportunities were not originally planned.

CONCLUDING COMMENTS

We have embarked on a program to redesign geometry education in the primary grades so that young children have the opportunity to develop a mathematics of space even as they are developing a mathematics of number. Including the mathematics of space and geometry early in schooling and maintaining it at the center of teaching and learning mathematics are critical for developing understanding of mathematics. Much like the case of algebra (see Kaput, chapter 8, this volume), forms of instruction that ignore the role of geometry (until a concentrated dose is administered at the secondary level) are apt to be lethal to the prospects of developing mathematical understanding for all. Such an approach favors analysis at the expense of space and geometry, with little apparent justification other than (comparatively recent) tradition.

Children's everyday experiences of space provide fertile grounds for developing mathematics. Understanding space, however, is not simply a matter of building on children's intuitions, just as building a structure is not simply a matter of accumulating sufficient material. Teachers in these classrooms assisted children in a number of ways. They encouraged children to invent their own ways of representing what they saw. These representations were not merely displays but were tools for developing understanding. Consider how children used net representations to better comprehend aspects of 3-dimensional structure, developed a conceptual foundation for measure by inscribing length in several ways, and drew maps modeling position and direction in both large- and small-scale spaces.

Teachers also orchestrated classroom conversation. Although talk and the mathematics of space may seem unrelated, in these classrooms talking about objects and forms and the space in which they resided helped children develop a mathematical language that fixed and anchored mathematically important elements of space (e.g., properties of figures). Language was also a tool for transforming what was first known perceptually and shared by common visual regard into mathematical objects that could be transported, shared, and manipulated to "see what happens if." The first steps in this transition often occurred in conversations like the one in this chapter involving triangles, where aspects of figures first known in natural language became fixed and recruited for purposes of mathematical definition.

Because understanding also includes developing a stance toward what we know and how we come to know it, teachers often concluded lessons by asking students to narrate first understandings and their judgments about significant transitions in their learning. For example, talking about nets of solids in the third grade, Adrian recalled: "Last year, we thought we knew all about nets, but, really, we didn't know much about nets." Melissa added: "Like, I did not really think about using a system and now using a system [algorithms the class developed to exhaustively search for all possible nets of a solid] makes it easier to figure out all the ways." Classroom reconstructions like these helped students to develop a sense of the history of their learning and to build identities as mathematical thinkers.

NOTES

1. Logo is a computer programming language for children with a turtle (a screen icon) that encourages a local or intrinsic geometry. For example, children can define a quadrilateral by programming the turtle's movement.

FOR FURTHER READING

Lehrer, R., & Chazan, D. (Eds.). (1998). *Designing learning environments for the development of understanding of geometry and space*. Mahwah, NJ: Lawrence Erlbaum Associates.

Lehrer, R., Randle, L., & Sancillo, L. (1989). Learning pre-proof geometry with Logo. *Cognition and Instruction, 6*, 159–184.

Chapter 6

Promoting Learning in Middle-Grades Mathematics

Judith Sowder
San Diego State University

Randolph Philipp
San Diego State University

The vision we present of classrooms where students learn with understanding requires that teachers understand the mathematics they are teaching and that they understand their students' thinking about that mathematics. For teachers in the middle grades, this means that they themselves must have a deep understanding of a rich, interrelated set of concepts and the ways in which children develop understanding of these concepts. First, students must extend whole-number concepts and reasoning to rational number concepts and reasoning. This extension in turn depends on a deepening understanding of the role of the unit (whole number) and mathematical consequences of partitioning the unit, of the many ways we represent rational numbers, and of the ways these representations are connected and can be used to perform operations on rational numbers. Second, recognition of situations that are multiplicative rather than additive in nature and, therefore, demand a different type of reasoning plays a central role in mathematics at this level. Third, another central but closely related idea is understanding the role of proportionality in many mathematical situations. When teachers understand this complex of concepts and related forms of reasoning, and have had opportunities to form appropriate expectations of students' growth of understanding and reasoning about these ideas, they are able to deal with students' insights and misconceptions, to recognize and seize opportunities for fruitful digressions, and to choose appropriate tasks, tools, and representations for promoting understanding.

When teachers have this knowledge, what happens in their classrooms is often radically different from the mathematics classes most of us experienced in these grades. To demonstrate the effects of teachers' knowledge of mathematics on the development of student understanding of the mathematics, we focus on what happens in middle-grade mathematics classrooms when teachers have reconceptualized the mathematics they teach. The teachers of classes described in the two vignettes were armed with both an understanding of the interrelatedness of the concepts and an understanding of ways to plan and undertake instruction that leads students to develop the concepts and skills needed to progress mathematically.

The school settings for these vignettes are quite disparate, and as a consequence there are many differences that can be noted: The level of the mathematics discussed, the management of the classrooms, and the interactions with the students, among others. But there are also fundamental similarities: (a) students are challenged with pedagogically appropriate mathematical tasks and provided opportunities and encouragement to grapple with them; (b) the classroom climate is nonthreatening and student ideas and methods are respected and valued; and (c) the teachers select the tasks for particular purposes related to the curricular frameworks they develop for their classes. (Note: All names are pseudonyms.)

VIGNETTE 1

Setting and Background

The first vignette took place late in the school year in Ms. A's sixth-grade classroom in a small suburban K through 6 school. In this school, administrative and parental support was provided to all the teachers. The children were from middle-class families, and although there was a sprinkling of minority students, the student population was not diverse. Ms. A had been teaching for about 15 years, and for many of those years she was involved in a variety of professional development activities related to the teaching of mathematics. In the class described in this vignette (typical of the many we observed in Ms. A's classroom), she demonstrated a deep knowledge of the mathematics she taught and built her lessons around the responses of her students and her understanding of what they were capable of achieving. In this vignette, Ms. A was teaching a lesson on division of fractions by whole numbers. She understood division to be an operation appropriately used when a situation involved repeated subtraction (e.g., How many 3s are in 12?) or partitioning and sharing (e.g., If 12 is partitioned into three equal parts, how many are in each part?). In this lesson she had decided to represent division as partitioning and sharing. Ms. A also understood that the fractional representation of a rational number can be thought of as a quotient, that is, it can indicate a division. She knew that recognizing a fraction as a quotient is rarely a focus in the middle grades, but she wanted her students to come to understand this meaning for a fraction. She knew that division of fractions by fractions is a particularly difficult operation for students to understand, and she had decided to approach this topic by considering, first, whole numbers divided by fractions (in an earlier lesson), then fractions divided by whole numbers (this lesson), and, finally, fractions divided by fractions (in a future lesson). In each case, she had students consider problems by relating them to an everyday situation. Students then worked through a sufficient number of problems to generate a pattern, formulate rules based on the pattern, and, finally, test their rules with other problems.

This series of tasks went beyond the more traditional instructional treatment of division with fractions to include situations that allowed students to explore division involving sequentially more difficult problems in both partitioning and repeated-subtraction contexts. The notation involved was particularly interesting because it contained an element of surprise: Because fraction notation for division was used here, complex fractions (i.e., fractions where either the numerator or the denominator or both are fractions) make a natural appearance.

In the previous lesson on whole numbers divided by fractions, Ms. A had used standard division notation, $2 \div \frac{1}{2}$, and used the subtraction notion of division: How many halves are there in 2? On the day previous to the lesson described here, for the last 5 minutes of class, Ms. A had written

$$\frac{\frac{1}{2}}{2}$$

on the board and asked students to write down what they thought it meant. They had never before encountered complex fractions. There was some discussion, and several meanings for the expression were suggested, but no consensus was reached. Ms. A wanted her students to think first about division problems involving fractions without resorting to a rule. The answers suggested by the students (e.g., "It's a fraction: one half over two wholes," "I think it's two and one half," "I think it's a fourth or a half of two," "The ratio of one half to two") indicated that they did not fully understand the concepts involved in the notation Ms. A was introducing. This information guided her focus in the lesson described in the following section.

The Lesson

The portion of the mathematics lesson included here lasted about 25 minutes. Ms. A began the lesson by writing the numbers

$$\frac{3}{1} \quad \frac{2}{1} \quad \frac{1}{1}$$

and asking students to "find a natural number for each of the rational numbers." She then asked: "What's another way to look at each of those rational numbers as an operation?" When some students said, "1 divided by 3" rather than "3 divided by 1," she reminded them of earlier problems. Sharing one cookie among three people was symbolized as $\frac{1}{3}$ or $1 \div 3$, leading students to understand that in this case $\frac{3}{1}$ should, therefore, mean $3 \div 1$. Students were then shown

$$\frac{\frac{1}{2}}{1}$$

and told to use the same logic on this. At this point, the following discussion took place:

Vicki: So it means if you have one cookie and a half a person—no, I mean, if you have half a cookie and one person, how much cookie does the person get? And the person gets it all.

Ms. A: What do you mean by "all"?

Vicki: That the person gets the whole half.

Ms. A: Well then, what is meant by $\frac{1}{2}$ over 2? We're going to keep half a cookie and share it with a greater and greater number of people and see what happens. So what is $\frac{1}{2}$ over 2? [Pause] How much cookie would each person get, Jack?

Jack: One cookie. [Pause] No, two parts of a cookie.

Ms. A: Two parts of a cookie? Does that mean each person gets a half?

Jack: Each person gets a fourth of the cookie.

Ms. A: Good. Now let's try $\frac{1}{2}$ divided by 3.

Karen: It's 6, because the other half would be three pieces too.

Ms. A: Let's make a drawing, like we did with cookies before, to check that out. [She waits to give students a chance to draw, walks around to observe their drawings, then draws the figure shown in Fig. 6.1 on the overhead projector.]

Lisa: One-sixth, 'cause the other half has three pieces too.

Ms. A: The other half could have three pieces too, so six pieces or one-sixth. Each person gets one-sixth of a cookie. Now take the same half and share it with four people. Pretend it's a big cookie, like a pancake.

FIG. 6.1. Illustrating $\frac{1}{2}$ divided by 3.

[The students solve this problem, then are asked to predict $\frac{1}{2}$ divided by 5, by 6, by 7, by 8, and to state some informal rules for what they have done.]

Sheena:	I just did double the number of people.
Robert:	Just add itself to it.
Ms. A:	Anyone else? [Pause] I'm interested in a rule, no matter what the denominator is, what is $\frac{1}{2}$ over N?
Billy Jean:	Double the N.
Ms. A:	So what would I say mathematically to double this?
Sandy:	Multiply by 2!
Ms. A:	So the answer is $2N$? Each person gets $2N$ pieces?
Karen:	No, each person get one two-Nth piece.
Ms. A:	Like this? [Writes

$$\frac{\frac{1}{2}}{N} = \frac{1}{2N}$$

on the board and students all agree with this expression after checking it with their examples.] We've just written an algebraic rule for this sequence. Let's see then what $\frac{1}{2}$ over 100 would be . . .

As the class proceeded, the teacher changed the numerator to $\frac{1}{3}$, and students divided this by 1, by 2, by 3, using cookie drawings as needed, and by N. After generalizing a rule for N for each of these cases, they then formulated the rule:

$$\frac{\frac{1}{K}}{N} = \frac{1}{K} \div N = \frac{1}{KN}$$

They were then given a challenge problem:

Find a rule for $\dfrac{\frac{2}{3}}{N}$

Students worked on this problem until the end of class. Ms. A walked around the class during the entire lesson, noting what students were writing down and drawing and stopping to talk to students when she thought the students were on the wrong track.

Follow-Up

Students had by now divided fractions by whole numbers and whole numbers by fractions. Ms. A told us that she felt that most if not all of her students by this time had a good understanding of what it meant to divide and of writing division in fractional form. They were ready to tackle fractions divided by fractions. After discussing all three cases (i.e., a fraction as divisor, a fraction as dividend, and fractions as both divisor and as dividend), she designed a lesson that would lead them to the generalization that division by a number, whether it is a fraction or a whole number, leads to multiplication by the reciprocal of that number (the reason we invert and multiply to obtain the correct quotient).

DISCUSSION OF THE MATHEMATICS
OF THIS LESSON

This lesson dealt with rational numbers expressed as fractions and with division. Students had learned previously that division could be appropriately used in two kinds of circumstances: situations that involve either fair sharing or repeated subtraction. In the first, something is partitioned and shared. For example, to share candy fairly among friends, they can pass the candies out one at a time to find how many each friend gets. Eventually, children learn that if they divide the number of candies by the number of friends, they will know how many candies each friend receives. This is the most common way of introducing division to children. In the second situation, which does not involve fair sharing, we might want to know, for example, how many of one thing are in another, as when candies are counted out, so many per basket. In this case, we can subtract the number per basket until we can no longer subtract; the number of times we subtracted will tell us how many baskets. In this setting, division is seen as repeated subtraction, just as multiplication can be thought of as repeated addition.

These students had earlier become familiar with these two kinds of division situations with whole numbers. This series of lessons extended the division situations to include fractions. Traditionally, children are taught division of fractions without attention paid to either setting, and they learn the rule that when either number (meaning either the dividend or divisor) is a fraction, the rule is to invert the second number (the divisor) and to multiply. The rule is easy to carry out, but it is not at all easy to understand the rationale behind this rule. Very few teachers can provide an explanation because they have not themselves acquired an understanding of why this rule works: They themselves were probably never taught why, and textbooks traditionally gloss over explanations for this rule. In classrooms such as this one, in which students have come to expect to be able to make sense of the mathematics they are learning, this is a particularly troublesome rule. Students are unable to figure it out on their own. They need a carefully arranged sequence of tasks and assistance in forming the generalizations needed to formulate this seemingly innocuous and handy little rule.

Although either meaning of division could have been used in this lesson, Ms. A chose partitioning and sharing (of parts of cookies) for students to reach the generalization that

$$\frac{\frac{1}{K}}{N} = \frac{1}{KN}$$

(or alternately,

$$\frac{1}{K} \div N = \frac{1}{KN}),$$

where $\frac{1}{K}$ was the part of the cookie to be shared by N people. The previous day, Ms. A had used the repeated-subtraction notion of division to consider whole numbers divided by fractions, so when presented with $3 \div (\frac{1}{2})$, students were asked how many halves there were in three. They found the answer, 6, by continued subtraction of $\frac{1}{2}$ until nothing was left (i.e., $\frac{1}{2}$ was subtracted 6 times). After a series of such problems, with different denominators, a generalization was made:

$$K \div \frac{1}{N} = KN$$

Textbooks also tend to overlook the different meanings a fraction can take. The fraction $\frac{3}{4}$ is commonly used to represent three out of four parts of one whole, and students are rarely provided opportunities to think about other meanings. In this lesson, Ms. A provided students with another meaning for the fraction: a common way of representing division. The problem, "If 2 people share $\frac{1}{2}$ of a cookie, how much does each person get?" can be represented either as

$$\frac{1}{2} \div 2 \text{ or as } \frac{\frac{1}{2}}{2},$$

where the second complex fraction represents the division by 2, also represented in the first notation.

Finally in this lesson, students were confronted with a situation that forced them to think about the referent unit for each number:

What is the referent unit for

$$\frac{\frac{1}{2}}{2} \text{ (i.e., for the quotient } \tfrac{1}{4})?$$

First, we ask: "What is the referent unit for $\frac{1}{2}$?" The answer is the whole cookie—we have $\frac{1}{2}$ of a whole cookie. "What is the referent unit for the 2?" The 2 refers to the number of people, so the referent unit is a person—we have two persons. "And the quotient $\frac{1}{4}$? What is the referent unit for this number?" The cookie again—$\frac{1}{4}$ of a cookie, but this time with reference to the person: $\frac{1}{4}$ *cookie per person*. Whereas the $\frac{1}{2}$ of a cookie is independent of the number of people sharing the cookie, the $\frac{1}{4}$ is arrived at only after considering the number of people who will share the $\frac{1}{2}$ cookie. (Note: Problems that involve cookies per person, or candies per bag, or miles per hour lead to the concept of rate).

Many of the difficulties associated with division stem from a lack of understanding of the referent units for each of the numbers involved. Ms. A's awareness of this difficulty was demonstrated by the manner in which she helped students keep track of the referent unit for each number: "Well then, what is meant by

$$\frac{\frac{1}{2}}{2} ?$$

We're going to keep *half a cookie* and *share it* [between 2 people]. *How much cookie* would *each person get?*" (italics added). The partitioning and sharing meaning of division used here affected the way in which the units could be described. Had Ms. A used the repeated-subtraction meaning for division, the referent units would have looked different. For example, suppose the label on a package says that there are 2 cookies in one serving and that I have 6 cookies. How many servings do I have? Because I can take away 2 cookies 3 times, I have 3 servings. But suppose instead of 6 cookies, I have only $\frac{1}{2}$ cookie to begin with. How much of a serving do I have? Now I am asking, how many 2s are in a $\frac{1}{2}$? This is also expressed as

$$\frac{\frac{1}{2}}{2} \text{ or as } \frac{1}{2} \div 2.$$

The referent unit for $\frac{1}{2}$ is again the whole cookie, the referent unit for 2 is now *cookies in a serving,* and the referent unit for the quotient $\frac{1}{4}$ is not cookies but the part of a total serving of cookies (2) that I have. So I am talking about $\frac{1}{2}$ of 2 cookies, not $\frac{1}{4}$ of 1 cookie: I have $\frac{1}{4}$ of one serving of cookies. The differences in these two situations are subtle, and unless Ms. A fully understood both situations, she would be likely to confuse her students.

MENTAL ACTIVITIES OF STUDENTS

Carpenter and Lehrer (chapter 2, this volume) discussed five forms of mental activity that lead to understanding: constructing relationships, extending and applying mathematical knowledge, reflecting about mathematical experiences, articulating what one knows, and making mathematical knowledge one's own. To show how these mental activities developed within Ms. A's classroom, we first examine the tasks, tools, and normative practices in the classroom and then consider this lesson within the context of the preceding and follow-up lessons, looking specifically at these five forms of activity.

In the Classroom: Tasks, Tools, and Normative Practices

Tasks and Tools. Ms. A clearly selected tasks that would guide classroom discussion over several days and lead finally to the generalized rule for dividing fractions. In this particular case, Ms. A was not guided by the textbook because the textbook tasks, in her mind, would not lead students to understand the rule for dividing fractions. She, therefore, designed and sequenced tasks in a manner that would assist students in constructing their own knowledge of dividing fractions. In addition, she decided to include contexts that embodied both meanings of division and presented tasks that would show how situations both of sharing and subtracting lead to division. Finally, she seized the opportunity to represent division itself through fraction notation as a reminder to students of this interpretation of fractions. This notation was an important tool in this lesson. Writing and drawing were also tools for this lesson; the students wrote and drew during the sequence of tasks presented, and Ms. A wrote and drew on the overhead projector to illustrate and summarize the points being made.

Normative Practices. As noted in chapter 2 by Carpenter and Lehrer, tasks and tools alone do not foster understanding; the normative practices for a particular class determine the types of responses engendered by the tasks and tools. In Ms. A's sixth-grade class, normative practices were well established by the time of this particular observation. Students all knew that the questions they were asked often did not have only one right answer; that they were expected to be able to provide reasons for answers they gave; that they could at any time go to the cupboards and take manipulatives and calculators if those tools would help them in their thinking; that all answers and reasons were to be considered and respected; that they would rarely be told whether they were right or wrong but would instead have to convince themselves and each other through good reasoning; and, finally, that they would be expected to write about the mathematics lesson after class, all in the service of the overriding norm that mathematics was supposed to make sense to them. Many of these practices were illustrated in the vignette.

The Lesson as Part of a Sequence

Constructing Relationships. This lesson was one of a sequence of lessons in which students constructed an understanding of fractions, division, the way division takes place within the realm of fraction numbers, and the way a fraction itself can denote a division of the numerator by the denominator. In each lesson, a situation familiar to the students was used to ground the lesson and make it understandable to the students; students used what they knew from previous lessons to construct an integrated knowledge of division with fraction numbers. As pointed out in chapter 2 by Carpenter and Lehrer, not all relationships are productive. The more traditional linking of division of fractions with multiplication through the inversion of the second number, for example, leads only to a rote rule with no basis for understanding and is, therefore, unproductive.

Extending and Applying Mathematical Knowledge. Ms. A devised the tasks to link and expand students' former knowledge of types of division situations to include situations where fractions described the quantities being considered. Because division of fractions was learned by taking a simple situation, sharing cookies, and formulating more and more complex situations for that sharing, students would be more likely to recognize future sharing situations that called for division of fractions. Skill in dividing in either sort of fraction situation was developed hand in hand with conceptual understanding of fractions and of division. The generated rule incorporated the former rules and would eventually lead to a rule or algorithm that could be used more generally to divide fractions.

Reflecting About Mathematical Experiences. The situations presented to the students required that they reflect on the problem most recently solved and try to extend it to the new situation. Ms. A helped them in this process by reminding them, when necessary, of previous applications. For example, she reminded them at the beginning of the lesson of what it meant to divide one cookie among three people and of the notation used to represent this situation. When a generalization was formed, the students needed to reflect on the rule stated to see if it fit all the situations previously considered. At one stage, their reflection on a problem led them to recognize an error—each person did not get $2N$ cookies, but rather $\frac{1}{(2N)}$ cookies. The students' struggle to find a rule for

$$\frac{\frac{2}{3}}{N}$$

forced them to reflect on what they had done and prepared them to understand the eventual generation of the invert and multiply algorithm.

Articulating What One Knows. Throughout the class period, students were required to articulate their present understandings by answering the questions asked—questions that led students through each change of denominator to an eventual generalization. Students also wrote their thoughts down and drew pictures to help them understand each problem in the sequence of problems presented. While circulating, Ms. A looked at what they were writing and drawing and noted the kinds of errors being made and the extent to which the children were understanding the lesson as it proceeded. Finally, the students were asked to find a rule for

$$\frac{\frac{2}{3}}{N}$$

Their thinking about this problem was first articulated in writing and on the following day was further articulated in discussion.

Making Mathematics Knowledge One's Own. The students all thought through the sequence of problems presented by Ms. A. Her careful questioning led students to provide answers to increasingly complex tasks. The fact that they were all writing down each new problem and trying to represent it with a drawing provided each the opportunity to construct a personal understanding of the generalizations made. For example, all agreed with the generalization that

$$\frac{\frac{1}{2}}{N} = \frac{1}{2N}$$

only after checking this out with their previously worked-out problems. It had taken Ms. A a good part of the school year to reach the point where students had formed the expectation that they could understand the mathematics—that mathematics was not a set of rules to be memorized. This expectation allowed her students to take ownership of the mathematics they were learning because they themselves had made sense of it: They understood it.

VIGNETTE 2

Setting and Background

Mr. K taught fifth grade in an inner-city classroom. He had 32 students, 17 of whom had recently moved to the United States from Mexico, Somalia, Haiti, and Southeast Asian countries and spoke English as a second language; 3 spoke practically no English. Because Mr. K was well liked by students and had excellent classroom management skills, he was given more than the usual number of students who were known to create difficult-to-manage classroom situations (in addition to the challenge presented by the fact that English was often not their first language). Yet there was a good learning climate in his classroom. Whenever possible, students whose English skills were poor were paired with students who spoke the same first language. Many of Mr. K's students had short attention spans; he used whole-class discussions and small-group work to keep students involved and working on the task at hand.

Mr. K was not certain where his students were in terms of their understanding of the mathematical tasks he had selected for this lesson. Mr. K was convinced, however, that, based on what he had learned in seminars associated with a teacher-development project, students in elementary school are provided too few experiences that prepare them to be able to reason multiplicatively and that, as a result, they tend to treat all situations as additive in nature. For example, they will say that a mixture of 2 cups of orange juice and 3 cups of water will taste the same as a mixture of 4 cups of orange juice and 5 cups of water because in each case there is one more cup of water than orange juice. They tend to make an additive comparison (resulting in equal differences of one in each case) rather than a multiplicative comparison (resulting in nonequivalent ratios of $\frac{2}{3}$ and $\frac{4}{5}$).

Mr. K had been thinking about appropriate tasks he could present to his students that would help them to make the transition from reasoning additively to reasoning multiplicatively and to recognize which type of reasoning was appropriate for a particular situation. On the previous day, Mr. K had given this problem to the students:

> Samantha invested $20 in her bank, and 3 months later she received $40 back. Jermaine invested $30 in his bank, and 3 months later he received $55 back. Who got the better deal?

All the students had thought Jermaine had the better deal, either because he received more money in addition to his original investment (an example of additive reasoning) or simply because he had more money at the end of the 3 months. Then one student noticed that Samantha's investment doubled (multiplicative reasoning), whereas Jermaine's did not, and said that Samantha got the better deal. This student explained his reasoning to the class, but the others remained convinced Jermaine received the better deal. Mr. K decided not to pursue the problem further until he had had time to think about it.

The Lesson

In the lesson described here, Mr. K changed the problem task:

	Investment	In Three Months
Jackie's bank	$20	$40
Jolanda's bank	$10	$30

You have $60 to invest. Will you invest it in Jackie's bank, in Jolanda's bank, or does it not make any difference in which bank you invest your money?

After presenting the problem to the class, Mr. K solicited answers from the students:

Lake:	Jackie's bank!
Kali:	Yes, Jackie's bank.
Jessica:	Jackie's bank, 'cause you get $20 more.
Lawrence:	Jolanda's bank. In Jolanda's bank, you get more. If you put two 10 dollars in Jolanda's bank, you get $60, but in Jackie's bank you only get $40.
Mr. K:	I don't think some of the others understood you, Lawrence. Could you make a table for us?

(Note: Lawrence had been in the class for only a few days. He was previously in a special education class. Mr. K thought the previous placement had been because he was considered disruptive rather than because he was slow to learn. He had so far not been disruptive in Mr. K's classroom.

In fact, he had said little up to this time. Mr. K told us later he "grabbed" at this chance to give Lawrence an opportunity to participate in class discussion.)

Lawrence walked to the board and hesitantly listed $20 three times in one column and $40 three times in a second column, then added the $40s to obtain $120. Mr. K helped him by summarizing:

Mr. K: So if you invest three $20 in Jackie's bank, you get $120. Can you do a table for Jolanda's bank?

Lawrence was confused about making a second table, but with assistance listed $10 six times in one column and $30 six times in a second column. He added the six $30s and wrote $180:

Mr. K: So if you invest your $60 in Jolanda's bank, what do you get?
Lawrence: $180.
Mr. K: And so where would you put your money?
Lawrence: In Jolanda's bank.
Mr. K: Lawrence, ask the others if they agree with you.

Some students agreed and some disagreed. Mr. K had them all give Lawrence a "quake" (a recognition of good work by pounding feet on the floor). He then labeled the tables as "Lawrence's solution" and asked the students who disagreed to give their solutions. As was his custom, Mr. K allowed several answers with solutions to be placed before the class before stopping for discussion:

Jermaine: In Jackie's bank you get $180 if you put in $10 a week.
Lake: No. I changed my mind. I agree with Lawrence's answer. The money doubles in Jackie's bank, but it triples in Jolanda's bank.
Sully: Jackie's bank is better, 'cause there's a slow way and a fast way. $20 to $40 is the fast way.

Others chimed in, insisting that it took too long to save in Jolanda's bank, so Jackie's bank was better. Mr. K told them that they could invest as many $10s at a time in Jolanda's bank as they wanted. He then asked them to work in groups to figure out how much they would make if they put $100 in each bank. There was a great deal of animated discussion. Students were very much on task and had strong feelings about their solutions. By the end of class, most students had decided to invest in Jolanda's bank, but four still thought Jackie's bank was better.

Follow-Up

Mr. K realized that some students were beginning to reason multiplicatively in this situation, comparing the ratios involved (2 to 1 versus 3 to 1) rather than the differences involved ($20 in each case). He felt they had made more progress on this problem than they had on the one the previous day. Based on his discussions with them during their group work, he felt that students now all understood that they could put more than $10 at a time in the bank. He was taken by surprise, however, at the number of students who continued to focus on the final amount rather than how that amount related to the initial amount. He decided to introduce in later classes other growth situations calling for multiplicative reasoning but to plan ahead of time exactly what comparisons to make and to choose the numbers carefully.

DISCUSSION OF THE MATHEMATICS
OF THIS LESSON

Mr. K recognized that growth situations can be viewed more productively as multiplicative rather than additive, and he decided to use an example of growth to help students begin to reason multiplicatively. He realized that bank investments were not everyday experiences for his students, and he had first considered several other situations involving growth. He decided, however, that investments in interest-bearing accounts would be a good example because he thought he could clarify what was involved in making a bank investment and because he knew that making money was a topic of great interest to his students. He had not, however, previously used these or similar tasks with any students and could not anticipate their thinking. Students who considered only the final amount were reasoning neither additively nor multiplicatively; they were at a yet more primitive level of reasoning. It is difficult, with an untried task, to foresee all of the cognitive difficulties that students will encounter while working on the problems presented by the task. This is particularly true when entering a territory that is not a usual feature of the curriculum, such as was true of the two forms of reasoning that were the focus of this lesson.

Yet children must be able to reason multiplicatively if they are to understand problems involving proportionality, a staple topic of the middle grades. Unfortunately, proportional tasks are rarely understood by students. Students learn a rule, just as for division of fractions, which they attempt to apply to all situations where a proportion is involved: They equate two ratios, fill in three of the four spaces, then cross multiply and divide to obtain the answer. In fact, many students do not recognize the two quantities equated as ratios—rather, they perceive the problem as involving four numbers, three of which are given and the fourth to be found. Very few students have a conceptual understanding of proportion. Perhaps they would be more prepared for proportional reasoning tasks if they first worked with the kinds of tasks Mr. K was using here.

MENTAL ACTIVITIES OF STUDENTS

In this section, we again look at the tasks, tools, and normative practices associated with this lesson and then consider it as part of a sequence, looking specifically at the five forms of mental activity discussed in chapter 2 by Carpenter and Lehrer. Note that although each of these activities occur in this lesson, they do not take place in the same way as in Ms. A's lesson.

In the Classroom: Tasks, Tools, and Normative Practices

Tasks and Tools. It is worthwhile to compare the two tasks Mr. K used. In the first task, dealing with Samantha's and Jermaine's savings, Mr. K had thought, not unreasonably, that some students would recognize that Samantha had doubled her money whereas Jermaine had not and that they could convince the others of their reasons. But only one student recognized this fact. Most students said that Samantha made only $20, whereas Jermaine made $25. A few, to Mr. K's surprise, insisted that Jermaine had the better deal because at the end of 3 months he had a total of $55, whereas Samantha had only $40. The problem as stated does not lend itself to further discussion because it asks a simple question ("Who got the better deal?"). Mr. K could have changed the question or made up a new problem on the spot, but he wisely chose to think more about the task and to design a new one that would draw the students into thinking more about the situation. The new task was the focus of the lesson described in this vignette.

The phrasing of the question personalized the problem: Each student had to decide which bank she or he would invest in. Mr. K selected the numbers carefully so that, although the differences ($20 in both cases) could be compared, the final amounts (twice the first and three times the first) would also be easy to compare. Also, the second investment was twice the first, making it easy to compare doubling and tripling effects; that is, the $20 investment could be thought about as two $10 investments. The doubling and tripling here were easier to discuss and compare than the ratios in the former problem. Although Mr. K eventually wanted his students to be able work comfortably with more difficult number combinations, he believed that when students first wrestle with multiplicative learning, the numbers should not distract from the students' sense-making. This problem could be extended to group work by simply changing the amount of money to invest. On the surface, the tasks do not look significantly different, but, in reality, the second leads to more investigation on the part of the students and to opportunities for more questions, more solutions, and extensions to new problems, slightly changed. The second task was rich enough for an entire class period and led to changes in students' thinking.

It is also important to note that the problem is accessible to a wide range of students. In fact, a special education student was the first to come up with a correct answer, with an accompanying rationale. The diversity of students in this class could be problematic for a teacher, but Mr. K was consistently able to hold their attention through the careful selection of instructional tasks.

The blackboard was an important tool for this lesson. Mr. K usually used only the overhead projector, but here he wanted several solutions placed on the board and left there for future comparison and discussion. For the first solution (by Lawrence), Mr. K encouraged the production of two tables, one for each bank, so that the amounts could be more easily compared. When working in small groups, the students also used tables of values to organize their thinking.

Normative Practices. The normative practices in Mr. K's classroom were a blend of practices designed for discouraging behaviors considered inappropriate and disruptive while allowing for open discussion and sharing by the students. What was particularly interesting in Mr. K's case was that he was able to accomplish all this while focusing on tasks designed to develop deep mathematical understanding rather than on the more traditional tasks (e.g., algorithm drills, individual seatwork, etc.) usually selected because they allow more classroom control of students with a history of disruptive behavior. Mathematics classes in Mr. K's room were marked by a high degree of student involvement and interest. Learning mathematics was almost synonymous with problem solving. Students learned that they were expected to explain their answers, and they became somewhat less impulsive in calling out completely unreasonable answers. Whole-group discussions and small-group work were often both in progress in the classroom. Not only did this allow a change of pace, but it allowed the non-English-speaking students a chance to discuss and ask questions of the students appointed as their translators, and it allowed Mr. K time to circulate and see what each student was doing, providing help as needed.

The Lesson as Part of a Sequence

Constructing Relationships. Most of the children in this class probably applied additive reasoning when they encountered situations calling for multiplicative reasoning. The earlier-mentioned orange juice problem and many similar problems have been extensively used with children, and there is abundant evidence that children of this age and even older use additive reasoning rather than multiplicative reasoning to answer related questions and thus arrive at incorrect answers. In this class the children are only beginning to understand the multiplicative nature of the problem; it is not the difference between the amounts nor is it the final amount alone that matters. Rather, it is the multiplicative relationship between the initial and final amounts that matters; tripling your money is better than doubling it. Mr. K could have told his students that tripling is better than doubling in this situation, but he believed that in order for his students to develop ways of reasoning that they could apply to other multiplicative situations, his students would need to recognize the pertinence of tripling versus doubling themselves. A new type of knowledge structure is being born in this lesson. Connections to other multiplicative situations will be formed in later lessons and eventually will lead to formulating ratios to express what is happening (in this case, the ratios are 2:1 and 3:1).

Extending and Applying Mathematical Knowledge. Mr. K was very careful in selecting a setting for today's lesson. Choosing a problem with connections to a real world setting, one that is of interest to the students because it involves money, will not only help in constructing appropriate mathematical relationships, but the problem also can act as a prototype for other growth problems yet to come.

Reflecting About Mathematical Experiences. The challenge of getting students to reflect on their learning was difficult in Mr. K's class; he was dealing with a high number of non-English speaking students and students with a record of behavioral problems. He knew that having them work alone, writing about what they had learned, would not be successful. He found alternate ways to help them to think about what they were learning. By having several students present their answers together with their reasons and by placing these on the blackboard with names attached, Mr. K could then ask students which method they thought was better. Students had to reflect on the reasons given for the different solutions in order to decide which they preferred. They then worked in small groups to solve a similar problem; this was an opportunity to reflect again on why it was better to invest in Jolanda's bank.

Articulating What One Knows. Students were very involved in this lesson, except for the few whose English was too poor to follow what was happening. Students were asked to place their solutions on the board, and when several solutions were available, the class discussed which were correct and which were not, and why. In the small group problem, discussions were intense and heated; it appeared that everyone wanted to have a say in how the problem ought to be solved.

Making Mathematics Knowledge One's Own. At the beginning of the class, most students appeared to believe that Jackie's bank gave the better deal. All but four students were, by the end of class, convinced that Jolanda's bank gave the better deal. This transformation came about not because Mr. K told them which was better but because they had to reason through the situation, making tables to figure out what would happen with the same amount invested at each bank. Although it is not clear that they would be able to generalize this conclusion and apply it to other situations, they have at least made a good start in that direction. Their convictions by the end of the class period were personal, and they were willing to argue and provide evidence that they were right. Most realized that simply looking at differences in the initial and final amounts was insufficient.

LOOKING BACK

In each of the vignettes, the mathematical task that was the focus of the lesson was devised by the teacher to develop particular mathematical understanding. In both vignettes, one carefully designed task, with appropriate extensions, guided the activities of the class for the entire period and led to a conclusion that in almost all cases became the students' personally constructed knowledge. In neither case was the task from a textbook. This is not to say, however, that textbook problems cannot be provocative and designed to develop mathematical understanding. What is important, whether the task is teacher designed or textbook selected, is that the teacher knows what mathematical understandings she or he wants to see developed and how the task in question can lead to these understandings. Both of these vignettes, although in dramatically different settings, illustrate how teachers who understand both the mathematics and the manner in which their students learn that mathematics can provide appropriate tasks and tools within established classroom norms to provide opportunities for their students to undertake the mental activities that lead them to develop mathematical understanding.

Because these two teachers had a deep understanding of the mathematics they were teaching, what happened in their classrooms is radically different from the mathematics classes most of us experienced in these grades. It is also different from what most teachers themselves experienced. It seems reasonable then that in order to teach a conceptually based curriculum in the middle grades, teachers must themselves have opportunities to revisit and reconceptualize the mathematics of these grades and to come to understand the nature of the mathematical knowledge and activity that are necessary for pedagogical effectiveness.

FOR FURTHER READING

Philipp, R., Flores, A., Sowder, J. T., & Schappelle, B. P. (1994). Conceptions and practices of extraordinary mathematics teachers. *The Journal of Mathematical Behavior 13*(2), 155–180.

Sowder, J. T., Philipp, R. A., Armstrong, B. E., & Schappelle, B. (1998) *Middle-grade teachers' mathematical knowledge and its relationship to instruction.* Albany: State University of New York Press.

Sowder, J. T., & Schappelle, B. P. (Eds.). (1995). *Providing a foundation for teaching mathematics in the middle grades.* Albany: State University of New York Press.

Chapter 7

Understanding of Statistics[1]

Susanne P. Lajoie
McGill University

When compared to other mathematical topics, statistics is rather new in the mathematics curriculum. Recent activity has been directed toward identifying what and when to teach statistical content as well as to how to teach and assess statistical understanding of such materials. In view of the junior status of statistics in the mathematics classroom, this chapter provides only a sketch of what statistical teaching and learning can look like in adolescents, along with some pastels for creating a classroom that can promote such understanding. One purpose in providing this sketch of statistical understanding is to foster better instruction and to stimulate further research in this area. The Authentic Statistics Project (ASP), described next, is an example of how statistical understanding can be fostered in classrooms. All classroom examples are taken from one Grade 8 classroom that implemented ASP. These descriptions are followed by a more detailed look at how Carpenter and Lehrer's (chapter 2, this volume) dimensions of understanding are supported in ASP.

THE AUTHENTIC STATISTICS PROJECT

The ASP was created as a response to the reform movement's suggestion that statistics be incorporated in Grades K through 12. One premise is that if statistics is introduced in the K through 12 period, students will be better prepared for decision making in the real world. The goal of ASP is to provide students with statistical knowledge and skills that can foster their independence in generating meaningful statistical investigations. ASP classrooms have been designed for Grade 8 mathematics students who work cooperatively in groups of three at their own computer work station (generally eight per class) on a unit that takes 2 weeks to complete. The role of the teachers (the mathematics classroom teacher and graduate research assistants involved in ASP research) is to facilitate students' progress by answering their questions or ensuring that they move forward in their investigations.

ASP is generally introduced to students following a unit on graphing during which the teacher builds on students' prior knowledge of graphing by relating it to data presentation. In order to facilitate the learning process, ASP anchors statistical concepts and the statistical investigation process through examples that model the use of concepts in a variety of real-world problems. The instructional sequence is set up in a progressive manner during which students learn the skills they will need to conduct statistical investigations with the use of technology. Figure 7.1 highlights the instructional components of ASP as well as the way they are sequenced. Learning in ASP is described within two phases: (a) the knowledge acquisition phase, during which students acquire knowledge through a tutorial and through a library of exemplars; and (b) the production phase, during which students design and conduct their own statistical investigations.

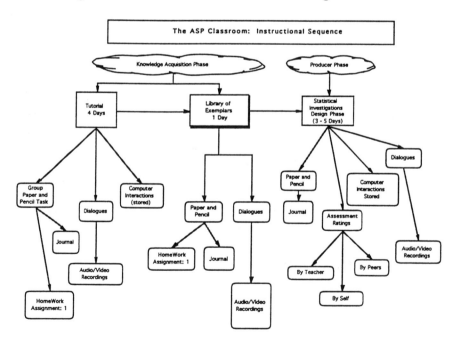

FIG. 7.1. The ASP classroom: Instructional sequence.

Knowledge Acquisition

The Tutorial. The tutorial is designed to help students learn new statistical concepts and procedures as well as how to use specially designed computer software to graph and analyze data. The computer software used to exemplify graphing procedures and statistical analysis, CricketGraph™ and MyStat™², respectively, were used in tandem with a hard copy of a tutorial we designed to lead students through a series of tasks using the computer for statistical purposes. We are currently designing and testing a HyperCard™ stack, Descriptive Statistics. This software leads students through these same tasks, using Excel for both graphing and analyzing data, and combines demonstrations with practice problems for students to solve.

In the tutorial, instruction is standardized in that each student sees the same examples and works through the same problem sequence. The primary instructional technique is to model the types of knowledge and skills students will need to produce their own projects. Concepts are defined, and examples modeling the use of such concepts in a variety of contexts are illustrated. Providing learners with concrete examples that clearly illustrate the meaning of concepts is an important feature of the tutorial, particularly given student difficulties with the abstract nature of such content. Concepts such as statistics, for instance, introduce the notion of describing and making predictions about data, which are collected to answer a particular question. An example research question is given to help learners situate the process of doing statistics in the context of a problem.

Statistical procedures are modeled through examples taken from newspapers and computer software. For instance, histograms, pie graphs, and percentages are demonstrated in the form of voter polls, sports statistics, and box office grosses for popular movies. Software applications enable students to represent the data in a multitude of ways: statistically, numerically, and visually. Generally, the teacher demonstrates how to solve the problem so that students can observe and build a representation of how to solve a task. Once statistical concepts and procedures are modeled, students apply their knowledge and skills to new problems. Multiple contexts are provided so that students can extend their knowledge.

Library of Exemplars. Once students have acquired the relevant knowledge and skills, they are required to demonstrate their understanding of statistics and the investigation process by designing and conducting their own statistics projects. To ensure that students understand this task and how they will be evaluated, they work through a Library of Exemplars, available on the computer. (This software we designed using Hypercard 2.1 and Quick Time software.)

The Library demonstrates how other students have performed on these abstract components and how they were assessed (see Fig. 7.2 for the table

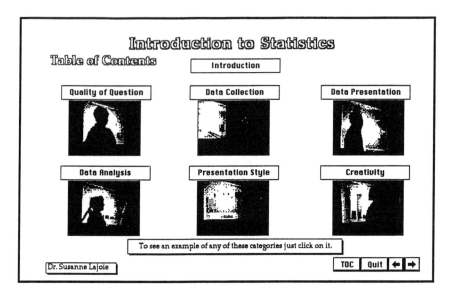

FIG. 7.2.   Hypercard table of contents for the performance standards for statistics.

of contents of the statistical components and Fig. 7.3 for an example of the data-analysis component). Through the available digitized videoclips of student performance, each student has the opportunity to examine the statistical process and think about his or her own knowledge in regard to these processes. Clicking on the average performance button, for example, allows the student to see a videoclip of a student from another class presenting the following acceptable research question: "What is your favorite fast food restaurant?" The videoclip of an above-average performance example shows a group restating the question as "What is your favorite fast food restaurant between Harvey's, Burger King, McDonald's, and Lafleur's?" The later videoclip demonstrates stronger performance on the criterion: Rather than presenting an open-ended question, which could have an infinite number of responses, the students added clear categories to the sample. After groups view these exemplars, they respond to textual prompts by discussing and reasoning about performance differences. Students have opportunities to internalize such criteria before they start their own statistics projects and can return to the computer at any time to refresh their memory of what a particular statistical concept means. Our assumption was that learning would be facilitated by making assessment criteria transparent through exemplars of student performance. When students are made aware of what is expected of them, it is easier for them to meet those expectations, to assess their own progress, and to compare their work with others. Armed with this knowledge, students then work in groups to conduct their own projects.

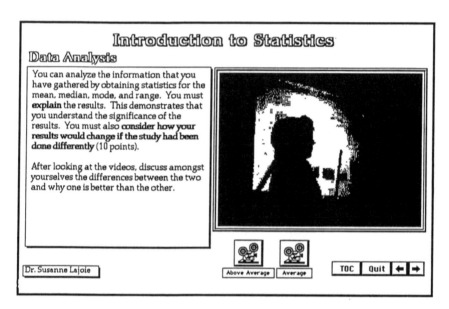

FIG. 7.3. Exemplars for data-analysis performance standard.

Producer Phase

Design teams of three students work together to plan, conduct, and present the results of their statistical investigations to the whole class. Students use computers to graph and analyze their data and to demonstrate their findings. During the production phase, students learn to work as a team to construct clear research questions, which can then be used to drive their data-collection procedures. Students communicate their understanding about the statistical investigation process and in so doing facilitate the reasoning and problem-solving process within the team. Opinions are debated, and actions are taken based on such discussions. After a consensus is reached regarding the research plan, decisions are made as to how each individual team member will contribute to the overall process, even though many of the tasks are shared. One team member, for example, might control the data entry into the computer, but all team members contribute to how the data should be collected, entered, graphed, analyzed, and interpreted. Data collection is usually a team effort during which students construct questionnaires and interviews, collect data based on these materials, conduct hands-on experiments (e.g., taste tests for favorite soft drinks), and–or use computer databases (e.g., a hockey database to make predictions about which team is more likely to win in the playoffs). Many ideas are tested before the group reaches a decision about the graphical representations and statistical results they prefer to use for their oral presentations to the class. Turn-taking decisions are preplanned so that every team member has a responsibility during classroom presentations.

The teacher facilitates the production phase by either answering student questions or prompting students to consider certain consequences of their actions. For example, as students brainstorm about what research question to ask, they often seek approval from the teacher. At other times, the teacher intervenes when she or he hears that the group is blocked about ways to answer their research question. In such a case, a teacher might suggest different ways of wording a question or of clarifying the types of people who should be asked (i.e., the sample) to answer a question. Other student inquiries involve how to organize data entry, what types of graphs are most appropriate for their data, and how to modify their graphs. The teacher often shows students different ways of addressing their questions. Most important, the teacher is able to draw student attention to the meaning of their results as it connects to the sample, the type of representations selected to describe the data, and the types of interpretations made of the statistical findings.

In ASP classrooms structured using design teams, the teacher attends to only three students at a time. This 1-to-3 student–teacher ratio enables teachers to give more individualized attention to students and facilitates their roles of monitoring, modeling, coaching, and fading. The teacher models the knowledge and skills for the students and coaches the students as they practice what they learn. The teacher monitors the teams as they design research questions and collect, graph, or analyze the data. Coaching learners requires assessment of their level of skill acquisition so that the right level of assistance can be provided. This assessment is done mainly through listening to the team's discussions and observing their work. Because one important goal of instruction is that learners become increasingly independent, the teacher gradually reduces his or her coaching and allows his or her help to fade as the group becomes more competent.

Computer as a Classroom Tool

The complex interplay among students, teachers, and computers exemplifies how classrooms can be designed to promote statistical understanding. The computer can help both the teacher and the learner in the ASP classroom by supporting the statistical investigation process. Computers can facilitate each stage of this investigation and help promote understanding. The computer provides students with opportunities to generate and test their statistical hypotheses about questions that are meaningful to them. The flexibility of the computer allows students to quickly find answers to the multiple hypotheses they might have at any particular time. Thus, instead of graphing and computing data by hand, students can experiment with how data can be graphed and whether it makes sense to represent their data as a pie chart or as a column graph. The immediate feedback students get from computers allows them to make the connection between what they think is correct and what actually is correct. The speed and accuracy of computers has many benefits. It reduces the memory problem students might have from day to day. Instead of spending an entire day drawing six graphs to represent their data, they can spend 15 minutes computing these graphs, thus allowing more time for reflecting on the meaning of the visual representations. It is this extra time for interpreting the meaningfulness of such graphs that the computer provides in the ASP classroom, thereby fostering understanding in an efficient manner. Furthermore, the teacher can spend more time helping students interpret data rather than helping them with the mechanics of statistics.

ASP AND TEACHING AND LEARNING WITH UNDERSTANDING

ASP was designed specifically to provide students with opportunities to engage in the various mental activities that are required if mathematics is to be learned with understanding. I now turn to a discussion of how ASP facilitates students' construction of relationships, extension and application of their knowledge, the use of tools for reflection, and the articulation of their thoughts and what they have learned. I illustrate these in action by providing vignettes from actual classrooms and discussing what the students are doing.

Constructing Relationships in ASP Classrooms

In ASP, students construct new relationships with assistance from the teacher and computer. Teachers foster statistical understanding by identifying prior knowledge that can be used to help students construct relationships with statistical concepts. When learning new concepts, students constantly try to construct an understanding based on what they know. If students lack this knowledge, they actively seek information to fill in the gap. Teachers help students fill in the gaps with appropriate information. What follows are several vignettes that illustrate the way classroom practice can help students construct relationships and enhance understanding. (All names are pseudonyms.)

One mathematics teacher, for example, helped students construct statistical understanding through their prior knowledge of graphing. The teacher did this by introducing students to statistical and graphical information found in newspaper clippings and by scaffolding classroom discussion that linked these representations to new concepts (i.e., data). In doing so, the teacher helped students establish a framework for new learning in the subsequent unit on statistics.

Classroom Example: Average Versus Mean. In the following excerpt, the teacher drew on students' prior knowledge of mathematical concepts to make a connection between average, a mathematical concept learned by eighth grade, and the statistical concept mean. The connection is facilitated through the use of graphs, such as scatterplots, constructed by students with the help of computer software. Some background information is needed to understand this dialogue. The graph shown in Fig. 7.4 was constructed by a pair of students during the tutorial phase of ASP.

Students were asked to use a computer database to construct a scatterplot of the temperatures, which included the minimum, maximum, and mean temperature by day for the month of May. Students selected the appropriate file from the database and used software to create a scatterplot for representing the data. The teacher instructed students about using the computer function Interpolate, which was an option for drawing a line between the mean temperatures for the month of May. The group seated at a computer consisted of a teacher and two students:

Teacher: Interpolate. Do you know what that means?

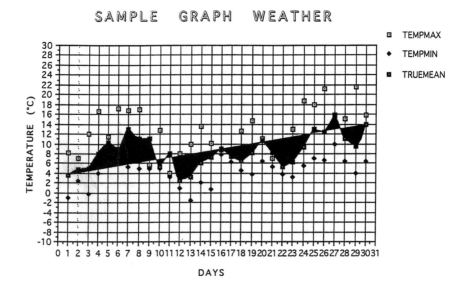

FIG. 7.4. Use of interpolation within a scatterplot to find mean temperatures for days in the month of May (computer-assisted student work).

Wade: No.

Teacher: OK, when you see the line come up, you'll know what it means.

Wade and Tyrone: Ohhhh.

Teacher: OK, why do you think it connected the middle line? What's that middle line?

Wade: Ah, so that you see the mean temperatures.

Teacher: Right, it's the mean temperatures. So it's taking the average of these two, the max and the min. That's what interpolate means.

Tyrone: Oh, OK.

Wade: 'Cause the max and min together make the average?

Teacher: Yeah, great.

Tyrone: So, anything in the middle [referring to points in the scatterplot] means average?

Teacher: OK, that's the average, the mean [points to middle line in the graph].

This dialogue provides an example of the complex interplay between the teacher, students, and computers in the context of learning about statistics. This interaction took place in the tutorial phase of ASP, which is relatively early in the instruction. The teacher led the discussion by asking a series of questions. When students responded that they did not understand interpolation, the teacher coached students to observe what happened to their graph when they selected this function. By asking pertinent questions, the teacher provided the necessary guidance for students to construct meaningful relationships on their own. The other half of the teacher-driven dialogue provided confirmation and feedback to students that they were on the right track. As students became more competent, the teacher reduced her coaching.

The computer acted as a partner in the learning process because it generated the scatterplot from the information students put into the computer. It provided the mechanism, interpolate, that allowed students to construct relationships between old and new knowledge. The computer served as a cognitive partner in the sense that it supported lower-level cognitive skills, such as graphing, so that learners could use higher-order thinking skills, in this case constructing relationships between the average and the mean. The interpolation function enabled students to make the connection that interpolation represented the mean scores. This connection is seen when the teacher asked the students, "What's that middle line?" and Wade responded, "So that you see the mean temperatures." Tyrone elaborated on this, "Anything in the middle means average."

The scatterplot itself provided a context for constructing relationships because it allowed students to see both the ungrouped (minimum and maximum data points) and grouped (the interpolate line representing the mean) data on one graph. In this sense, graphs such as scatterplots can be used to help students construct the meaning of statistical concepts as well as the relationships among concepts. Construction of such relationships can facilitate the integration and structuring of knowledge and, consequently, foster conceptual understanding of statistics. Once these basic statistical concepts are acquired through the computer tutorial, students can extend this knowledge to their self-designed statistics projects.

Extending and Applying Knowledge in ASP Classrooms

Once basic concepts and skills are mastered and practiced, students extend understanding developed during the tutorial by applying this knowledge to student-designed experiments. Classrooms with a problem-solving focus help students learn about statistics as well as what to do with them. In this regard, students learn to extend what they have learned in one situation to a new situation.

Classroom Example: Exploring Pulse Rate.   In ASP, realistic problems are provided to engage students in the problem-solving context. For instance, concepts related to measures of central tendency (i.e., mean, median, and mode) and variation (i.e., range) were taught in this vignette within a pulse-rate task during which mean was connected to mode, median, and range. Students' knowledge expanded through a problem-solving context in which each student could actively participate. Students worked in groups to collect their pulse data and calculate the mean pulse rate for their group using computer software. Once students understood the concept of mean within their working group, the task was extended to full classroom participation so that students could apply their knowledge to a broader context. Each student's pulse rate was recorded on the chalk board. The teacher led classroom discussions about the individual group means; the median and mode for the class data followed, along with a discussion of the range for the class. Each group calculated the class mean using their computer so that comparisons could be made between group means and the class mean. After that, students had to compare their results with the class data, which meant graphing and analyzing the class data with software. A student, for example, who thought a pie chart a more effective representation than a bar graph could test this hypothesis by quickly generating the two graphs and comparing them. The teacher facilitated the discussion about the differences in the data representations, encouraging students to reflect on the meaning of their data. Ultimately, however, the students themselves had to make the appropriate connections and relationships and extend their knowledge to new problems.

Classroom Example: Comparing Hockey Teams. The real test of students' ability to extend their knowledge of statistics is their performance on self-generated projects. Provided here is an example of how one ASP group extended its knowledge to the data-analysis component of statistical investigation. This particular group was interested in comparing two National Hockey League (NHL) teams, the Montreal Canadiens (the Habs) and the Boston Bruins, in terms of number of wins each team had over a 24-year period. The data for these teams was provided in a computer database for NHL statistics, which has information on 12 variables for 21 hockey teams. This group created a new database file that listed the number of wins the Habs and the Bruins had over 24 seasons. The fact that students understood the technology well enough to select the appropriate data and copy it into a new data file is not trivial. Students demonstrated both knowledge of the software and knowledge about the statistics:

Teacher: How do we find the mode?

Litsa: I know—you have to put it in order or something.

[Discussion ensues about how to sort the data columns using the software.]

Teacher: Okay, so now what do you want to do with the data once you are done with it? Like now you have it sorted, so what are you going to do?

Litsa: Gonna go to Analyze. [Analyze is an option that allows students to do several types of statistics.]

Teacher: Okay, and do what?

Litsa: Now, we find the mean, and the mode, and all that stuff.

Teacher: Okay, but can we find the mode when we analyze in Mystat?

Litsa: We don't have to 'cause we could just look.

Teacher: Exactly. But you can calculate the mean and the range if you wanted to analyze. So since you have the data there, you can try to determine what the mode is for the Habs and then do your analyses. And once that's done—

Litsa [to Jessie]:   Okay, go to analyses.

Jessie: Mean, min, and max—

Litsa: You didn't select anything yet.

Jessie: Huh?

Litsa: Now, press Select. Go to Habs, and Select. Go to Habs to Bruins. No, we are going to have to go to Clear Variable.

Jessie:	Okay.
Litsa:	No, go to Clear, press it. Go to Select. Okay, now go to Habs. Now go to Select.
Jessie:	Here?
Litsa:	You didn't press Select, go press Select.
Jessie:	What does SD mean?
Litsa:	I dunno.
Teacher:	Standard deviation.
Litsa:	We don't know what that is, so take it off. Okay, now go to, ah, okay.
Jessie:	Mean.
Litsa:	Ha, ha, Canadiens have more!
Jessie:	We gotta find a graph now. We gotta make a graph.

Of the 25 exchanges in this dialogue, 76% were made by students and 24% by the teacher. Notice the sharp increase in student-generated dialogue from the tutorial phase, demonstrated in the first vignette, to this one, which is situated in the context of student-generated statistics projects. The student dialogue illustrates the connection that students had made with data-analysis concepts and data-analysis software tools. The establishment of this relationship is not surprising, given that concepts and computer tools were taught simultaneously, within a problem-solving context. The dialogue reveals that these students understood concepts such as sorting data, finding the mean through the Analyze function, and finding the mode by just looking at the data, and that they knew how to compare two means. Students understood that in order to find the mode number of wins for the two hockey teams, they had to sort the data in ascending order so they could see which number was most common in the number of wins in each team. Using the software, they sorted the teams individually and saved their new sorted file before they performed subsequent analyses. Litsa said, "Go to Analyze." There was much discussion on what to do with Analyze once it was selected. Litsa realized that she did not need the computer to find the mode: "We could just look." Jessie said mean, min, max, but Litsa realized that nothing had been selected yet and that these analyses could not be run until the variables Habs and Bruins were selected. Figure 7.5 demonstrates that the types of statistics requested were indicated by an X; thus, Mean, Minimum, Maximum, and Range were selected. The outcome of their analyses is also visible in Fig. 7.5, and Litsa said, "Ha, ha, Canadiens have more!" meaning that the mean number of wins per season for the Habs was higher than for the Bruins. Also note that the last comment by Jessie, "We gotta make a graph," illustrates her understanding of the overall process of statistical investigation (i.e., We have

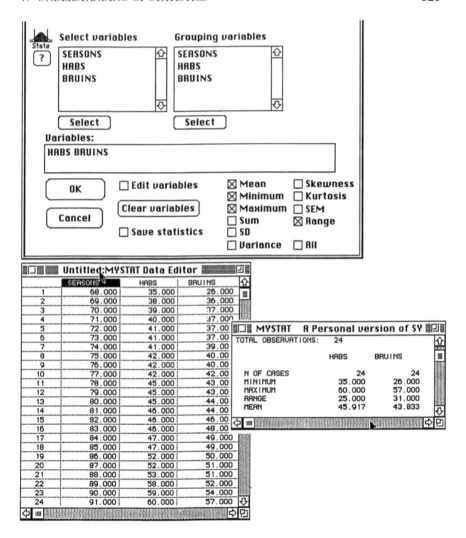

FIG. 7.5. Finding the mean number of wins for two hockey teams using the Analyze and Stats functions of MYSTAT.

done analyses; now how are we going to represent this information graphically?) Of the six teacher entries, four were questions that prompted students' next actions, one was a confirmation that students were on the right track, and the sixth was filling in information that students did not know (i.e., SD means standard deviation).

The students definitely demonstrated that they understood when the computer was helpful for analysis purposes and when it was not. They eased their task of finding the mode by using the computer to sort the data before they eyed the data to find the most frequent data point. They demonstrated understanding of how to use the technology to find the mean and they demonstrated that the means supported their assumption that the Canadiens was a better team than the Bruins. Because the students were from Montreal, they wanted the Habs-Canadiens to be the best. What the students did not understand was the term standard deviation. Without this knowledge, their interpretation of the means was limited.

Later in their investigations, after students had experimented with graphing their data, the following dialogue occurred:

Teacher: Well, what does this show you?

Jessie: It shows there that the Canadiens got more wins at this time, here they were about the same, and here they're much higher than the Bruins.

Teacher: OK, so in terms of variability or range, is that small or large?

Litsa: Small.

Teacher: Right, and what does that mean?

Litsa: It means they are pretty close together.

These dialogues reveal that, as students progressed in their investigations with graphing, their understanding was more complete. Earlier, the students did not know what standard deviations referred to and boldly stated that the Habs were better. Once they graphed the data, they realized that the two teams were closer together in terms of number of wins than they had thought previously.

Jessie and Litsa communicated their ability to apply and extend their knowledge and skills learned during the construction of their projects to their discussion of data analysis in their classroom presentation. Jessie and Litsa involved their classmates in the data-analysis process by asking them to eyeball their raw hockey-data file, to identify any outliers, and to predict and estimate which team had the higher mean wins of the two NHL teams. Classmate estimates were then compared with their own analysis. Notice that this strategy is similar to the way the pulse-rate task was used in the tutorial to introduce various statistical concepts in the classroom: Students first worked together in groups to solve problems, and then the classroom data was collected and compared to see if the results from all the groups were similar. Jessie and Litsa extended the knowledge they acquired in the pulse-rate task by applying it to a new context, that of creating their own statistics project and involving the class in their problem-solving activity. The strategy they used to present their findings paralleled that used in the instruction.

Tools for Student Reflection

In the ASP work, students reflect on their statistical understanding through the many opportunities for self-monitoring. The Library of Exemplars (described earlier) is a tool that provides a context for reflecting on the overall statistical process and for extending statistical understanding to new problem situations. To assist in the reflection process, journals are also used.

Prompting Reflection Through Structured Journals. External record keeping helps students reflect on their thinking. Journals provide a mechanism for focusing the learners' examination of their statistics work. They are designed with embedded prompts to support students' statistical knowledge, reasoning, planning, and reflection during the design of a statistical investigation, and students are required to record their reasoning at specific points during the problem-solving activity. Knowledge prompts, such as "What does 'population' refer to?" "What is a mean, and how is it calculated?" and "Why do we need to calculate the range?" encourage students to reflect on the new terms that they acquire in class during the tutorials. Other prompts encourage students to articulate their understanding of statistical procedures (e.g., "Name five steps involved in conducting a statistics experiment"). Reasoning prompts encourage students to think about data and graphs (e.g., "Of the graphs that you have tried, which one does your group think will be better for presentation purposes?"). Planning prompts focus on the ideas generated for the statistical investigation (e.g., "List some ideas your members have for the group's project"; "How many people does your group need to make your sample representative?" "How is your group going to demonstrate the data you have collected?" "What statistical procedures does your group want to use?" "What analyses has your group tried?"). Reflection prompts encourage groups to evaluate their own understanding (i.e., "What questions does your group have?" "What does your group not understand?" "What future research could your group do, based on the results of your study?").

The responses to these prompts are varied and to some degree demonstrate the depth of the groups' reflection on the overall process of statistical investigation. One group, whose project involved a survey, reflected that they needed to know the number of people who liked a particular product, who did not like it, and the average. Another group focused on how they would represent their data once they had collected it, what types of graphs would be useful, and what their information meant. This type of external reflection is important to learners because it demonstrates their thinking processes and is helpful to teachers because it demonstrates student understanding and how it changes over time.

Reflection can also take place after a task is completed. After observing others perform, one group decided they could improve their own performance and wanted an opportunity to do so—a good demonstration of the way self-monitoring and reflection assist students in becoming independent learners.

Articulation in the ASP Classroom

The classroom provides the context for making statistical problem-solving skills visible. Groups presents their projects to the classroom by discussing how they met each of the performance standards modeled in the Library of Exemplars. Students use a liquid- crystal-display (LCD) overhead projector to demonstrate their data files to the class, the graphs they selected to represent their work, and the analyses they conducted. Finally, students interpret their data for the class and answer questions. Each group demonstrates their skills of argumentation through their handling of key questions. The classroom provides the community setting for articulating knowledge and discussing alternative strategies for explaining conjectures and conclusions.

Students are often asked to explain their assumptions and their reasons for pursuing the strategies they have chosen. It is crucial that students are allowed to articulate their knowledge in a manner that is conducive to their strengths. Each student should be given optimal opportunities to demonstrate his or her statistical understanding. Some students tend to be better at articulating their knowledge verbally rather than in writing, in drawing rather than in formal dialogues, and so on. Others may do better on a written task than when asked to speak in front of his or her peers. Even in open-ended tasks, reasoning capabilities can be masked when writing tasks restrict the amount of information to be documented.

Articulating one's knowledge of statistics also involves constructing graphs or conducting analyses. These products, in and of themselves, demonstrate students' understanding of statistics. Requiring that students explain the assumptions underlying the use of particular graphs and analyses, as well as what those graphs convey, however, provides students with additional opportunities to articulate their knowledge.

New technologies are also changing the ways in which problem situations, methods of representations, and strategies are used. ASP is an excellent example of the way new signs and symbols evolve in the context of technology. Students articulate their understanding through their use of computer software. They construct data files, generate graphs, and perform analyses. These notations of statistical understanding become computer files of the representations. Every action that students take on the computer can also be stored as a computer-screen recording, an actual

computer-screen video of all on-computer activity. With this use of technology, an entire session on the computer—each step or function a student
carries out on the computer—can be stored for later replay (like a video-
tape) and analysis. Screen recordings are a notational form of statistical
investigation in progress in that student actions are visible representations
of their statistical problem solving. When we examine this technological
form of articulation in addition to students' verbalizations, their reasoning
can be better understood.

Audiotapes of the group, taken when the screen recordings are made,
add other forms of evidence to serve as a basis for our understanding of
a group and allow us to develop a better picture of students' reasoning
processes as they use the computer to develop their statistics projects. The
group's responses to pre- and post-paper-and-pencil tests, homework assignments, and journals can also be used to build a more robust picture
of the groups' statistical understanding (e.g., "Does the group elaborate
on the design of their research question in their journal?" "Do their verbal
protocols reveal their understandings or misunderstandings of graphical
and statistical manipulations?").

*Classroom Example: Oral Presentation of Results of Survey on Favorite Fast
Food Restaurants.* Students in this example were successful in articulating
their knowledge in oral presentations, during which they explained how
they conducted their surveys. The most revealing aspect of the oral presentations (in terms of examining students' understanding of statistics),
however, was the question period that followed the oral presentation. During such question periods, the classroom teachers and peers were free to
ask presenters any questions requiring clarification or elaboration. It was
during these question periods that students' misunderstandings or confu-
sions were revealed. Students in one group, for instance, used a bar graph
with frequency data to discuss results of the group's survey on favorite fast
food restaurants (see Fig. 7.6). The results, however, were discussed in
terms of percentages.

Classmates watching the presentation were confused by the incongruity
between the information depicted in the graph and the information presented verbally by the group. The following dialogue illustrates this confu-
sion:

Teacher: How did you know there was a certain percent? Is there a
label on the chart? Um, that [graph] says the numbers along
the bottom are percentages. Is that what it means? You were
saying—I was trying to follow you—you were saying percent,
but I don't see percentage signs or labels of percent. I was
wondering, uh, were you giving that have a label along the

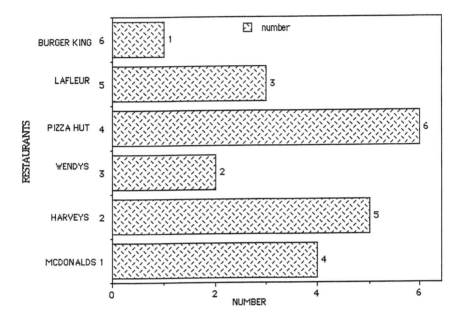

FIG. 7.6. "Favorite Restaurant" survey represented by a bar graph (computer-assisted student work).

bottom of the graph, along the *x*-axis, uh, that says "number"—Does it really represent percent?

Kevin: Uh—

Teacher: Because there was a relationship between what you are saying and the numbers that are at the bottom of each of those bars there.

Jim: Um, yeah, um, yeah, I guess so.

[As the discussion continues, it becomes clear that this group has calculated the percentages by hand and that errors have been made in the process.]

Teacher: Well, then, 4 out of 21 is not 40%.

Kevin: Show him what you got [to Jim].

Teacher: If 4 people chose McDonald's—Is that what you're showing here? Then 4 out of 21 is not 40%.

Kevin: Eh, Jim?

Teacher: The numbers here can't be percent because they don't make 21, see what I mean? [The teacher is referring to that fact that 21 is not a percentage but a number count.]

Kevin: Jim?

Gord: Well, what I have here are the original positions that we have—uh, on our graph there. Ah—for Burger King, there is 19%.

Teacher: Yeah?

Gord: And for Lafleur's, 24%.

Teacher: That's not what Kevin was saying though.

Gord: Pizza Hut is 10%—ah—Wendy's is 29%, Harvey's is 14, and McDonald's is 4.

Jim: Excuse me, Gord. Pizza Hut can't be 10, especially when Wendy's is 50%—or whatever you said—25.

This dialogue illustrates the need to probe students with questions so that they are given every opportunity to articulate their knowledge. In this case, students made calculation errors that could have been avoided had students used a pie graph in addition to, or rather than, a bar graph. These students used a bar graph to demonstrate their data, and bar graphs only provide frequency counts on categories. For some reason, the students computed the percentages by hand and presented them during the presentation. It is unclear why they decided to discuss percentages rather than frequencies or why they had selected a bar graph instead of a pie graph, which has percentages built into the visual representation. The assumptions and reasoning behind the choice of graphs was revealed only when questions were asked and answers articulated. Moreover, without such probing, a teacher might erroneously assess a student as not having acquired the relevant knowledge when, in fact, the student could either have had difficulty with graph interpretation or with calculating percentages.

Also, in oral presentations, students might simply forget to discuss certain aspects of their project. Students, for example, might understand that the representativeness of categories selected for a survey of favorite fast food restaurants (e.g., Burger King, Harvey's, Lafleur's, McDonald's, and Wendy's) has implications for drawing conclusions (e.g., "Quebec market differs from other markets in Canada") but may neglect to discuss this in their presentation unless they are prompted for such information. When asked whether the results would be different if the data had been collected in Toronto, students were able to respond in a knowledgeable way (e.g., "Ah, I'm sure it would because maybe they promote different restaurants down there, more than we do here. It depends on the age group that you ask."). During these question periods, many of the students also demonstrated knowledge that was not evident during their presentations. Omission of information is not necessarily an indication that students lack an understanding of the concept but may simply be due to oversight. For this reason, developing scripted questions for assessing students' performance on verbal tasks is crucial.

Making Knowledge One's Own in ASP Classrooms

The personal nature of understanding involves the construction of knowledge by individuals through their own activity. In ASP, students decide on their own research questions, automatically personalizing their quest for knowledge rather than having ideas imposed on them. They personalize their group work by naming their team, (e.g., the Wiseguys), and labeling their data and graph files on the computer with their group name. Their research project is their own creation, and they are responsible for the knowledge they have to use to develop it and the types of representations they select for depicting their results. How students personalize their projects in terms of their own interests is reflected in their research questions. For example, one group was interested in whether or not people preferred having curly or straight hair. This interest stemmed from one student's frustration with his curly hair and comments made by others (having straight hair, of course) that they thought he was lucky to have curly hair. Others were interested in favorite music, foods, and basketball teams. Students' desire to personalize their projects, however, was most evident in groups that were asked to construct their research questions by selecting data from one of five computer databases. Student groups often supplemented the computer database with data they collected independently. For instance, one group used hockey data from the database but supplemented it with data for subsequent seasons, which they collected from city newspapers. Another group used computer data on regular and diet colas taken from a database and compared this data with data they collected based on their own taste test (same categories of colas used, but a smaller sample). In each case, students were making knowledge their own.

DEVELOPING A COMMUNITY OF LEARNING

Communities of learning can be developed in classrooms by making articulation a normal classroom practice. Individuals need to share their understanding of statistics with others by articulating how they problem-solve and reason with statistics. Sharing of alternative strategies is part of the social norm for an ASP group. In the example that follows, the group involved conducted a survey of favorite fast food restaurants. Each student in the group collected his or her own data and represented them in a different manner. In doing so, individual impact on the overall group project could be seen, but the group was still able to reach consensus on data interpretation:

Marco:	Ooooh. You can ahh and ooh any time. This is a pie graph. I, ah, took a survey on "What is your favorite fast food restaurant?" I only asked kids that attended this high school. And as you can see, Harvey's came up the big winner, 31.71%, and second place was Others, with 26.83%. And third place was Lafleur's with 19.5%. And in fourth place was McDonald's with, umm, 9.76%. And in fifth place was Burger King with 7.33%, and in sixth place was Wendy's with 4.88%.
Teacher:	How many people did you ask?
Marco:	I asked a total of 41 people.
Teacher:	The other graph, compared everybody. How come you don't compare everybody on that one?
Marco:	Ah, I, ah, I did another one like that and, ah, I did pie Kyle, pie Sylvie. This is mine, and this is Bob's [points to screen]. And as you can see, they're, ah, very different. Ah, ah, that's it. Are there any questions?
Teacher:	Are there any similarities between the data that you all collected?
Marco:	Yes, as you can see, Harvey's, ah, was in all of them, ah, the winner overall.
Teacher:	Great! How 'bout the second place? Was that the same overall?
Marco:	Ah, I don't think so.
Teacher:	Why did you choose to use a pie graph rather than a bar graph?
Marco:	'Cause in a pie graph you can, ah, like see the results better—like you can compare them better.

[Discussion continues. At resumption of excerpt, a stacked bar graph is presented on screen with the entire group data.]

Bob:	All right. As again, as all my other students said, Harvey's has won. As you can see, you can tell by the different patterns. As you can see, Harvey's has won there, with Kyle's. Mine, Harvey's has won again. Between McDonald's, Lafleur's, and Burger King, it looks pretty tied. Wendy's comes out second, and, ah, okay. Marco, it's very close between Harvey's and others, but at the end Harvey's wins. With, ah, Others next, followed by Lafleur's, McDonald's,

Wendy's. Harvey's wins. And, in conclusion, Harvey's is the
best restaurant in the most general population.

These classroom dialogues engaged all students in reflecting on the
importance of the way data was collected, graphed, and analyzed. Sharing
group projects in the classroom provided an opportunity for a community
of statistical problem solvers to emerge. This dialogue also demonstrates
that individuality can survive within a small group. Such individuality is a
crucial step in understanding, as is reflected in the next section on making
knowledge one's own.

FUTURE CONSIDERATIONS

The ASP project is currently being updated to consider different uses of
technology for encouraging student reflection about the statistical investigation process. One change in our instructional techniques is the broader
use of models of statistical performance. We have found modeling to be
a powerful instructional tool because students do engage in performances
that reflect the standards modeled: In essence, you get what you model.
For example, in our examination of student performance on the performance standard establishing a research question, we found that 93% of
groups constructed a question similar to the one modeled in the Library
of Exemplars. In order that students acquire a broader understanding of
what exemplars can be, we recognize the need to provide, in this instance,
a variety of statistical designs and models of these designs, as well as examples from statistical investigations that use different graphs and analyses.
By increasing the number and variety of statistical performance standards
that we model, we anticipate that students will acquire a broader range of
applications of statistical knowledge.

CONCLUSION

The ASP illustrations given in this chapter provide a vibrant view of a
mathematics classroom that creates statistical understanding by (a) providing appropriate tasks and social norms and (b) engaging students in
statistical dialogues. A central theme in ASP is to situate instruction in tasks
that are authentic or meaningful to the learner. The tasks used in ASP,
whether a survey concerning fast food restaurants or an analysis of data
on hockey teams, interest and engage the students. In addition, because
ASP is an inquiry-based approach to learning and understanding statistics, student consensus (in small groups) is sought for each step of

the statistical investigation: the type of research question posed; the type and amount of data collected; the ways to organize, represent, and interpret the data; and the best way to present their group project to the classroom. Teachers assist by modeling and coaching students in constructing statistical relationships with the goal that once students understand such relationships, they will be able more easily to extend and apply their newly acquired knowledge to statistics projects they themselves design.

In ASP classrooms, opportunities for student reflection and articulation of knowledge are provided within instructional practice so that multiple methods of assessment can take place. Through this process, every individual is provided with ample opportunity to demonstrate his or her understanding in a manner conducive to individual strengths, thereby truly meeting the equity standard described in the NCTM *Assessment Standards* (1995). Computers and other technologies are used as tools both to help students understand statistics and to provide benchmarks of statistical performance that students reflect on, model, and apply in new situations. In effect, technology helps clarify the goals of instruction as well as the criteria by which students are assessed: Modeling the performance standards for each of the components of the statistical process of investigation in one context provides a schema for applying this investigation process to new contexts constructed by students.

Carpenter and Lehrer, in chapter 2, this volume, make a strong case for learning with understanding. In our experiences in ASP, we have found that when students work on tasks they find engaging and are expected not merely to give the "right" answers but to understand the statistical relationships they use and manipulate, they own that knowledge, stay interested in the mathematics, and do not fear working on problems in new contexts.

NOTES

1. Preparation of this document was made possible through funding from the Office of Educational Research and Improvement, National Center for Research in Mathematical Sciences Education (NCRMSE). Special thanks to Dr. Thomas A. Romberg for his support and encouragement of this research endeavor. Additional thanks to Phil Knox, a gifted teacher, who made our data collection possible. I especially would like to acknowledge my graduate assistants Nancy Lavigne, who continues her research in this area and has been central to all phases of work, and to Steven Munsie and Tara Wilkie, who have worked tirelessly on this project over the years. Special thanks to André Renaud for his programming skills. Further acknowledgments to Marlene Desjardins, Cindy Finn, Bryn Holmes, Jody Markow, Tina Newman, Litsa Papathanasopoulou, and Steve Reisler for volunteering their time throughout the study.
2. Cricket Software Inc. (1989). Cricket Graph Version 1.3.1 [Computer program]. Valley Stream Parkway, PA: Author.
   Systat Inc. (1988). Mystat Version 1.0: A personal version of Systat [Computer program]. Evanston, IL: Author.

REFERENCE

National Council of Teachers of Mathematics (1995). *Assessment standards for school mathematics.* Reston, VA: Author.

FOR FURTHER READING

Here are several seminal readings that helped formulate the ideas presented in this chapter, the two most important ones being the National Council of Mathematics Teachers documents on Curriculum and Evaluation, Teaching, and Assessment.

Gal, I., & Garfield, J. B. (Eds.). (1997). *Handbook on assessment in statistics education.* Amsterdam: IOS Press and the International Statistical Institute.

Garfield, J., & Ahlgren, A. (1994). Student reactions to learning about probability and statistics: Evaluating the quantitative literacy project *School Science and Mathematics, 94*(2), 89–95.

Garfield, J. B., & Burrill, G. (Eds.). (1997). Research on the role of technology in teaching and learning statistics. *Proceedings of the 1996 IASE Round Table Conference.* Vooburg, The Netherlands: Interbational Statistical Institute.

Lajoie, S. P. (Ed.). (1998). *Reflections on statistics: Learning, teaching, and assessment in Grades K–12.* Mahwah, NJ: Lawrence Erlbaum Associates.

Lajoie, S. P., Jacobs, V. R., & Lavigne, N. C. (1995). Empowering children in the use of statistics. *Journal of Mathematical Behavior, 14*(4), 401–425.

Lavigne, N. C., & Lajoie, S. P. (1996). Communicating performance standards to students through technology. *The Mathematics Teacher, 89*(1), 66–69.

National Council of Teachers of Mathematics (1989). *Curriculum and evaluation standards for school mathematics.* Reston, VA: Author.

National Council of Teachers of Mathematics (1991). *Professional teaching standards.* Reston, VA: Author.

Scheaffer, R. L. (1988). Statistics in the schools: The past, present, and future of the quantitative literacy project. *Proceedings of the American Statistical Association from the section on statistical education,* 71–78.

Shaughnessy, J. M. (1992). Research in probability and statistics: Reflections and directions. In D. Grouws (Ed.), *Handbook for research in mathematics teaching and learning* (pp. 465–494). New York: Macmillan.

Chapter 8

Teaching and Learning
a New Algebra[1]

James J. Kaput
University of Massachusetts–Dartmouth

To discuss the teaching and learning of algebra with understanding, we must first look at the algebra that students too often encounter in their classrooms. The traditional image of algebra, based in more than a century of school algebra, is one of simplifying algebraic expressions, solving equations, learning the rules for manipulating symbols—the algebra that almost everyone, it seems, loves to hate. The algebra behind this image fails in virtually all the dimensions of understanding that Carpenter and Lehrer (chapter 2, this volume) have taken as a starting point for reform in the classroom. School algebra has traditionally been taught and learned as a set of procedures disconnected both from other mathematical knowledge and from students' real worlds.

Construction of relationships and application of newly acquired knowledge are not at the heart of traditional algebra: The applications used are notoriously artificial (e.g., age problems and coin problems), and students are neither given the opportunity to reflect on their experiences nor the support to articulate their knowledge to others. Instead, they memorize procedures that they know only as operations on strings of symbols, solve artificial problems that bear no meaning to their lives, and are graded not on understanding of the mathematical concepts and reasoning involved but on their ability to produce the right symbol string—answers about which they have no reason to reflect and that they found (or as likely guessed) using strategies they have no need to articulate. Worst of all, their experiences in algebra too often drive them away from mathematics before they have experienced not only their own ability to construct mathematical knowledge and to make it their own but, more important, to understand its importance—and usefulness—to their own lives.

Although algebra has historically served as a gateway to higher mathematics, the gateway has been closed for many students in the United States, who are shunted into academic and career dead ends as a result. And even for those students who manage to pass through the gateway, algebra has been experienced as an unpleasant, even alienating event—mostly about manipulating symbols that do not stand for anything. On the other hand, algebraic reasoning in its many forms, and the use of algebraic representations such as graphs, tables, spreadsheets and traditional formulas, are among the most powerful intellectual tools that our civilization has developed. Without some form of symbolic algebra, there could be no higher mathematics and no quantitative science; hence no technology and modern life as we know them. Our challenge then is to find ways to make the power of algebra (indeed, all mathematics) available to all students—to find ways of teaching that create classroom environments that allow students to learn with understanding. The broad outlines of the needed changes follow from what we already know about algebra teaching and learning:

- begin early (in part, by building on students' informal knowledge),
- integrate the learning of algebra with the learning of other subject matter (by extending and applying mathematical knowledge),
- include the several different forms of algebraic thinking (by applying mathematical knowledge),
- build on students' naturally occurring linguistic and cognitive powers (encouraging them at the same time to reflect on what they learn and to articulate what they know), and
- encourage active learning (and the construction of relationships) that puts a premium on sense making and understanding.

Making these changes, however, will not be easy, especially where the new approaches involve new tools, unprecedented applications, populations of students traditionally not targeted to learn algebra, and K through 8 teachers traditionally not educated to teach algebra (neither the old algebra nor some new version). Despite these challenges, this chapter suggests a route to deep, long-term algebra reform that begins not with more new-fangled approaches but with the elementary school teachers and the reform efforts that currently exist. This route involves generalizing and expressing that generality using increasingly formal languages, where the

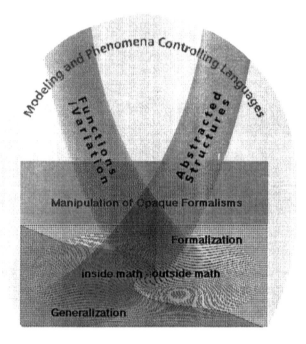

FIG. 8.1. The overlapping and interrelationships of the five forms of algebraic reasoning.

generalizing begins in arithmetic, in modeling situations, in geometry, and in virtually all the mathematics that can or should appear in the elementary grades. Put bluntly, this route involves infusing algebra throughout the mathematics curriculum from the very beginning of school.

Although this chapter is designed to show this route to teaching for understanding in greater detail, I have chosen to organize the material around the five different forms of algebraic reasoning as I see them (see Fig. 8.1) in order to demonstrate how algebra can infuse and enrich most mathematical activity from the early grades onward. These five interrelated forms, each discussed in the sections that follow, form a complex composite. The first two of these underlie all the others, the next two constitute topic strands, and the last reflects algebra as a web of languages and permeates all the others. All five richly interact conceptually as well as in activity—to understand this algebra is to make a rich web of connections. The classroom examples in these sections are based in actual student work and language and are taken from across many grade levels and mathematical topic areas. Together, the forms of reasoning and the classroom examples discussed in this chapter emphasize where we need to go rather than where we are or have been.

ALGEBRA AS THE GENERALIZATION
AND FORMALIZATION OF PATTERNS
AND CONSTRAINTS

Although pure computational arithmetic of the sort that dominates elementary school mathematics, the kinds of counting and sorting involved
in combinatorics, and pure spatial visualization need not inherently emphasize generalization and formalization, it is difficult to point to mathematical systems and situational contexts where mathematical activity does
not involve these two processes. The manipulations performed on formalisms (which I identify in this chapter as the second kernel aspect of algebra
and which sometimes yield general patterns and structures—the essence
of the third, structural, aspect of algebra) typically occur as the direct or
indirect result of prior formalization. Generalization and formalization are
intrinsic to mathematical activity and thinking—they are what make it
mathematical.

Generalization involves deliberately extending the range of reasoning
or communication beyond the case or cases considered, explicitly identifying and exposing commonality across cases, or lifting the reasoning or
communication to a level where the focus is no longer on the cases or
situations themselves but rather on the patterns, procedures, structures,
and the relations across and among them (which, in turn, become new,
higher-level objects of reasoning or communication). But expressing generalizations means rendering them into some language, whether in a formal language, or, for young children, in intonation and gesture. In the
case of young children, identifying the expressed generality or the child's
intent that a statement about a particular case be taken as general may
require the skilled and attentive ear of a teacher who knows how to listen
carefully to children.

We distinguish two sources of generalization and formalization: reasoning and communication in mathematics proper, usually beginning in arithmetic; and reasoning and communicating in situations based outside
mathematics but subject to mathematization, usually beginning in quantitative reasoning. The distinction between these two sources (mathematics
proper and situations outside mathematics) is especially problematic in
the early years, when mathematical activity takes very concrete forms and
is often tightly linked to situations that give rise to the mathematical activity.
Whether the starting point is in mathematics (and therefore arising from
previously mathematized experience) or from a yet-to-be-mathematized
situation, the source is ultimately based in phenomena or situations outside
mathematics proper because, after all, mathematics thinking inevitably
begins in experience and only becomes mathematical on appropriate activity and processing. Failures to teach for understanding are most often

the result of breaking the link with meaningful experience. I now illustrate with an example of students building generalizations both from within and from outside mathematics.

A Classroom Example of Early Generalization and Formalization

The following example from a third-grade class was observed and documented by Bastable and Schifter (in press). The teacher began by asking how many pencils there were in three cases, each containing 12 pencils. After the class arrived at a repeated-addition (12 + 12 + 12) solution, the teacher showed how the result could be seen as a (3 × 12) multiplication. She expected to move on to a series of problems of this type, but one student noted that each 12 could be decomposed into two 6s, and that the answer could be described as 6 + 6 + 6 + 6 + 6 + 6 or six 6s and could be written as 6 × 6. Another student observed that each 6 could also be thought of as two 3s, yielding twelve 3s or 12 × 3. Another student realized that, "This one is the backwards of our first one, 3 × 12." What follows is a description of the extended investigation that occurred.

Task. The students continued to find ways of grouping numbers that totaled 36. One student, looking at the column of 3s, suggested four groups of three 3s, or 4 × 9. Another student noted that, "We can add another one to the list because if 4 × 9 = 36, then 9 × 4 = 36, too." One student objected, asking a question the teacher found interesting: "Does that always work? I mean, saying each one backwards will you always get the same answer?" When the teacher asked her what she thought, the student said, "I'm not sure. It seems to, but I can't tell if it would always work. I mean for all numbers."

For homework, the teacher asked them to explore ways to prove (or disprove) the student's question. The next day, the students explained their thinking, noting various number pairs such as 3 × 4 and 4 × 3 and sometimes using manipulatives to illustrate their examples. Although the original objector was still not convinced that this would work for all numbers, the teacher decided to leave the issue unresolved temporarily and continue exploration of multiplication by introducing arrays. Two weeks later, however, the teacher reintroduced the problem, suggesting students use what they now knew of arrays "to prove that the answer to a multiplication equation would be the same no matter which way it was stated." The class worked on this for a while, alone and with partners. Finally, one student decided she could prove it. Holding up three sticks of 7 Unifix cubes, she said,

See, in this array I have three 7s. Now watch. I take this array [picking up the three 7-sticks] and put it on top of this array [turns them 90 degrees and places them on the seven 3-sticks she has previously arranged]. And look—they fit exactly. So 3 × 7 equals 7 × 3, and there's 21 in both. No matter which equation you do it for, it will always fit exactly.

At the end of this explanation, another student eagerly explained another way to prove it:

I'll use the same equation as Lauren, but I'll only need one of the sets of sticks. I'll use this one [picks up the three 7-sticks]. When you look at it this way [holding the sticks up vertically], you have three 7s. But this way [turning the sticks sideways], you have seven 3s. See? . . . So this one array shows both 7 × 3 or 3 × 7.

At this explanation, the class objector agreed: Although both students had used a 3 × 7 array to explain their points, the final, simpler representation convinced her of the general claim. As she noted: "That's a really good way to show it . . . It would have to work for all numbers."

Discussion. In this example, students were attempting to generalize what they saw in a few cases of multiplication to all cases of multiplication and (because they had not yet worked with formal language in mathematics) to articulate their generalization through a variety of notational devices in combination with natural, informal language. The basic issue was the range of the generalization—Did it hold for all numbers? The students used cubes and sticks to generate their ideas, to show one another their thinking, and to justify claims that were clearly theirs, not their teacher's. The questions of certainty and justification arose as an integral aspect of the process and were interwoven in their use of notations. Thinking of this activity merely as the children developing the concept of commutativity of multiplication (of natural numbers) trivializes what happened during this extended lesson. The students were actually constructing both the very idea of multiplication (although only two aspects: repeated addition and array models) while beginning to develop the notion of mathematical justification and proof.

Although the episode began in a concrete situation, it quickly became a mathematical exploration. Pencils and cases were the stepping-off point that (inadvertently) led the students to the grouping and decomposition of whole numbers and, after some reflection, to the articulation of their newly constructed knowledge (the equivalence of alternative groupings) through use of concrete arrays of cubes. Students found ways to articulate the invariance of the amount, or total, first under alternate groupings of 21 and then under alternate orientations of the same physical grouping.

In the end, despite the fact that they did not have a formal language available, the generality was not only realized, but made explicit: "It would have to work for all numbers." It is easy to imagine that this property might be given a more formal expression later, first perhaps as "box times circle = circle times box," and then later as $a \times b = b \times a$.

Summary. The Bastable–Schifter study (in press) study from which this case was taken includes several examples of such episodes (across Grades 1–6) involving properties of numbers (odd–even, zero), operations, extensions to other number systems beyond the natural numbers, and so on. Many important questions remain unanswered about these tasks and how to organize them, including what the role(s) of language and special notations might be, how to discern generality in students' informal utterances, what the interplay between generalization and justification might be, what the role of concrete situations might be, and so on.

One other aspect of this situation deserves attention: This is certainly not traditional symbol-manipulation algebra. Although this was clearly an excellent teacher doing a good job in an arithmetic, this extended lesson focusing on generalization rather than computation took place in what many teachers would regard as the normal course of mathematical concept development in an ordinary mathematics classroom (ordinary in the sense of fitting the NCTM *Professional Standards for Teaching Mathematics*, 1991).

ALGEBRA AS SYNTACTICALLY GUIDED MANIPULATION OF (OPAQUE) FORMALISMS

When we deal with formalisms, whether traditional algebraic ones or those more exotic, our attention is on the symbols and syntactical rules for manipulating those formalisms rather than on what they might stand for, with much of their power arising from internally consistent, referent-free operations. The user suspends attention to what the symbols stand for and looks at the symbols themselves, thus freed to operate on relationships far more complex than could be managed if he or she needed at the same time to *look through* the symbols and transformations to what they stood for (see Fig. 8.2). To paraphrase Bertrand Russell, (formal) algebra allows the user to think less and less about more and more.

The problem is that our traditional algebra curriculum has concentrated on the less and less part, resulting in many students' inability to see meaning in mathematics and even in their alienation from mathematics. The power of using the *form* of a mathematical statement as a basis for reasoning is lost when students practice endless rules for symbol manipulation and lose the connection to the quantitative relationships that the symbols might

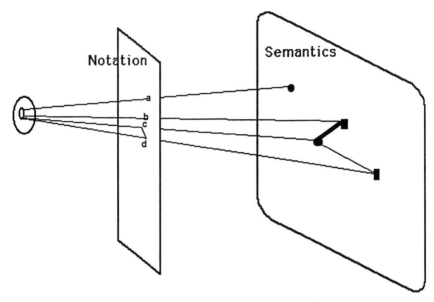

FIG. 8.2.   Looking *at* versus *through* symbols.

stand for (coming, along the way, to believe that this is what mathematics really is). What happens too often in traditional mathematics classrooms is less learning with understanding than learning with misunderstanding. Research provides many examples of the difficulties into which students have been led when they do not construct their own knowledge or are not given sufficient time to reflect on what they have learned. (One common problem involves students' overgeneralizing patterns such as linearity, believing, for example, that $(a + b)^2 = a^2 + b^2$ for any a and b. Reflection and trials would convince most students that this pattern does not hold for real numbers except when a or b is zero.) The classroom examples that follow suggest comparison. The first illustrates what can (and too often does) happen when students do not construct relationships among pieces of mathematical knowledge. The second describes a task taken from a reform curriculum that supports learning with understanding.

Classroom Examples

Common Symbol-String Misunderstandings.   The example discussed here was documented by Harel (in press). The high school student in this example was attempting to solve the inequality $((x - 1)^2 > 1)$. When asked to explain how she arrived at $x > 1$, she responded that "The solution to the equation $(x - 1)(x - 1) = 0$ is $x = 1$, $x - 1$." She then crossed out the three equality signs and above each wrote an inequality sign $>$, noting that "x is greater than 1." When she was then asked to solve $(x - 1)(x - 1) = 3$, she wrote: "$(x - 1) = 3, (x - 1) = 3$." Harel noted that:

> [her] mathematical behavior suggests that she was not thinking about the situations [or quantities] that these strings of symbols may represent; rather, the strings themselves were the situations she was reasoning about. That is, Patti's thinking was in terms of a symbolic, superficial structure shared by the three strings. . . . From her perspective, these strings share the same symbolic structure and, therefore, the same solution method must be applicable to them all.

Although this example concerns a high school student (mis)solving an inequality ($[x - 1]^2 > 1$) because she assumed that equality and inequality behave essentially in the same way, the application of similar procedures to symbols that look alike is common. (Another such example involves cross-multiplying, a procedure often used blindly without regard to whether the two fractions involved are separated by an equal sign or a plus sign.) For students who reason this way, who appear to be in the majority, not only is the surface shape of a symbol string a call to perform a certain procedure, but dealing with symbol strings (without attaching meaning) is what mathematics is all about. For them, understanding is remembering which rules to apply to which strings of symbols. Unfortunately, understanding algebra requires being able to connect knowledge of procedures with knowledge of concepts.

Meaningful Operations on Opaque Symbols. The example discussed next is taken from a fifth-grade unit, "Patterns & Symbols" (Roodhardt, Kindt, Burrill, & Spence, 1997), in *Mathematics in Context* (National Center for Research in Mathematics and Science & Freudenthal Institute, 1996–1998), a National Science Foundation–funded reform curriculum. Among the tasks it contains is one involving transformations on sequences of the letters *S* and *L*, where the letters represent rectangular blocks standing on end (*S*) or lying on their sides (*L*). In this task (see Fig. 8.3 for an example), students work with various transformation rules (e.g., $SS \rightarrow L$ and $LL \rightarrow S$) to act on such arrays, interpreting their results in terms of strings and vice-versa (e.g., What happens if you repeatedly apply these rules to the above array of blocks?) The students make up their own rules, apply them to their own designs and to those of others, and then interpret them (in both realms). Students gradually move toward more abstract substitution rules, which they can apply to arbitrary strings of symbols (e.g., sequences of their own initials).

Summary. Work on (opaque) formalisms is necessary throughout mathematics, independent of topic or students' use of modeling. Tasks such as the one just described both encourage students to work comfortably within

FIG. 8.3. Block array represented by letter sequence (*LSLLSSLSLSS*).

a world of opaque symbols not at all based on or referring to numbers and allow students to experience mathematics in ways that encourage understanding rather then alienation.

(TOPIC-STRAND) ALGEBRA AS THE STUDY OF STRUCTURES ABSTRACTED FROM COMPUTATIONS AND RELATIONS

Acts of generalization and abstraction based in computations (where the structure of the computation rather than its result becomes the focus of attention) give rise to abstract structures traditionally associated with abstract algebra, which, in turn, is traditionally regarded as fancy university-level mathematics. This side of algebra, beginning with computations on familiar numbers, has some roots in the 19th-century British idea of algebra as universalized arithmetic but has deeper roots in number theory. Indeed, this aspect of algebra is precisely what many professional mathematicians mean when they refer to algebra.

In structural-abstract algebra taught for understanding, structures arise from students' mathematical experience: from matrix representations of motions of the plane, symmetries of geometric figures (see next), modular arithmetic, manipulations of letters in words, or other, fairly arbitrary, even playful contexts. Such structures (a) can be articulated in preformal, natural language, (b) enrich student's understanding of the systems from which they are abstracted, (c) provide students intrinsically useful structures for computations freed of the particulars those structures were once tied to, and (d) provide them a base for yet higher levels of abstraction and formalization. What follows are two classroom examples, one illustrating the use of natural language to articulate the structures students discover, and the second, a class inquiry into dihedral group structures.

Classroom Examples

The Use of Natural Language to Articulate Algebraic Structure. In their study of students working a task again from the fifth-grade unit Patterns & Symbols (Roodhardt, Kindt, Burrill, & Spence, 1997) in *Mathematics in Context* (National Center for Research in Mathematics and Science & Freudenthal Institute, 1996–1998), Spence and Pligge (in press) cited the powerful understanding exhibited by students and their articulation of that understanding in preformal, natural language.

The students had just completed a task on the concept of even and odd. During this task, they played a game of Once, Twice, Go: Two players, on a signal, display a certain number of fingers from one hand. One player wins if the sum of the fingers is even; the other, if the sum is odd. In recording their games, students also used arrays of dots to represent odd and even numbers as well as sums of those numbers. At the end of this task, they were asked to explain the patterns they could see in these sums. One student explained:

- An even number and an odd number is always odd. Even always has pairs. Odd always has an extra. Putting them together will still leave that extra, so it's always odd.
- An odd number and an odd number is always even. Odds always have 1 left over, so 2 left over form a new pair.

This student's highly articulate response indicates the power of natural language (even in a fifth grader) to express and justify general relationships, in this case that "an even plus an odd is always odd" and "an odd plus an odd is always even."

Exploration of Dihedral Groups. In their study of children's natural ability to construct algebraic reasoning, Strom and Lehrer (in press) described a second-grade class using a quilting activity based in a curriculum unit, *TexTile Math* (Franco, 1997). This task engages students in a series of ideas customarily associated with the courses in abstract algebra offered to university mathematics majors. The activity begins with students designing a core square, which is then flipped or rotated to produce four versions of itself in a 2×2 array, the foundation design to be repeated to produce a quilt. Although the students cannot be said to be doing group theory, they are working in what we could regard as the concrete group of rigid motions of the square. Students working on this task confront many of the issues that university students confront initially when dealing with dihedral groups such as, What is the operation? When do I know two elements are the same? What is the result of repeatedly multiplying an element by itself? Will I ever get the identity element—the same as not doing anything at all? (This last question leads to the standard group-theory question, "What is the order of the elements of the group?")

Prior to the episode described next, the students had dealt with the issue of when two elements are the same. The class had determined that an up-flip (bringing the bottom of the quilting square forward and up) led to the same result as a down-flip (bringing the top forward and down) and had decided to call these two actions by the same name, up-down flip.

They then tried to determine how many up-down flips were needed to return a core square to its original position (identified as having the small *x* in the upper-left corner of the side facing them). With teacher scaffolding, they determined that it took two up-down flips to return the core square to its original position. The class then explored what happened when this flip was repeated. Notice that although the teacher (CC) scaffolded the discussion in the next example (and in the ones that follow), it was the students who actually drove the exploration forward, with their own extensions of the ideas and their own conjectures:

CC: And there's her little "x," to mark the top of the core [square], so I know this isn't the flip side. So two up-down flips gets it back right to where it started from.

Na: And zero, um, zero flips.

CC: Zero flips. Yeah, not flipping it.

Br: And four!

CC: Four? Let's try that.

Br: Four, six, eight, ten!

CC: Why would two, four, six, eight and ten flips make—

Br: Because, um, because, like, one's an odd number, and two's an even number. So if you just flipped it once it would be—

St: Different!

Br: It'd be the back. So try it four times.

CC: OK. This is Ka's beginning position, the "x" is in the top left. I'm gonna do up-down flips, four of them. Watch what one up-down flip makes it look like [flips the square.] Does it look the same or different?

Br: Different.

CC: OK, now instead of just doing one flip, I'm gonna try four flips. Do you think it will look the same or different?

All: Same.

CC: [Flips the square four times] One. Two. Three. Four.

BR: Brrr-di-doo di-doo! The same!

All: Same, same! [More trumpet sounds and clapping.]

(Strom & Lehrer, in press)

At this point, one student, Br, further conjectured that flipping the square any even number of times would make the square look the same as when they started:

CC: Um, what do you think about this idea of Br's? Br's idea is that I could do *any even* number of flips on this core square—

Br: Can't do eleven, but you can do twelve—

CC: Meaning two, four, six, eight, ten, twelve—Any *even* number of flips, and it would look the same.

Br: One's odd, two's even, three's odd, four's even.

CC: [Repeating Br to the class] And then she said for you, "One's odd, two's even, three's odd, four's even." OK, that's her idea. Ke has a question for you, Br, about your idea.

Ke: Well, you can go besides by ones, by twos. But if you go by ones, it'll just, like, the square will be on the other side. By twos, you could go up, like, as far as you wanted, and it would still be the same as when it was started, if you go by twos—if you flip it two times.

CC: So if I flip it two times, what will happen, Ke?

Ke: It will be the same.

CC: OK, so you're saying I could do what Br was saying, count by twos, as high as I wanted—

Ke: Then [what I mean is that at any counted number] it would be the same as it is now.

CC: So, no matter how big that number got, if I just counted by twos and then stopped at that number, and then I flipped it that many times, it would look just like this?

All: Yeah. Yes!

(Strom & Lehrer, in press)

Summary.   The second graders in the last examples not only dealt with concrete forms of issues and concepts important in elementary group theory, but, in episodes not shown here (see Strom & Lehrer, in press), they also dealt head-on with questions of argumentation, moving between the particular and the general and, specifically, the eternal problem of induction from examples. Clearly, the highly skilled orchestration over a long period of time by their teacher is critical to this class's culture of careful inquiry and open discussion. Her pedagogical style created a classroom where students learned mathematical concepts with understanding. The individual quilts created by the students in later extensions of this task not only focused the mathematical thinking, encouraged reflection on what they saw, and provided a common set of tangible, discussible objects, but also made tangible each student's ownership of the problem and the knowledge they themselves constructed. Even more, by design, their quilts shared an underlying structure that was gradually defined and elaborated through their guided discussions. As with the previous examples, this kind of algebra foundation-building is within the reach of most students and teachers, given a classroom culture of teaching and learning for understanding—despite the fact that the mathematics that they are building toward is currently regarded as appropriate for university-level mathematics majors. Finally, the reader may notice that part of this classroom's work appears in Lehrer et al. (chapter 5, this volume), a fact that underscores our point that learning algebraic reasoning is intimately connected to learning other important mathematics.

(TOPIC-STRAND) ALGEBRA AS THE STUDY OF FUNCTIONS, RELATIONS, AND JOINT VARIATION

The idea of function has perhaps its deepest conceptual roots in our sense of causality, growth, and continuous joint variation—where one quantity changes in conjunction with change in another. Although for most of the 20th century reform of high school mathematics has called for using function as a central, organizing concept, functions have traditionally been introduced in U.S. schools in precalculus courses at the high school level, and the traditional notation for representing functions has been symbolic (algebraic formulas). Recently, however, headway has been made, primarily in the new reform curricula being developed for middle and high schools.

As the following example illustrates, the concept of function can be fruitfully approached in the early grades, using familiar quantities that change over time (e.g., heights of plants or people, temperature, numbers of people who are eating or asleep at various times throughout the day) and representing them both pictorially and with time-based graphs. Similarly, students can work in familiar contexts. To explore, for example, the cost of beans as a function of the number of packages of beans purchased, students can package the beans themselves and, with appropriate teacher scaffolding, develop along the way their own methods of describing the cost of different numbers of bags of beans.

The two ideas of correspondence and variation of quantities, which underlie the concept of function, cut across and unify many different kinds of common mathematical experiences that can readily be introduced in elementary-school classes, including those involved with counting, measuring, and estimating. The idea of function embodies multiple instances, all collected within a single entity (e.g., a list, table, graph), a process that also involves generalizing—answering the question, "What is it that all these instances have in common?"

In the example discussed next (Tierney & Monk, in press), fourth-grade students analyzed graphs of plant height over time, graphs that represented functions of time. Several big ideas associated with interpreting functions came alive in this classroom—without numerical values and without formulas.

A Classroom Example of Functional Thinking

The example described here was taken from Tierney and Monk (in press). Students, working on a task in the unit "Changes Over Time" (Tierney, Weinberg, & Nemirovsky, 1994) from the curriculum series *Investigations in Number, Data, and Space* (TERC, 1994), were studying height versus time functions to compare both the changes in the plants' heights and the rate of change of height. Through a symbol system, in this case a graph, and in their own language, students were able to communicate what they learned as they thought, reflected, and talked about vertical height of familiar objects. In so doing, they began to make important distinctions between two ways of looking at functions: the value of a function versus the rate of change of that value (i.e., height vs. growth rate).

The children grew plants from seed, recorded the growth, and graphed plants' heights each day for 2 weeks. In the exchanges I cite in this section, they were interpreting qualitative graphs (provided by the instructor) of plant height over time. In these, only the shapes of graphs were known; no quantities were shown on the axes. In this particular class, all the students interpreted the steeper graphs as meaning the plant was growing faster and the higher graphs as showing a taller plant. At the point of the discussion I cite next, students were working on a problem with two graphs: the first above the second, but not as steep; the second lower but steeper (see Fig. 8.4a). This crossing-difference between the respective height and steepness properties of the two graphs provoked disagreement based in distinguishing height from change of height and change from rate of change. Some students focused on change in height (depicted by the slope of the graph), whereas others focused on current height and the growth of the plant that yielded the beginning height (before the growth shown on the graph [see Fig. 8.4b]). What follows is a description of the exchanges as students worked to understand what they saw and resolve it with what they already believed.

When the teacher asked which plant was growing faster, one student compared the growth of the plants by comparing the changes in height in a fixed amount of time (the rates of growth): "The light line. It started really small and got bigger and bigger and took the same amount of time to get to the same height." Two other students, however, responded directly to the shape, interpreting it in terms of comparative change: "The light one [grows faster], because it's always going up. The dark one is kind of steady and kind of going across"; and "The dark one is slightly going up and it's not going fast."

When questioned by a peer, this last student changed to another student's approach: "It didn't grow high in a short time." When the teacher questioned him ("Tell me about the changes"), he based his answer on the shape of the line, describing it in a language appropriate for the plant it depicted, "The dark line is only growing a little bit over a long time. The light line, the changes are bigger over the same amount of time."

Two other students then talked about the plant before and after the time depicted on the graph (see Fig. 8.4b): "I chose the dark line. The

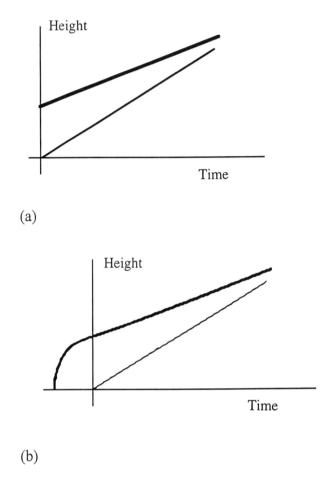

(a)

(b)

FIG. 8.4. Using height versus time functions to compare both changes in
the plants' heights and the rate of change of height. Note that (b) shows
the time before the beginning of (a).

light line takes time to grow up. It's going to take it a long time to catch
up with the black line"; and "The dark line grew faster at the beginning,
before the graph."

The teacher asked the second of these students to come up to the board
and draw the dark line as he thought it might have been before the graph
began. He started at the left end of the dark line and extended it leftward,
making a line that curved down to the horizontal axis, almost vertically.
The student, moving his finger along the line he drew, said, "It grew fast,
then still fast, then started to get steady."

Summary. These excerpts were part of what Tierney and Monk (in press) described as a spirited discussion among students exploring the concept of function: in this case, the properties of the functions describing the height over time of plants they themselves had grown and how those properties might relate to what the functions stood for. The many ways of comparing change and interpreting graphs (explored as well in university calculus courses) appeared in the informal language and graphical notation of these fourth graders. Their understanding of how plants grow, refined in the 2 weeks of recording the growth of their own plants (previous to this discussion), was extended and applied to make sense of the graphs and relations among sizes of plants, changes in size, and rates of change. To decide which plant was growing faster, some children focused on visual aspects, such as steepness, whereas others focused on implicit quantitative information.

One student's belief that "the dark line grew faster at the beginning, before the graph" (i.e., that part of the graph was missing) raises an important issue in the use of symbols, in this case, the representation or model: "Is it a complete record, the only source of available information about the event, or is it like an illustration that tells part of the story to be supplemented by other things we know and believe?" (Tierney & Monk, in press).

How do the ways we organize the representation system (into parts and wholes) relate to the way we organize the experience being represented? Does the whole graph always stand for a whole situation, or, if not, when does it stand for only part of one? (And how can we tell when it does?) Does the labeling of the graph give it absolute meaning or range? Or can we assume, as this student did, that there is a before-the-beginning and an after-the-end? These are deep, subtle matters—and, importantly, elementary school students, in an extended exploration in an investigative classroom culture (i.e., a classroom where students learn with understanding) can begin to make sense of such mathematical issues.

ALGEBRA AS A CLUSTER OF MODELING AND PHENOMENA-CONTROLLING LANGUAGES

Quantitative reasoning, as well as the use of functions and relations, involves building mathematical systems through, usually, several cycles of improvement and interpretation, which act to describe phenomena or situations and to support reasoning about them. Put more simply, quantitative reasoning involves modeling, and many have argued that the modeling of situations is the primary reason for studying algebra.

In modeling, we begin with phenomena and attempt to mathematize them. But the use of computers and graphing calculators, increasingly common in nontraditional and some traditional classrooms, enables us to rethink how we explore and model phenomena—and how we can assist students in coming to understand the mathematical concepts behind those phenomena. For example, we can now use mathematics to simulate phenomena within the computer and even drive physical devices such as motorized cars on a track using data from a computer or graphing calculator. In fact, computer languages amount to an algebra-like language within which we can create, explore (to some degree experience), and extend mathematical environments. Similarly, coordinate graphs can create–control phenomena. Whether these technological environments are used to model or create–control phenomena, they change in fundamental ways how we relate the particular to the general and how we can state and justify mathematical conjectures. But more important, they can change how we teach and learn mathematics—even, in fact, how we relate to the mathematics itself. The following example suggests a new level of intimacy between students' activity and the mathematical notations that they use and interpret.

Example of Mixed Modeling and Phenomenon-Controlling Interactions in Physical and Computer-Based Motion

Background. As part of a 5-week summer program for economically disadvantaged children, 15 students, who had recently finished either third or fourth grade, were involved in a program conducted by two teachers and the principal from the students' (urban) school and who were assisted by the author and two SimCalc[2] project staff members. Students were involved in an extended exploration first of their own physical movement and then of related movement issues in a computer simulation (developed as part of the SimCalc project, directed by the author). Students' work began with creating a 50-foot path with masking tape in the gymnasium and then marking it at 2-foot intervals, with double marks at the 10s places. Over a period of 3 days, they studied their own motion, using a combination of the marked masking-tape path and stopwatches. Although (as expected) they were unable to quantify their velocity numerically, they were quite able to distinguish three values of their own speed: slow, medium, and fast. They also accepted the fact that one person's medium might be close to someone else's slow or fast. They timed one another's trips down the path and recorded these in three tables, one each for slow, medium, and fast. The fact that they were able to move, measure, count, and record their data was a source of delight and fascination for them.

Students then moved to a motion-simulation software system, Elevators, part of the SimCalc MathWorlds software system (Kaput, Roschelle, De-

Laura, Burke, & Zeppenfeld, 1997). Through elevators that they themselves were able to control, using velocity versus time graphs, students were able to reenact a number of the tasks that they had engaged in physically. The sections that follow describe how they related their own physical and kinesthetic experiences to their computer-based ones (elevator simulations) over eight sessions spread over 2 hot (and un-air-conditioned) summer weeks.

Building Understanding. On the third day (after they had recorded the lengths of time they took to move the entire 50-foot pathway at their slow, medium, and fast paces and had discussed how these rates differed from student to student), students engaged in planned movements: to walk or run for given lengths of time (timed with a stopwatch) at various paces. For example, a student might be asked to go for 2 seconds each at slow, fast, and medium, or to go fast for 2 seconds, slow for 3, and medium for 2 more. Several students repeated a given set of directions, stopping and standing at the end of their trip as a way of recording and comparing (with their peers) how far they had gone under the given stipulations. The boys, more than the girls, tended to value higher speeds, hence distances, particularly early in the tasks. The issue of competition arose as some students came to realize that the purpose of the task was not to go as far as possible under the given velocity constraints, but to be as precise as possible in carrying out the motion instructions. These tasks helped the students develop a perspective on their own motion and a sensitivity to relationships among time, speed, and distance—although they were not expected to quantify these relationships until much later, after substantial experience.

On the third and fourth days, students engaged in a paired activity in which one student of the pair was to move at a constant rate while the other moved according to directions similar to ones that they had previously enacted. After a couple of trials, during which the students started and ended at the same times, the constant speed student was asked to travel at a perfectly constant rate in such a way as to end up at exactly the same place as the other student by the end of the given time interval. Thus, if successful, the constant-speed student would be moving at the average speed of his or her counterpart, whose speed would vary according to the given instructions (some of which were provided by other students).

Bringing out the notion of constant speed in this very concrete, visible way directly confronted students' tendencies to want to catch up. Those students who were not in the currently moving pair lined the pathway, observing the motion closely. When a student who was supposed to be traveling at a constant speed sped up or slowed down (usually in fear that he or she would not reach the endpoint simultaneously with his or her counterpart), the audience shouted its disapproval or corrections. This led to considerable concentration on the part of those moving to maintain a constant pace.

For students who cycled through this task and variations of it (eventually all students), the notion of constant rate became constructed knowledge, a notion of speed they were acutely sensitive to and were able to reflect on and articulate. Students discussed and were concerned, for example, that the moving person reach the given constant speed as soon as possible and that, at the end of the trip, the moving stop abruptly. Because other students were timing them as they carried out the publicly announced slow–medium–fast instructions, they also became more aware of the length of a given time interval: The quantities and concepts associated with constant speed and time interval were made their own in an intimate, deeply felt kinesthetic sense and at the same time were connected to their emerging knowledge of graphs and functions.

Using Computer Simulations and Dynamic Graphs to Represent Quantitative Relationships. At first, the quantitative relationships and concepts arising from these tasks were described using preformal language and numbers. Beginning on the fifth day, however, the students moved to the computer simulations: buildings with two elevator shafts each. The screen had three draggable icons on the toolbar: one each for slow, medium, and fast (see Fig. 8.5). These students could drop on a velocity versus time graph and get a horizontal line segment that represented either 1, 2, or 4 floors per

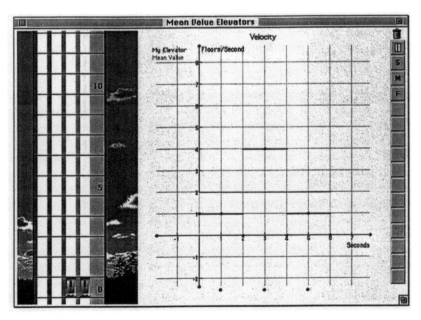

FIG. 8.5. Slow, medium, fast velocity graphs controlling the elevators in SimCalc task.

second in the simulation. They could then stretch these segments horizontally as needed to determine the length of time the elevator traveled at the indicated speed. (Thus, students could create and manipulate piecewise constant velocity functions.) When the students ran the elevators (by clicking on the big arrow in the Controls window), the elevators moved according to the velocity graphs that the students had created. Working in pairs at the computer over the fifth and sixth days, the students worked through a series of tasks that paralleled and then built on the work they had done physically in the gymnasium.

The point of the computer side of the task, however, was to continue the process of quantifying, or mathematizing, motion. Physical and cybernetic environments differ in a fundamental way: The physical is kinesthetically rich but quantitatively poor (or, perhaps more accurately, inaccessible); the cybernetic is kinesthetically vacuous but quantitatively rich. For example, the floors in the building are numbered, and the graphs are numbered and labeled in such a way as to help students establish a close connection between the graphs and the building floors. Thus, a student creating a medium velocity graph (2 floors per second), with the elevator traveling a given direction for a given length of time (6 seconds—as in the flat graph in Fig. 8.5) would be asked, "Where will the elevator finish its trip?" Rather quickly, the students came to see that the area (a rectangle) under the flat-topped graph segment gives the answer, and that, if the velocity is composed of several segments, they could predict the final position by adding up the areas under the appropriate segments.

In the final 2 days, the students returned to the physical context to deal with the issues of changing direction and negative velocity—repeating the cycle of physical and then computer-based motion. Somewhat surprising was the ease with which students made the transition between horizontal and vertical motion. (At that time, we did not have a horizontal motion simulation available.) It appears that the natural motion-talk, which occurred in both contexts, served to link the two motions. Discussions about speeding up, slowing down, turning around, and so on applied to both realms, and these terms were used to describe both the graphs and the motion (both the motion on the computer screen and their own physical motion).

Summary. Students were quite clearly personally invested in the simulation and the motions they were creating. Almost unanimously they chose to name the elevators after themselves (the program allowed them to both color and name the elevators, and new versions of the software allow students to modify actors in the simulations even further). When pairs of motions were involved, such as in the average-speed task, they took ownership of their respective elevators, often referring to them in the first person (as in "I'm ahead" or "I'm slowing down"). Additionally, the fact that they worked on the computer in pairs allowed them to continue to communicate informally—an extension of the conversational mode employed in the physical context.

The development of understanding in this situation involved intimate connections between students' physical actions and the motion simulations, connections that were mediated by the students' own talk about both sides of the connection and by the not-quite-standard graphical notation, which proved a powerful form of expression for the students, both as a modeling language and as a phenomenon-controlling language. I feel that the structure of the task and students' own (similar) physical exploration of motion were the foundations both for their understanding and their investment—their making this knowledge their own. Without that prior physical exploration, which built the concepts and kinesthetic sense of what these velocity graphs were all about, this would have been an empty exercise in symbol manipulation.

REFLECTIONS

The five aspects of algebra except for the second (symbol manipulation) that we have examined in this chapter are not well represented in standard algebra courses. Some may be tempted to say that what we have described here is not algebra, to which we would reply, "Yes," if "algebra" is what commonly occurs in standard Algebra I and Algebra II courses. But the assumption of this chapter is that algebra must be much broader, deeper, and richer than that. Algebra writ large cuts across topics and adds a conceptual unity, depth, and power that in our K through 8 curriculum, especially in the earlier grades, has been difficult to achieve. Although in this chapter we have deliberately chosen illustrations that exhibited young students led by sensitive teachers, the algebra we have shown here is neither a mystery nor out of reach of most teachers and most students. Indeed, elementary and middle-school students *can* make sense of complex situations while simultaneously building big mathematical ideas. It is my premise that this "fancy" algebra, taught, I hope, *in classrooms that promote understanding*, will prove more accessible than the traditional algebra that everybody loves to hate.

NOTES

1. Funded by the NSF Applications of Advanced Technology Program, Grant #RED 9619102 and the National Center for Improvement of Student Learning and Achievement, University of Wisconsin–Madison, U.S. Dept. of Education Prime Grant #R305A60007.

2. SimCalc is a technology and curriculum research and development project intended to democratize access to the basic ideas underlying calculus beginning in the early grades and extending to AP calculus and beyond.

REFERENCES

Bastable, V., & Schifter, D. (in press). Classroom stories: Examples of elementary students engaged in early algebra. In J. Kaput (Ed.), *Employing children's natural powers to build algebraic reasoning in the content of elementary mathematics.* Mahwah, NJ: Lawrence Erlbaum Associates.

Franco, B. (1997). *TexTile Math.* Worth, IL: Creative Publications.

Harel, G. (in press). Symbolic reasoning and transformational reasoning and their effect on algebraic reasoning. In J. Kaput (Ed.), *Employing children's natural powers to build algebraic reasoning in the content of elementary mathematics.* Mahwah, NJ: Lawrence Erlbaum Associates.

Kaput, J., Roschelle, J., DeLaura, R., Burke, J. & Zeppenfeld, K. (1997). SimCalc MathWorlds [Software]. Berkeley, CA: Key Curriculum Press.

National Center for Research in Mathematics and Science Education & Freudenthal Institute. (Eds.). (1996–1998). *Mathematics in context.* Chicago: Encyclopaedia Britannica.

National Council of Teachers of Mathematics. (1991). *Professional standards for teaching mathematics.* Reston, VA: Author.

Roodhardt, A., Kindt, M., Burrill, G., & Spence, M. (1997). Patterns and symbols. In National Center for Research in Mathematical Sciences Education & Freudenthal Institute (Eds.), *Mathematics in context.* Chicago: Encyclopaedia Britannica.

Spence, M., & Pligge, M. (in press). The algebraic eye of middle grade students. In J. Kaput (Ed.), *Employing children's natural powers to build algebraic reasoning in the content of elementary mathematics.* Mahwah, NJ: Lawrence Erlbaum Associates.

Strom, D., & Lehrer, R. (in press). Springboards to algebra. In J. Kaput (Ed.), *Employing children's natural powers to build algebraic reasoning in the content of elementary mathematics.* Mahwah, NJ: Lawrence Erlbaum Associates.

TERC. (1994). *Investigations in number, data, and space.* Palo Alto, CA: Dale Seymour.

Tierney, C., & Monk, G. S. (in press). Children's reasoning about change over time. In. J. Kaput (Ed.), *Employing children's natural powers to build algebraic reasoning in the content of elementary mathematics.* Mahwah, NJ: Lawrence Erlbaum Associates.

Tierney, C., Weinberg, A., & Nemirovsky, R. (1994). Changes over time: Graphs. In TERC, *Investigations in number, data, and space.* Palo Alto, CA: Dale Seymour.

FOR FURTHER READING

Algebraic thinking [Focus issue]. (1997). *Teaching Children Mathematics, 3* (6).

Algebraic thinking[Focus issue]. (1997). *Mathematics Teaching in the Middle School, 2* (4).

Algebraic thinking [Focus issue]. (1997). *Mathematics Teacher, 90* (2).

Part III

DEVELOPING CLASSROOMS THAT PROMOTE UNDERSTANDING

Chapter 9

Assessment in Classrooms That Promote Understanding

Mary C. Shafer
Thomas A. Romberg
University of Wisconsin–Madison

Other chapters provide compelling evidence that teachers can and have used a domain-based approach to create classrooms that promote student understanding. Yet these teachers also must assess student understanding and performance as a consequence of instruction and be able to trace the growth of that understanding over time. Using a domain-based approach to the development of understanding requires a close look at the ways we can appropriately assess students and still provide sufficient evidence of student learning for parents, administrators, and the general public. Our purposes in this chapter are threefold: (a) to examine ways of documenting students' understanding, using a domain-based approach to assessment; (b) to describe examples of assessment items related to this approach; and (c) to discuss difficulties that have arisen as teachers have implemented such an approach to assessment.

DESIGNING AN APPROPRIATE ASSESSMENT PROGRAM

The difference between a domain-based approach to assessment and traditional assessment lies in the meaning attributed to understanding in a mathematical domain. Understanding the concepts of a domain involves more than accumulating a set of facts and procedures. Rather, understanding develops as new relationships among pieces of existing knowledge are sought, tested, and realized, or as new information is connected to and integrated with existing knowledge. As understanding grows, the facts, relationships, and procedures in a domain become resources that aid reasoning in solving ordinary problems in routine ways and in generating insights for making sense of unfamiliar situations. This growth in understanding in a domain occurs intermittently and sporadically in periods of progression and regression, rather than in linear increments or stages. Assessment using a domain-based approach, therefore, is not limited to checking whether students have acquired mathematical facts and procedures emphasized during instruction. Assessment focuses on the new relationships that students are forming among mathematical ideas, their use of existing knowledge in new situations, and the levels of reasoning applied in solving problems. Assessment examines the ways students' knowledge is changing over time during instructional units related specifically to the domain, as well as in instructional units focused on other domains, during one grade level and across grade levels.

The ideas expressed in this chapter are based on other assumptions:

- Assessment should be viewed as an ongoing process that is integrated with instruction.
- Multiple sources of evidence are needed to assess students' developing knowledge in a domain.
- Assessment should involve the deliberate documentation of information derived from classroom interaction as well as from written work.

In this chapter we examine one assessment program using a domain-based approach to documenting student understanding in mathematics and point out the possibilities of its implementation. We focus on assessment of the growth in mathematical knowledge through attention to the mental activities that promote learning with understanding described in chapter 2 by Carpenter and Lehrer (i.e., constructing relationships, extending and applying mathematical knowledge, reflecting on mathematical experiences, articulating what one knows, making mathematical knowledge one's own) at varying levels of complexity.

Key Aspects of Design

Because learning mathematics with understanding develops gradually over time through active engagement in mathematical thinking, assessment using a domain-based approach requires changes in thinking about and planning assessment opportunities. Understanding the instructional sequence for the development of the concept throughout the curriculum is essential, especially in domain-based curricula designed to enhance gradual formalization of mathematical concepts. In such curricula, understanding of formal mathematical symbols and procedures develops through students' informal reasoning strategies and the use of mathematical tools (such as the fraction bar) over several units in one grade level or across grade levels. Evidence of individual students' knowledge in a particular domain should, therefore, be gathered during all instructional units related to the domain as well as when opportunities arise during other instructional units in which the concepts of the particular domain are used.

The development of a domain-based assessment program involves creation of numerous opportunities for informal and formal assessment that involve mathematical reasoning at increasingly complex levels and that document growth over time.

Informal Assessment. The assessment program should capitalize on the information that teachers gather through informal assessment methods during instruction rather than assessing only written responses on assignments, quizzes, or tests. Items embedded in instructional materials can be used to focus classroom assessment. The instructional goals of selected items might vary in focus from more narrow levels (e.g., whether students appropriately apply a particular mathematical tool, such as a fraction bar) to a broader application of concepts and reasoning in solving nonroutine problems. Observation of students as they work can provide opportunities for teachers to learn about students' understanding of mathematical concepts, thought processes, and solution strategies. Classroom discussions offer numerous opportunities for teachers to gather information about students' reasoning. Questions can be posed that involve students in seeking patterns, stating and testing conjectures, and moving toward generalizations. The information gained through such informal assessment can enhance instructional decisions. Teachers might, for example, change a familiar problem slightly to stimulate thinking, approach instruction on a concept in a different way, encourage students to make connections among mathematical ideas, or ask students to articulate their thinking in oral or written presentations.

Formal Assessment. Items for formal (end-of-unit or end-of-grade-level) assessments can be selected or created in ways that enable students to demonstrate what they know and can do rather than determine what they do not know. End-of-unit assessments ask students to select and apply appropriate mathematical tools for problem situations that are frequently set in contexts different from those posed during instructional units. Such items provide teachers opportunities to monitor the flexibility with which students use their knowledge of the same concept in a variety of contexts. Also, because end-of-unit assessments are often completed without interaction between students or between students and teacher, the items offer opportunities for students to explain and communicate, in writing, their own solutions and thinking processes.

End-of-grade level assessments offer a different perspective about students' developing mathematical knowledge. Because they do not rely on direct connections to particular instructional units, end-of-grade assessments can provide specific evidence of students' increased and more powerful use of concepts, procedures, reasoning, and abilities at the end of a yearlong period of study. Although in theory all domains should be assessed at the end of a school year, no single assessment can contain the quantity and quality of assessment items needed to assess all concepts and procedures. As a result, items on end-of-grade-level assessments are generally designed to provide evidence about the depth of students' understanding related to some of the more important domains addressed in the curriculum. These assessment items present especially good opportunities to assess thinking that involves more than one domain as well as students' abilities to make mathematics their own.

Growth Over Time.   Because understanding in a domain is acquired over a long period of time, assessment should reflect the continued development of understanding. Growth in understanding is a gradual process in which the student progresses and regresses in abilities to use the concepts in a domain. Assessment, then, involves the creation of both informal and formal assessments that require attention to relationships the student has constructed at particular points in time, the variance in these relationships over time, the use of knowledge in the domain as resources in approaching novel situations, and the complexity of reasoning applied by the student in the domain. The evidence gathered can be used to inform instructional decisions that further promote learning with understanding, for example, to encourage connections among the concepts of the domain or to provide different contexts for the application of these concepts.

Attention to Levels of Reasoning

As understanding in a particular domain grows, the concepts and procedures of the domain are used in more powerful ways. A domain-based approach to assessment of knowledge in the domain therefore includes attention to the levels of reasoning students apply in using the ideas of the domain. Assessment opportunities involve students in using the mental activities described in Carpenter and Lehrer (chapter 2, this volume) while providing attention to increasingly complex levels of reasoning: reproduction, connections, and analysis.

Reproduction. Mental activities involving reproduction include recall of facts and definitions and routine, efficient application of standard procedures such as performing a particular calculation, solving an equation, or constructing a graph. Assessment items that elicit reproduction are frequently presented without connections to real or imaginable situations in such formats as fill-in-the-blank or short answer. Because basic facts, definitions, and procedures are also used in solutions of complex problems, they can be assessed in student responses for complex problems as well.

An approach to assessment that includes only items that elicit reproduction limits the assessment of knowledge in a particular domain because these items cannot assess the extent to which a student uses the resources in the domain in mathematical reasoning and communication. Assessment items that involve connections and analysis present situations for students to think about and apply mathematics in new situations and provide opportunities for students to develop deeper understanding of mathematical concepts and procedures in a domain.

Connections. Making connections among mathematical ideas involves connections within and across mathematical domains, integration of information, and decisions about the appropriate mathematical tools needed to solve nonroutine problems. Connections among mathematical ideas are formed as students reflect on their existing knowledge in light of new information or new situations. In making connections, students construct relationships between new ideas and existing knowledge. Students also construct relationships as they extend and apply mathematical ideas already understood. Assessment items that elicit connections, therefore, engage students in three of the mental activities that promote learning with understanding and often include articulation of reasoning as well. Such assessment items are frequently set in real or imaginable contexts and, although there is generally only one answer to each problem, can be solved in multiple ways. Student responses, therefore, can show qualitative differences in approach and understanding.

Analysis. Mathematical thinking at complex levels in mathematics includes interpretation, analysis, and mathematical argumentation; development of the student's own models and strategies; and generalization. Often situated in real or imaginable contexts, assessment items that elicit analysis are open-ended and require that students determine appropriate strategies and select appropriate mathematical tools for the solution. Because students often develop innovative solutions for these items, their responses should include all assumptions and reasoning used and the mathematical arguments that support their conclusions. Assessment items that elicit analysis engage students in all mental activities that promote learning with understanding. Students must search their existing mathematical knowledge to make sense of the new situation. This involves reflection, construction of relationships, extension and application of mathematical knowledge, and solutions that involve articulation of mathematical ideas. Because assessment items that elicit analysis require students to determine the mathematical ideas and tools needed for appropriate solutions, they are especially useful for assessing the fifth mental activity, making mathematics one's own.

Summary

Understanding in a domain involves the use of concepts, procedures, and strategies in that domain as resources in thinking about and solving novel problem situations. Assessing that understanding will involve multidimensional approaches that make use of both informal and formal assessment, that examine growth of student understanding in a domain over time, and that pay particular attention to levels of reasoning. In the section that follows, we examine specific assessment items and point out the ways in which student responses demonstrate the mental abilities that promote learning with understanding. We then explore ways in which the evidence of students' knowledge produced in responses to these assessments can, in turn, inform instructional decisions for teaching with understanding.

EXAMPLES OF ASSESSMENT ITEMS

In this section, we discuss a variety of assessment items that can be used with the domain-based approach to assessment outlined previously. We present a series of examples from classrooms that show evidence of students' mathematical knowledge as they engage in the mental activities that promote learning with understanding at increasingly complex levels. In these classrooms, teachers are implementing *Mathematics in Context* (MiC), a comprehensive curriculum for Grades 5 through 8 funded by the National Science Foundation. The curriculum includes 40 instructional units (10 per grade level) organized into four domains, each encompassing related mathematical subdomains:

- Number: whole numbers, common fractions, ratio, decimal fractions, percents, and integers;
- Algebra: expressions about variation, graphs, and formulas for patterns and functions;
- Geometry: measurement, spatial visualization, synthetic geometry, and coordinate and transformational geometry; and
- Statistics and probability: data visualization, chance, distribution and variability, and quantification of expectations.

Each unit includes activities that move students toward making connections among subdomains in a particular domain and making connections among domains.

The assessment program for MiC was designed to make the goals of mathematics instruction operational. Teachers are encouraged to use a variety of assessment methods to gather multidimensional information about students' thinking processes, solution strategies, and mathematical knowledge. Assessments include ways for teachers to examine students' abilities to use basic skills; mathematize situations (i.e., extract the mathematics in a situation and use that mathematics to solve problems); reflect on mathematical strategies, discuss results, and formulate arguments that support their thinking; communicate using mathematical vocabulary, diagrams, symbols, and models; and form generalizations. In the example assessment items described next, students are asked to *construct relationships* between text and visual representations and to *extend* and *apply* their mathematical knowledge in making sense of the information provided. In explaining their work to the teacher and in participating in discussions, they are expected to *reflect* on their strategies and use of mathematics in order to *articulate* a mathematical explanation. By thinking about and applying mathematics in the context of a real or imaginable problem, students make strides toward *making mathematics their own*. Their strategies, solutions, and later discussions (both one-on-one and whole class) provide viable evidence of students' understanding of these concepts.

Informal Assessments

Although assessment of reproduction is often completed during informal assessment, in the sections that follow, we examine items that provide opportunities for students to engage in the five mental activities and assess reasoning at the levels of connections and analysis.

Extension and Application of Knowledge. In Fig. 9.1a, we present a problem from the sixth-grade MiC algebra unit Keeping on Track, in which students explore the connection between individual data points and the continuous nature of line graphs, interpret line graphs by examining both global features (such as regularity and slope) and point-specific information, and write stories that explain line graphs in relation to given contexts. As an assessment embedded in instructional materials, the problem allows students to extend and apply their knowledge of algebra within the subdomain of patterns and functions. To solve the problem, students must integrate their knowledge of minimum and maximum values, slope, and variance with information they have been given in text and graphical representation. The problem, therefore, provides a situation in which students make connections among mathematical ideas.

(a)

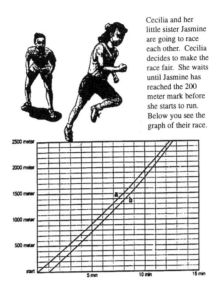

Cecilia and her little sister Jasmine are going to race each other. Cecilia decides to make the race fair. She waits until Jasmine has reached the 200 meter mark before she starts to run. Below you see the graph of their race.

20. a. Identify the names of runners a and b. How do you know?

b. Who won the race and how far behind was the other person when the winner crossed the finish line?

c. Who was running faster in this race? How do you know?

(b)

Christina's Response

(A) I think A is Jasmine, because it said that she started first, and A is exactly on the starting line. The book said Cecilia started 200 meters after, so that's the same as the graph. B is Cecilia.

(B) Jasmine won, and Cecilia was about 3 meters behind.

(C) Cecilia was running faster because when they started, she was 200 meters behind, and when they ended, she was only a little behind. Cecilia was able to catch up although she got a later start.

Julio's Response

(A) A is Jasmine because A started first and it said above that Cecilia gave her sister a head start.

(B) A won the race by 20 seconds.

(C) Cecilia was because she started one minute behind and ended up losing by 20 seconds.

FIG. 9.1. Assessment item from Keeping on Track. (a) The problem. (b) Student responses. Used with permission of Encyclopaedia Britannica Educational Corporation.

The responses from two students, Christina and Julio, are shown in Fig. 9.1b. Christina formed correct conclusions: Although Jasmine (the first runner) won the race, Cecilia (the second runner) ran faster. In Part A, Christina pointed out the ways in which the graph verified statements in the text. In her response to Part B, Christina noted that Cecilia was about 3 meters behind the winner rather than about 100 meters behind. Because Part B required an interpretation of specific information in the graph within the context of the problem, to further assess Christina's thinking and knowledge in algebra, the teacher might ask questions to ascertain Christina's strategy for determining the 3-meter difference and scaffold other questions to assist her in interpreting the graph correctly. The response to Part C, although correct, lacked an emphasis on mathematics, making it difficult for the teacher to assess the extension and application of Christina's knowledge of graphs. A more thorough response might have included the distance Cecilia gained on Jasmine during the race, an examination of the starting and finishing times, or an interpretation related to the differences in the slopes of the lines.

Julio also reached the same (correct) conclusion to Part A. His response, although correct, lacked a clear explanation of the connection between the graph and the text. Again, Julio's response to teacher questioning about his reasoning could provide evidence of understanding not available from his written response. In Part B, Julio chose to show the differences in finishing in terms of seconds (rather than meters), demonstrating a qualitatively different, but equally appropriate and accurate, interpretation of Part B. In his response to Part C, Julio used information from the graph to make an interpretation that supported his conclusion. Julio demonstrated his ability to extend and apply his knowledge of algebra in his responses to Parts B and C.

Classroom discussions can provide substantial evidence about students' developing knowledge and understanding in a mathematical domain. The student responses described do provide information about the students' abilities to obtain information about particular points and reason about global information in the graph. But the differences in these students' responses can also be brought out in whole-class discussions, during which students think about the problem situation from another student's perspective and ask questions that clarify various strategies. Expectations for thorough explanations that emphasize mathematics can then be fostered during such dialogue.

Reflection. The assessment item discussed here ("Describe what a shadow is. How are shadows and blind spots similar?") is from the MiC seventh-grade unit Looking at an Angle and was designed to engage students in reflection on geometric ideas in the subdomain of spatial orientation. Throughout the section preceding this problem, students explore the formation of a blind spot (or shadow) when a vision line (or the sun's rays) hits an opaque object and use a vision line (or representative light ray) as the hypotenuse of a right triangle in side-view representations. Through their explorations, students come to realize that differences in the type of light source (an artificial light source or the sun), the angle of the vision line (or the sun's rays), and the height of the given objects produce differences in the size of blind spots (or shadow lengths). To complete the item, students must consider the effects of the light source and the object blocking the view on the size and shape of the shadow or blind spot and then make inferences about the similarity of shadows and blind spots. In this item, students reflect on the mathematical activities engaged in during instruction and use analysis to mathematize the problem situation, develop their own solution strategies, and explain the mathematics in written form. They also decide whether to use diagrams or models to support their reasoning and–or assist their peers and teacher to understand the mathematics they are using to solve the problem.

Construction of Relationships. The problem shown in Fig. 9.2a is from the MiC sixth-grade unit Fraction Times and is designed to engage students in constructing relationships between number subdomains (fractions and percents) and across mathematical domains (number and statistics). Students interpret the visual representation (a pie chart) of the problem information, relate the (children's) statements to that representation, and compare those statements using their knowledge of fractions and percents. In so doing, they analyze and integrate the information given and apply their knowledge of number subdomains (fractions and percents) and statistics (analysis of representations of data). In each of the responses in Fig. 9.2b, students demonstrated understanding of the pie chart by accurately evaluating the children's statements about the fraction of people who were against construction of new nuclear power plants.

The written responses, however, might not have yielded enough information for the teacher to assess students' construction of relationships among mathematical ideas. If other evidence from classroom interactions is unavailable for these students, the teacher might further assess the relationships they are constructing between number subdomains. For example, the teacher might ask Students C and D how they determined that $\frac{2}{3}$ is about 66%. Their responses might indicate that this is a memorized fact or that they had used a calculator to convert the $\frac{2}{3}$ to an equivalent decimal representation. Other students might have used a number sense strategy such as the one shown in Fig. 9.3a. Still others might have used a visual tool, such as the fraction–percent bar in Fig. 9.3b, to support their reasoning. Further questions, therefore, could provide more evidence of the relationships students were constructing between fraction and percent representations of numbers.

(a)

19. Compare the statements and choose the one that you think best describes the pie chart. Explain your choice.

(b)

A. I think Mary's statement is the best one. Mary said that most of the people are against new nuclear plants and the pie chart shows that 2/3 of the people are against them. 2/3 is most of the people.

B. I think that Juan is the best one because Juan said 2/3 of the people are against it and that's the same thing that the pie chart shows.

C. I think Karen has the best statement. She said just over 60% of the people are against new plants. That is close to the 2/3 shown in the pie chart because 2/3 is about 66%.

D. I think Linda is the best. She said that almost 70% of the people don't want new nuclear plants and the pie chart shows that 2/3 are against new plants. 2/3 is about 66% which is closer to 70% than to the 60% Karen said.

FIG. 9.2. Assessment item from Fraction Times. (a) The problem. (b) Sample student responses adapted from teacher's guide. Used with permission of Encyclopaedia Britannica Educational Corporation.

(a)

1/3 of 100 is about 33

2/3 of 100 is double that or about 66

So 2/3 is about 66%

(b)

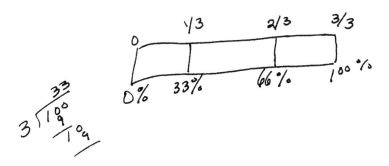

FIG. 9.3. Sample student strategies for determining the relationship between a fraction ($\frac{2}{3}$) and the percent it represents (66%). (a) Number sense strategy. (b). Fraction–percent bar.

Articulation of Relationships and Making Mathematics One's Own. The following problem, from the eighth-grade MiC unit Insights Into Data, is designed to engage students in articulating relationships among numerical and graphical representations of data and in articulating conclusions based on the data. Students are asked to write a report about their experiments dealing with the growth of bean sprouts over time. In this assessment item, students make a statistical summary of the data they have gathered. During this process, they raise the types of questions that should be asked when analyzing data sets: "What is the distribution of the data?" "Are there outliers or clusters?" "Which plot is most useful for initially picturing the data? For comparing data sets from different treatments?" "What statistic is most appropriate for summarizing the data?" These questions allow students to apply their knowledge of single-number statistics (mean, range, median, quartiles, mode) and representations of data (e.g., histogram, box plot, plot over time). For instance, if there is an outlier in the data, students might select the median to summarize the data because the effects of the outlier do not influence the median. Students might also use knowledge that box plots, although useful in looking at variation among different groups in the experiment, obscure individual data points and decide that a stem-and-leaf plot is more appropriate for developing an initial sense of the distribution of the data.

Ample evidence of students' abilities to articulate the relationships they are discovering can be gathered through listening to student interactions in small groups and observing all phases of their work: planning, selection of numerical and graphical representations, written support for their conclusions, and oral presentation to the class. Although the item elicits analysis, students also make connections when integrating information and making decisions about appropriate statistics and graphical representations and use reproduction when applying technical skills to accurately calculate the statistics and complete representations of the data. In addition to articulating their thinking and conclusions, students move toward making mathematics their own as they explore, represent, interpret, and analyze the data and develop mathematical arguments (statistical summaries, in this case) to support their conclusions.

Formal Assessments

End-of-Unit Assessments. In this section, we examine items from the end-of-unit assessments from Per Sense, a fifth-grade MiC unit. During this number unit, students think about percent as a means of standardization useful in making comparisons between quantities. Algorithms are not emphasized in the unit. Rather, students use mathematical tools such as the percent bar, the ratio table, and benchmark percents (e.g., 1%, 10%, 25%, 50%) to support their thinking, estimation, and calculation. This emphasis gives students opportunities to develop conceptual understanding of percent in realistic problems. The end-of-unit assessment, Jammin', shown in Fig. 9.4, is composed of three questions in the number subdomain of percent (and subdomains of fractions and ratios, if students use the relationships between fractions, ratios, and percent). Because the instructional unit did not include an emphasis on procedures or this particular context for thinking about percents, responses to the questions in this assessment provide evidence about the ways students are moving toward making mathematics their own. Although the end-of-unit assessments provided for MiC units address questions at all three levels of reasoning, these questions assess making connections and analysis.

The first and second questions of this assessment engage students in reflection and articulation of their understanding of the relative nature of percent. In the first question, students are asked to compare the quality of three kinds of jam. The solution requires that students consider the

Use additional paper as needed.

Jams can differ in quality. The quality often depends on the percent of fruit that is used for making the jam. The higher the percent, the higher the quality.

1. What can you say about the quality of these three cherry jams?

2. This black currant jam is sold in large and small jars. Someone forgot to put the percent of fruit on the smaller jar. Fill in this missing information. Explain your strategy for finding the percent.

3. How many grams of fruit does this jar contain? Explain how you got your answer.

FIG. 9.4. End-of-unit assessment from Per Sense. Used with permission of Encyclopaedia Britannica.

percent of fruit contained in each jar, not the size of the jars or the amount of fruit (in grams) contained in each jar. The second question, which asks students to find the percent of fruit in the small jar of jam, requires an understanding of the relative nature of percent: Because both jars contain the same recipe of black currant jam, the ratio of fruit to jam (and the percent of fruit in the jam) must be the same in each jar. In the third question, students determine the amount of fruit in a jar of jam when the percent of fruit and the total grams of jam are known. In their solutions, students apply their knowledge of percent to make decisions about appropriate ways to estimate or calculate the amount of fruit.

The students whose solution strategies for this assessment are shown in Fig. 9.5 used four different mathematical tools to support their reasoning and calculation: the percent bar for estimating percents, the 10% (bench-

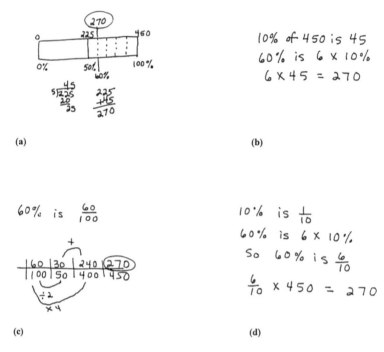

FIG. 9.5. Adapted student solution strategies for end-of-unit assessment from Per Sense. (a) Percent bar model. (b) 10% strategy. (c) Ratio table model. (d) Relationship between percents and fractions. Used with permission of Encyclopaedia Britannica.

mark) strategy, the ratio table, and the use of relationships between percents and fractions. The student response in Fig. 9.5a involved the use of a percent bar and number sense to determine that 50% is equivalent to 225 grams and that 10% is equivalent to 45 grams (by dividing 50% into five equal portions). The amount of fruit in the jam (60%) was then calculated by finding the sum of 225 and 45 grams (50% + 10%). Figure 9.5b shows the use of a number-sense strategy based on 10%. The student first determined that 10% of 450 is 45, and, using the knowledge that 60% is 6 times 10%, calculated the answer by taking 6 × 45. Figure 9.5c shows the connection the student was making between percent and ratio. This student wrote a ratio representation for 60% and then used the ratio table to organize calculations with equivalent ratios until a ratio involving 450 grams was found. The response in Fig. 9.5d demonstrates the student's understanding of the relationships between percents and fractions. In this case the student used knowledge that 10% is $\frac{1}{10}$ to write 60% as $\frac{6}{10}$ and then used multiplication with this fraction to calculate the number of grams of fruit contained in the jar of jam.

The questions posed in this assessment allow teachers to assess the flexibility of students' knowledge about percents through their selection and use of various mathematical tools to support accurate conclusions. Teachers might also use student responses to question 3 to look for changes in individual students' use of the concepts and procedures of the domain over the course of the unit. For example, "Did the student use a different strategy on the end-of-unit assessment than on assessments during instruction?" "Did the student apply a method she or he frequently used prior to the assessment, or was there a change to a more efficient or sophisticated solution strategy?" "Did the student make connections between various representations of numbers (percents, ratios, and fractions)?" As teachers reflect on the various pieces of information they gather about the work of individual students during classroom interactions and compare work done on informal assessments with that on end-of-unit assessments, they develop a clearer understanding about the growth in knowledge of particular domains for individual students.

End-of-Grade-Level Assessments.   In this section we look at an assessment designed to be given at the end of Grade 5 in the MiC curriculum. A photograph of a giant Ferris wheel taken at a neighborhood festival provides the context for the item. The first of five questions involves whole-number computation requiring reproduction: Given that each of 36 baskets on the Ferris wheel can each hold four people, students are asked to find the number of people who can ride the wheel when it is full. The calculation is straightforward, as student responses indicate: "144—I added 4 up 36 times" or "144 people because 36×4 equals 144."

The second question of the assessment directs students' attention to the photograph of the Ferris wheel, noting that it is impossible to count the number of baskets on the Ferris wheel (because of the background in the photograph and the activities at the festival). Students are then asked to describe a way to check if the number of baskets is accurate. Students extend and apply their knowledge of circles (the ways a circle can be subdivided using diameters or radii) and articulate their reasoning. Although fairly easy to solve, this question elicits analysis because it allows students to develop a variety of strategies for solving the problem. Student responses, for example, include: "You can divide the Ferris wheel in 2 [implicit use of the diameter], count the number of baskets on one half of the Ferris wheel, and multiply that by 2," and "Count half the baskets [implicit use of the diameter] and multiply by 2." Some students do find more direct ways of working the problem. The following student response involves only the domain of number: "When the Ferris wheel is full, count how many people come off. Then divide by 4 because that's how many people are in a basket."

In the third question of the assessment, students think about the Ferris wheel in more abstract ways. Visualizing the wheel as a large circle seen from a distance, students imagine they are seated in one of the baskets and are asked to draw the path they travel as their basket moves around the circle. This question elicits analysis because it involves interpretation and mathematization of the problem situation and allows students to develop their own solution strategies. The question provides an opportunity for students to extend their knowledge of geometry (circles) and engages them in making mathematics their own as they mathematize the problem situation.

Two solutions are shown in Fig. 9.6. In the first, a basket is drawn hanging from the center of the circle (Ferris wheel); another circle (of the same radius) is then drawn using the base of this basket as its center. In the second solution, the circle (Ferris wheel) is separated into equal arcs, a basket is drawn at each of the points where the arcs cut the circle, and a new circle is drawn using the bases of the baskets as a guide. These solutions demonstrate quite different yet equally appropriate interpretations and mathematizations of the problem situation and provide evidence of students making mathematics their own.

In the fourth question of the assessment, students are given a diagram of the Ferris wheel along with an enlarged drawing of one of the sections (see Fig. 9.7) and are asked to determine the measure of the angle formed by the bars of the Ferris wheel. Designed for students to make connections among mathematical ideas, students make a decision about the appropriate mathematical tool to use in solving the problem and then apply their knowledge of circles. In this case, students might use a protractor to measure the angle in the wheel, or they might determine the number of divisions

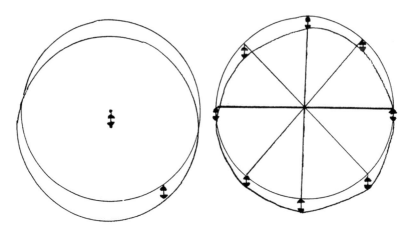

FIG. 9.6. Student solutions for the Ferris wheel item from end-of-Grade-5 assessment. Used with permission of National Center for Research in Mathematical Sciences Education.

In the drawing below you see a model of the front view of the giant wheel.

Part of this front view is drawn below. One basket is attached.

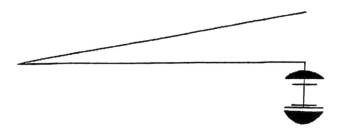

FIG. 9.7. Measuring angle and interpreting scale and ratio in the Ferris wheel item on end-of-Grade-5 assessment. Used with permission of National Center for Research in Mathematical Sciences Education.

made by the bars of the Ferris wheel and divide the total degrees in a circle by that number.

The fifth part of the assessment refers to the enlarged drawing of one of the sections of the Ferris wheel (see again Fig. 9.7): "Kathy says, 'I am sure the bars and the basket in this drawing are not drawn to the same scale.' Explain why her statement is true." The question, designed to elicit analysis, draws on students' interpretation of scale and ratio in the drawing, thus extending and applying their knowledge of number concepts: In constructing a response, students examine the relationship between the size of the basket and the size of the angle formed by the bars. Students typically give responses that do not fully describe their reasoning: "Because if it was true the basket from one bar would be hitting the basket on the bar below it" and "Because the basket is bigger." These responses do, however, provide some insight into the individual student's thinking and can be used in combination with other evidence of the student's knowledge gathered from different sources to assess the student's knowledge in the domain.

The assessment just described provides opportunities for students both to approach problems in a realistic context different from the ones used during instruction and to express their thinking about unfamiliar problem situations related to geometry and ratio. The five questions assess reproduction, connections, and analysis by providing situations for students to perform calculations, make decisions about appropriate mathematical tools, and interpret the situation. Students' responses to these questions can provide ample evidence of their abilities to apply their mathematical knowledge in new situations, to articulate their understanding of the concepts in a domain, and make mathematics their own as they mathematize the problem situations.

Assessment of Growth Over Time

In order to assess students' understanding of the concepts of a domain, assessment items at multiple points in the instructional sequence focus on students' use of existing knowledge in new situations, new relationships students are forming among mathematical ideas, and the levels of reasoning applied in solving problems. Assessment of rational-number concepts from a domain-based approach, for example, begins with items that build on students' intuitive notions of rational-number concepts and connect this informal knowledge to operations (e.g., ordering, comparison, and calculation) with fractions, decimals, percents, and ratios. Assessment items also include attention to relationships among these representations of numbers, the flexibility of calculation empowered by knowledge of such relationships, the mathematical tools for supporting reasoning with rational-number concepts, and articulation of that reasoning.

In order to illustrate this concept, we examine the responses of fifth- and sixth-grade students to assessments related to rational numbers. (Also consider in this discussion the evidence gathered about students' understanding of rational numbers shown earlier in this chapter from Fraction Times and Per Sense.) We then conjecture about questions that might guide thinking about growth in mathematical knowledge.

Figure 9.8a shows the response from a fifth-grade student, Jenna, at the end of the first instructional unit related to the number concepts, Some of the Parts. In this unit, students are introduced to addition, subtraction, multiplication, and division with fractions using number sense strategies rather than formal methods of calculation. In this problem, students are asked to determine if one submarine sandwich 78 inches long is enough to serve 25 people, given that each serving is $3\frac{3}{4}$ inches long. In her response, Jenna articulated a convincing argument that details her interpretation of the problem situation and solution of the (division) problem using a repeated-addition strategy. Jenna's solution involves determining the length

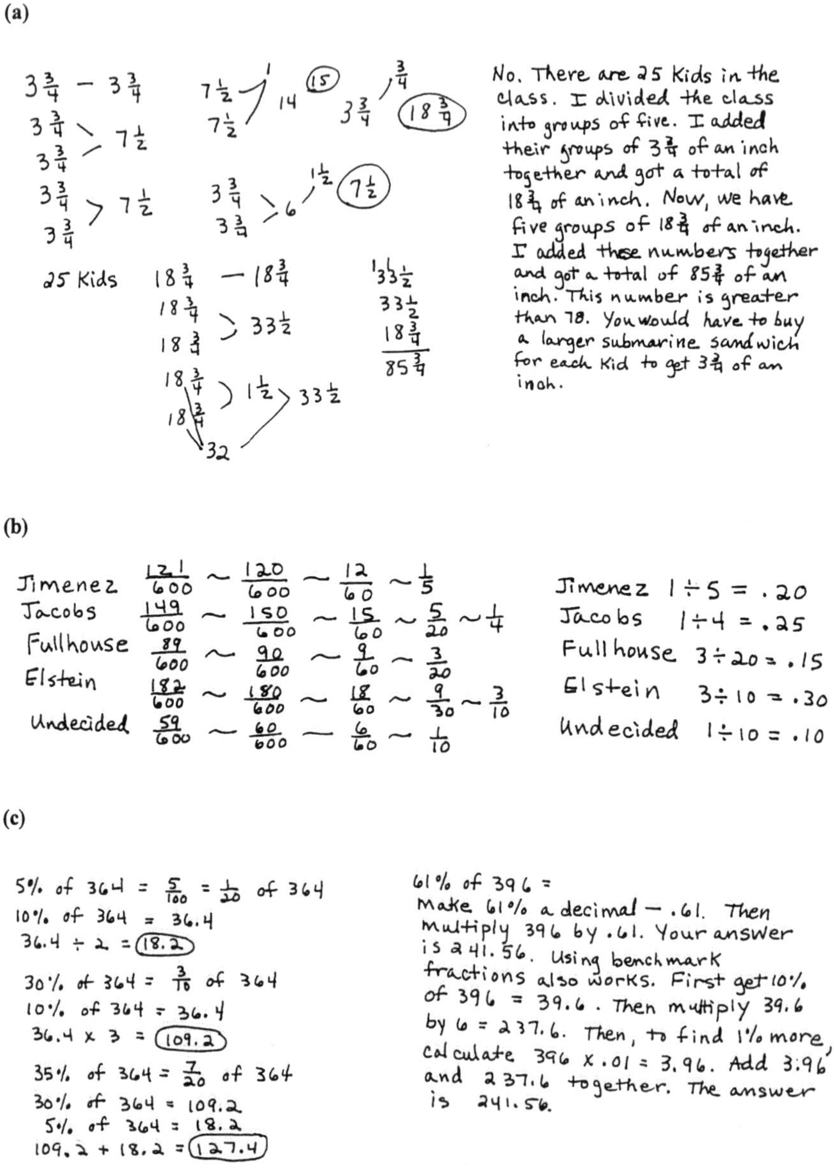

(a)

$3\frac{3}{4} - 3\frac{3}{4}$

$3\frac{3}{4} \searrow 7\frac{1}{2}$
$3\frac{3}{4}$

$7\frac{1}{2} \overline{)14}$ ⑮
$7\frac{1}{2}$

$3\frac{3}{4}\overline{)18\frac{3}{4}}$ $\frac{3}{4}$

$3\frac{3}{4} > 7\frac{1}{2}$ $3\frac{3}{4} \searrow 6 \overline{)7\frac{1}{2}}$ $\frac{1}{2}$ ⑦½
$3\frac{3}{4}$ $3\frac{3}{4}$

25 Kids $18\frac{3}{4} - 18\frac{3}{4}$ $33\frac{1}{2}$
$18\frac{3}{4}$
$18\frac{3}{4} > 33\frac{1}{2}$ $33\frac{1}{2}$
$18\frac{3}{4}$
$18\frac{3}{4}) 1\frac{1}{2} > 33\frac{1}{2}$ $18\frac{3}{4}$
$18\frac{3}{4}$ $85\frac{3}{4}$
$\searrow 32$

No, There are 25 Kids in the class. I divided the class into groups of five. I added their groups of $3\frac{3}{4}$ of an inch together and got a total of $18\frac{3}{4}$ of an inch. Now, we have five groups of $18\frac{3}{4}$ of an inch. I added these numbers together and got a total of $85\frac{3}{4}$ of an inch. This number is greater than 78. You would have to buy a larger submarine sandwich for each Kid to get $3\frac{3}{4}$ of an inch.

(b)

Jimenez $\frac{121}{600} \sim \frac{120}{600} \sim \frac{12}{60} \sim \frac{1}{5}$

Jacobs $\frac{149}{600} \sim \frac{150}{600} \sim \frac{15}{60} \sim \frac{5}{20} \sim \frac{1}{4}$

Fullhouse $\frac{89}{600} \sim \frac{90}{600} \sim \frac{9}{60} \sim \frac{3}{20}$

Elstein $\frac{182}{600} \sim \frac{180}{600} \sim \frac{18}{60} \sim \frac{9}{30} \sim \frac{3}{10}$

Undecided $\frac{59}{600} \sim \frac{60}{600} - \frac{6}{60} \sim \frac{1}{10}$

Jimenez $1 \div 5 = .20$
Jacobs $1 \div 4 = .25$
Fullhouse $3 \div 20 = .15$
Elstein $3 \div 10 = .30$
Undecided $1 \div 10 = .10$

(c)

5% of $364 = \frac{5}{100} = \frac{1}{20}$ of 364
10% of $364 = 36.4$
$36.4 \div 2 = \boxed{18.2}$

30% of $364 = \frac{3}{10}$ of 364
10% of $364 = 36.4$
$36.4 \times 3 = \boxed{109.2}$

35% of $364 = \frac{7}{20}$ of 364
30% of $364 = 109.2$
5% of $364 = 18.2$
$109.2 + 18.2 = \boxed{127.4}$

61% of $396 =$
Make 61% a decimal — $.61$. Then multiply 396 by $.61$. Your answer is 241.56. Using benchmark fractions also works. First get 10% of $396 = 39.6$. Then multiply 39.6 by $6 = 237.6$. Then, to find 1% more, calculate $396 \times .01 = 3.96$. Add 3.96 and 237.6 together. The answer is 241.56.

FIG. 9.8. Student responses to problems involving rational number. (a) Jenna's response. (b) Mark's response. (c) Marisol's responses. Used with permission of National Center for Research in Mathematical Sciences Education.

of sandwich needed for one group of 5 students and finding the sum of sandwich lengths for all 5 groups (25 students) in the class. A minor error in calculation ($18\frac{3}{4} + 18\frac{3}{4} = 33\frac{1}{2}$) led to an inaccurate total sandwich length needed, but because her answer was still larger than the given sandwich (although smaller than the actual length needed), her answer was not affected. After determining the length of sandwich needed for the entire class, Jenna wrote about the solution strategy, providing evidence that she had reflected on the solution strategy before articulating it to the teacher or other class members.

Figure 9.8b shows the response from a sixth-grade student, Mark, for a problem from Fraction Times, a unit taught during the first semester of his school year. The focus of this unit is on formal methods of addition, subtraction, multiplication, and division with fractions and relationships among fractions, percents, ratios, and decimals. In the problem, students are told that the newspaper staff of *Fraction Times* had conducted a survey of 600 people to determine the most popular mayoral candidate. Students are asked to describe with a fraction, then an alternative representation, the portion of votes received by each candidate. Mark's estimation strategy demonstrates the number sense he had developed. He chose to round the numerators either up or down to the nearest 10 and write equivalent fractions for each fraction until it was simplified to an approximation that made sense to him. For example, Mark wrote $\frac{182}{600}$ as $\frac{180}{600}$ and then as equivalent fractions, $\frac{18}{60}$, $\frac{9}{30}$, and $\frac{3}{10}$. Each simplified fraction was then used to express the results in decimal form. Mark showed distinctions between the fractions drawn directly from the data (e.g., $\frac{182}{600}$) and the approximations he used for understanding the data. The responses also demonstrate his knowledge of relationships among fraction, division, and decimal notations for numbers.

Figure 9.8c shows a pair of responses from a sixth-grade student, Marisol, for a problem from More or Less, the second number unit at that grade level. The unit uses everyday situations related to retail business transactions to provide opportunities for students to extend and apply their knowledge of fractions, decimals, and percents. The first set of responses are from a series of eight problems in which students are asked to use benchmark fractions in their calculations. In each of these calculations, Marisol noted the fraction equivalent for the percent, but her solutions involved her knowledge of strategies for calculating with percents. When calculating 5% of 364, Marisol chose to use a strategy based on the fact that 5% is half of 10%. Her calculation of 30% also relied on a strategy using 10% by multiplying 10% of 364 by 3. To determine 35% of 364, Marisol separated 35% into 30% + 5% and, using answers to the previous problems, simply found the sum of these components. The flexibility with which Marisol approached calculations with percents is also demonstrated in her response to determining 61% of 396. In this set of responses, Marisol clearly articulated two different solution strategies, both of which involved equivalent decimal representations of 61%: a single-step calculation multiplying 396 by 0.61 and a multiple-step calculation using a combination of 10% and 1% strategies. Those responses provide evidence of the relationships Marisol had constructed among fractions, decimals, and percents and the flexibility of calculation gained by applying her knowledge of such relationships.

In assessing the growth over time for individual students, the evidence gathered for each student can be summarized in terms of growth in mathematical knowledge. Suppose the evidence presented previously was gathered for one student over time. The following questions might guide thinking about growth in the domain: "Has the student acquired a variety of approaches and strategies for using mathematical concepts and procedures in the domain?" "How does the student's use of symbols and procedures vary over time?" "In what situations does the student use informal approaches? More formal symbols and procedures?" "Does the student have a solid foundation of informal reasoning to fall back on when faced with more difficult problems in the domain?" This list of general questions could be supplemented with more specific questions about particular domains. With respect to rational-number concepts, additional questions might include, "What relationships is the student constructing among fractions, decimals, percents, and ratios?" "How does the student use equivalent representations of fractions, percents, and decimals to solve problems?" "Which mathematical tool or strategy does the student use to represent and solve problems in which rational numbers are involved?" "Does the student clearly articulate the reasoning used to solve problems with rational numbers?" Such questions can guide later reflections by the teacher on students' growth of understanding and can establish comprehensive evidence of the growth of mathematical knowledge over time.

TEACHER-IDENTIFIED PROBLEMS
IN IMPLEMENTING A DOMAIN-BASED ASSESSMENT

Instruction that supports learning with understanding involves more-active roles for students: participation in whole-class or small-group discussion about the central ideas of the domain, the development of their own strategies for solving problems set in real or imaginable situations, and the articulation–communication of their own thinking. Such participation provides multidimensional opportunities for assessment unavailable in traditional mathematics classrooms; yet in order for this information to be useful it must be sought, gathered, and documented. This change in assessment, from solely monitoring the progress of the class toward developing an awareness of the ways individual students reveal their understanding of mathematics, represents a substantial shift in perspective and one that may require professional growth.

Using a domain-based approach to documenting student understanding, teachers shift their thinking away from mastery of skills at the end of an instructional unit to the development of concepts over time. This notion that students need not have complete mastery of concepts before moving on to the next unit (or sometimes grade level) presents a complex dilemma:

> That's always the tightrope you walk as the implementor. As much as we say that, we sort of always want [mastery of concepts] to happen. . . . The question remains, then, *is* there something I can or should do to make this better, or is this just one of those things where we should say, "Well, this is exposure and what happens, happens, and now let's go on to the next thing." You never quite know where to draw those lines. (Shafer, 1996, p. 98)

This teacher's reflection underscores the significance of considering the ways in which mathematics is learned with understanding, the manner in which a particular curriculum addresses this issue, and the instructional sequence of particular concepts (throughout the curriculum) when planning assessment opportunities.

Linkages in a domain in the curriculum and features of problems that permit assessment of developing knowledge of the concepts and procedures of a domain may not be readily apparent to teachers who are starting to implement domain-based curricula:

> During the unit itself, I don't think I was aware of the connections, or perhaps was as aware, as I might be now or next year. . . . Those things come slowly for most of us . . . It's more that I'm still immersed in the day-to-day struggle. But I do know that as we grow, those things become more apparent. (Shafer, 1996, p. 93)

Listing them in teacher guides is not enough, but as teachers teach mathematics for understanding, they become aware of these connections, build on them during instruction, and use them in assessing students' growth in knowledge in a particular domain.

The character of more formal assessments must also change in order to assess students' understanding of relationships among mathematical ideas and their use of mathematical analysis. As teachers focus more on understanding, they begin to recognize and look for differences in levels of reasoning applied in responses to each assessment item. When opportunities for connections and analysis are not present in publisher-provided materials, it falls to the teacher to write more complex items.

With the change in assessment, teachers face the new, more difficult task of scoring and interpreting items that assess students' abilities in increasingly complex situations—a sharp contrast to traditional mathematics tests in which little variation is expected in student responses, simple scoring rubrics (if any) are used, and grades are easily determined. Richer and more open problems (such as those in domain-based assessment) yield more information about individual students' understanding of skills and concepts than do traditional assessments. As a consequence, responses can be more difficult to interpret than those to (traditional) closed problems and problems not set in contexts. Complicating this is the range of students' abilities to express their own reasoning. Perhaps the most significant step in good assessment practice is the need to understand students' responses, not only by understanding what they actually communicate in writing or orally, but also by understanding what they mean to communicate:

> Naturally, the students should be able to communicate clearly about how they proceeded, and, as such, the communication should be taken into account when grading. On the other hand, however, having insight into a certain topic is not the same as being able to communicate about it. . . . This means that figuring out whether a student has understanding sometimes requires not being distracted by the clumsy wording of the student. (van den Heuvel-Panhuizen, 1995, p. 85)

Looking for reasonable answers is also often more appropriate than looking for correct ones. Again, this implies taking the position of the student in order to make decisions about what a particular answer meant or what the student's reasoning (behind a seemingly wrong answer) might have been. This method of interpreting students' responses allows for more equitable scoring in addition to providing more information about the knowledge of individual students in the domain. Although scoring rubrics and point assignments for partial credit can be composed in advance of grading, unexpected interpretations of the problem, which become evident during analysis of student work, should be added to the categories during the evaluation process.

Another problem in implementing domain-based assessment lies in the limits that teachers' reliance on mental record keeping for accessing information gathered during informal assessments can have on developing an understanding of students' knowledge over a series of units in a domain or across the curriculum. If such information is documented, however, it is available to the teachers not only to refer to and reflect on when assessing student growth in knowledge, but also to share with parents or with other teachers in collaborative discussions. Documentation (whether as notations on class rosters or as checklists in portfolios) also helps ensure that information is gathered for each student. Confidence in assessment of students' understanding is strengthened when the results of formal assessments can be shown to mesh with the information gathered during informal assessment. (In-depth examinations of informal instructional assessments and documentation of the information gathered are described in several of the readings listed at the end of this chapter.)

Finally, reporting systems that support, not undermine, the new assessment programs will need to be developed. We will need to find ways to create (and to inform audiences about) reliable comprehensive profiles that capture the multidimensional evidence acquired and documented about a student's knowledge and abilities and the processes through which the student's understanding is developing.

CONCLUSION

In this chapter, we have looked more closely at what it might mean to appropriately assess students who are learning mathematics with understanding. Looking for ways to measure the key cognitive activities of understanding requires more than the measurement of basic-skills mastery and rote-memory items provided by standardized tests. If we are to ensure that mathematical understanding is valued, we will need to design and implement ways of showing what such understanding means.

Certainly, assessment results must be reported to the students, parents, and other teachers in forms that are easily understood, and, if we hope to really understand what our students know, in ways that preserve the richness of the information gathered. It will do little good to replace traditional tests (and teaching) with multiple sources related to depth of understanding if this information is collapsed into a single grade or numerical score.

As teachers begin to document specific evidence of a student's knowledge in a domain at particular points in time (and in a student's education) and to record their assessment of the student's growth in knowledge, more comprehensive individual and group profiles of learning, achievement, cognitive processes, and understanding can be developed. Such profiles could provide not only a record of each student's accomplishments and growth but a source of information, far richer than transcripts and standardized scores, on which to base future instructional decisions for each student as well as provide an in-depth portrait of our achievement as a nation.

In this chapter, we have examined one possible assessment program and pointed to the problems and possibilities of its implementation. The program we have described is but a model, but it is a beginning. As we

move toward (and work in) classrooms that promote understanding, we
need to rethink, in terms of the next decades of vast, increasingly rapid
technological change, what we value as mastery of mathematics—mathematical understanding or rote memorization of formulae and procedures—
and retool how we measure and report "achievement."

REFERENCES

Dekker, T. (1997). *Enquiry project: Assessing Realistic Mathematics Education.* Unpublished manuscript, University of Utrecht, The Netherlands.
Shafer, M. C. (1996). *Assessment of student growth in a mathematical domain over time.* Unpublished doctoral dissertation, University of Wisconsin–Madison.
van den Heuvel-Panhuizen, M. (1995). *Developing assessment problems on percentage: An example of developmental research on assessment conducted within the Mathematics in Context project along the lines of Realistic Mathematics Education.* Unpublished manuscript, University of Utrecht, The Netherlands.

FOR FURTHER READING

Greeno, J. G. (1991). Number sense as situated knowing in a conceptual domain. *Journal for Research in Mathematics Education, 22* (3), 170–218.
National Center for Research in Mathematical Sciences Education & Freudenthal Institute (Eds.). (1997–1998). *Mathematics in context.* Chicago: Encyclopaedia Britannica.
Romberg, T. A. (Ed.). (1995). *Reform in school mathematics and authentic assessment.* Albany: State University of New York Press.

Chapter 10

Creating Classrooms
That Promote Understanding

Elizabeth Fennema
University of Wisconsin–Madison

Judith Sowder
San Diego State University

Thomas P. Carpenter
University of Wisconsin–Madison

The classrooms described in earlier chapters, which were developed by teachers and researchers working as teams over a long period of time, provide existence proofs that classrooms that promote understanding can and do exist. These classrooms were dramatically different from traditional ones, and students who studied in them did come to understand mathematics (see suggested reading list provided with each chapter for more information about student learning). Even with the evidence that such classrooms can exist, a critical question remains: In what ways can many more classrooms be developed so that all students have the opportunity to learn with understanding? The purpose of this chapter is to point the way toward such development.

A REPRISE

The Mathematics To Be Understood

Learning or understanding trivial, nonuseful mathematics makes no sense at all. Our concern throughout this book has been with presenting examples not only of students' learning with understanding but of students learning mathematics worthy of understanding. The definition of mathematics worthy of understanding is more complex than and different from what has usually been taught during the 20th century. Although the domains of concern appear to be the usual ones (whole numbers, fractions, geometry, etc.), the various instructional examples provided in this book make clear that these domains have been substantially redefined as being not only mathematical rules and procedures but also sets of intra- and interrelated processes and concepts.

Included in the definition of school mathematics is also the ways students think about it, understand it, and manifest their understanding. For example, in Cognitively Guided Instruction, one of the programs described in Carpenter et al. (chapter 4, this volume), addition and subtraction of whole numbers is not portrayed as two related operations but as an organized taxonomy of structurally different word problems that adults would probably solve using traditional addition or subtraction procedures. Although children solve the problems in their own invented ways, their solutions have recognizable similarities related to the taxonomy of word problems. Thus, students' thinking is clearly seen in the definition of the domain of addition–subtraction for the primary-school curriculum. In classrooms that promote mathematical understanding, students' thinking is an integral part of the mathematics curriculum.

The tasks that carry mathematics to the students portray mathematics as integrated and creatable. For instruction, the mathematics is presented in problem contexts that require mathematization and the creation of solution procedures by the students. As students engage in solving the various problems, they concurrently learn basic skills, concepts, and ways to engage in mathematical activity.

Students' Mental Activities

In the descriptions of classrooms where students are learning with understanding, instruction is not portrayed as the presentation of clear, precise explanations of procedures to be practiced by students. Instead, understanding is constructed by each student as she or he engages in the various mental activities we have found to be critical: actively constructing relationships between and among mathematical ideas by reflecting on problem solutions, extending knowledge by relating the new solutions to what has been known previously, and articulating thinking about the mathematics they have explored. By engaging in these activities, each learner assumes ownership of the mathematical knowledge that she or he has constructed.

Although each mental activity is described separately, in reality they are not isolated but integrated. *Constructing relationships* without thinking about or *reflecting* on those relationships is difficult. *Articulation* facilitates reflection because describing (or articulating) how a problem is solved requires thinking about (or reflecting on) what has been done. Because these mental activities are personal, the *understanding that develops becomes the learner's own.*

So we come full circle: Understanding is constructed, reflected on, and articulated by the learner and the knowledge that results is his or her own.

The School Curriculum

Children enter school with a rich understanding of whole numbers and an informal knowledge of space. The out-of-school environment continues to provide some school-age learners with experiences that are mathematical, but the knowledge gained from out-of-school experiences is limited and provides only a preliminary foundation for learning. Because of this limitation, the rich understanding of mathematics necessary to function in our modern society is almost always developed in formal schooling. Thus, it falls on school mathematics programs (aided and abetted by related courses) to provide the experiences necessary for learning mathematics. Although all students are dependent on school-based experiences for learning mathematics, traditionally underachieving populations, because they typically do not have a mathematically enriched environment outside of school, are even more dependent on classrooms to provide a curriculum that enables them to learn mathematics with understanding.

The Standards (NCTM, 1989) have provided as complete a description of a curriculum that would promote understanding as is available today, and it is unnecessary to provide another description here. However, there are a few critical elements of the curriculum that we wish to emphasize.

Because the goal of mathematics education should be the development of understanding by all students, the majority of the curriculum should be composed of tasks that provide students with problem *situations*. Two reasons support this claim. The first is that mathematics that is worth learning is most closely represented in problem-solving tasks. The second is that students are more apt to engage in the mental activities required to develop understanding when they are confronted with mathematics embedded in problem situations.

Tasks that students do in order to learn mathematics should be relevant to them and engage each student in a situation in which she or he can identify a problem and figure out her or his own solutions. The mathematics involved in doing the tasks should be related to other mathematical ideas in the curriculum, lead to model building, and require inquiry and justification.

Consider some of the tasks in which learners were engaged in the previous chapters. In Carpenter et al. (chapter 4, this volume), children constructed their own algorithms to solve word problems. Children in the Sowder chapter worked with division of fractions. Lehrer et al. (chapter 5, this volume) described children investigating geometric ideas, specifically the concept of triangle, which led to the study of quilt patterns. Lajoie (chapter 7, this volume) reported on students' use of a computer database to construct a scatterplot of temperatures. Students in one of the examples presented by Kaput (chapter 8, this volume) studied functions by comparing the changes in plants' heights and the height's rate of change. These tasks varied dramatically in their complexity, the amount of time needed to complete them, the mathematical domain in which they were situated, the tools selected to be used, and the representations used (symbols or words). But in each instance the tasks were embedded in problem situations, and the students were engaged in complex mental activities that would lead to understanding.

Normative Practices of Classrooms

Normative practices are the modus operandi of all classrooms, and some norms are particularly critical for classrooms that promote understanding. One is the establishment of understanding as the major characteristic of learning and doing mathematics. When this norm is firmly established, students, in part because they are aware of its importance to the teacher, develop a predisposition to gain understanding, and understanding becomes important to them. Another classroom norm that students come to expect is articulation of problem solutions or thinking. When thinking is articulated regularly, patterns of thinking develop that are iterative. Thinking cannot be articulated unless students reflect on the problem and the strategies they use to solve it; articulation, in turn, increases reflection, which leads to understanding. Students learn to anticipate sharing their strategies, and discourse about mathematics becomes commonplace. Particularly rich examples of discourse and sharing were described earlier in the Carpenter et al., Kaput, and Lajoie (chapters 4, 7, and 8, this volume).

TEACHERS AND DEVELOPING UNDERSTANDING

Although teachers and researchers collaborated on producing the classrooms described previously, it is clear that teachers hold the major responsibility for developing similar classrooms across the nation. They are the ones who decide what is done on a day-by-day basis in their classrooms. Even with the plethora of constraints that exist, the final decision making about instructional activities is done by teachers. In this section, we take a closer look at the responsibilities of the teacher for developing classrooms that promote understanding. We then examine one professional development program that supports teachers in developing their own understandings of instruction and of their students' thinking. An examination of teachers' responsibilities helps to define the teacher's role.

Teachers' Responsibilities

The Establishment of Classroom Norms That Encourage Learning With Understanding. Because groups of students vary from year to year, as do teachers' skills in classroom management, it is impossible to write a prescription that tells a teacher how to establish classroom norms for promoting understanding. However, just as students' learning is continually being assessed, teachers also need to continually assess the norms in their classroom to ensure that the norms being manifested enable students to engage in problem-solving, reflect, and articulate their thinking.

The Selection of Tasks That Lead to Understanding. Tasks carry the mathematics and provide opportunities for problem solving, reflection, and articulation. They have to be embedded in mathematics worthy of learning and be organized into a coherent set that leads to rich understanding of a domain. Not only must teachers select tasks appropriate for their students, they also must provide appropriate tools that enable students to solve problems and to develop understanding. These can range from very simple counters to paper and pencil to complex computer programs.

The Purposeful Incorporation of Equity Concerns. Ensuring that *all* students learn with understanding involves attending to individuals while at the same time being aware of group differences that may lead to differential participation in classroom activities and learning. Group differences may have to do with the relevance of the context in which each task is embedded (as illustrated by Secada and Berman, chapter 3, this volume), appropriate social–cultural norms (such as challenging or not challenging another's thinking in discourse), or the degree of competitiveness (e.g., some girls may be hesitant to compete, whereas some boys may be hesitant to work cooperatively). There are no simple guidelines for making instructional decisions about groups of learners. But the mental activities elaborated on in this book can be encouraged in a large variety of settings, and sensitive teachers can adapt tasks and norms so that all learners can engage in those mental activities.

The Assessment of Each Student's Understanding in Both the Short and Long Term in Order to Ensure That Understanding Continues to Develop. Assessment is done for at least two reasons: so that the teacher can learn whether the tasks and the classroom structure are effective in developing students' understanding, and so that the student can gauge her or his own understanding.

Assessment can be done formally through testing and informally as students articulate and share their thinking. Classrooms that promote understanding rely heavily on informal assessment. Assessing understanding is never particularly easy and usually requires combining knowledge from a number of sources: oral reporting or discussion, logs students might keep, daily homework, and–or formal tests. However, when students are aware that each assessment stresses understanding, not memory, they become more aware of understanding and exert greater efforts to understand.

Overall, the role of a teacher in a classroom that promotes understanding combines being very active sometimes with being almost passive at other times. The teacher must be active in establishing a classroom with norms that encourage a climate of understanding, in selecting tasks that incorporate important mathematics appropriate for each student and that will enable their understanding to grow, in assessing each student's growth, and in ensuring that all students are enabled to learn mathematics with understanding. However, sometimes a teacher must be passive and let students struggle either alone or with each other in the problem-solving process. It takes restraint on a teacher's part when the student appears to be heading in the wrong direction, but the best role of the teacher may be to just listen to what the student is doing and to ask questions that enable the student to find her or his own pathway to successful problem solving. On the other hand, sometimes the wise role for a teacher is to be active and lead the student to a solution. It takes a sensitive teacher to know when to be passive and when to actively help. She or he just needs to always remember that the goal at all times is to enable the student to increase her or his understanding.

Teachers' Knowledge

One of the most critical influences on the instructional decisions made by teachers is the knowledge that they have about mathematics and their students' mathematical thinking. These two kinds of knowledge are intertwined and their impact on students permeates the classrooms that have been described in this book. In each case, teachers had mathematical knowledge and understood their students' thinking.

Consider the case of Carmen Curtis (Lehrer et al., chapter 5, this volume) leading second-grade students to derive a mathematical definition of triangle. As she led the children in a lengthy discussion, her knowledge of mathematics and knowledge of children's thinking were manifest in the complex interactions that took place. It is clear from very early in the vignette that she knew that the mathematical definition of triangle included more than a triangle being a polygon with 3 sides and 3 angles (or a set of 3 nonlinear points connected by line segments). She also anticipated that most of her students' prior knowledge about triangles was probably limited to triangles that had 3 equal sides and 3 equal angles (an equilateral triangle).

By sensitive questioning, Ms. Curtis led the students to move in the direction of identifying relevant properties such as straight sides (rather than curved ones) and ignoring irrelevant ones such as orientation. She led them to reason about classes of triangles defined by sets of properties. She recognized the immature ideas of some children and worked with the ideas as building blocks as more mature ideas about triangles were developed. It should also be noted that this was not an isolated task but was embedded in an ongoing set of lessons. (Consider Romberg and Kaput's discussion (chapter 1, this volume) about the selection of tasks to make a coherent curriculum.) During the remainder of the school year, she continued to provide triangle-based tasks such as studying nets, building quilts, and constructing solids with triangles as components.

In the case of Ms. A, reported by Sowder and Philipp (chapter 6, this volume), the integration of the teacher's knowledge of mathematics and students' thinking is well illustrated. Her knowledge of her students can be seen in the thoughtful questions she asked, which elicited answers that revealed student thinking. Her knowledge of mathematics was particularly salient as she carefully led her students to an understanding of the referent unit of the fraction involved in fraction problems (see Sowder and Philipp, chapter 6, this volume, for a thorough discussion).

Professional Development of Teachers

The teachers of the classrooms described in earlier chapters gained their integrated knowledge of mathematics and children's thinking in a variety of ways that are beyond the scope of this book. In many cases, teachers participated in a professional development program consisting of seminars in which mathematics and research-based information about students' thinking within specific mathematical domains were discussed. Concurrently with attending seminars, teachers selected instructional tasks that required problem solving and had their students invent and report their solutions for the problems. The teachers discussed those solutions in the seminars that led to teachers' increased knowledge about their students' thinking.

Consider one such professional development program directed by Sowder and Philipp (chapter 6, this volume). In this program, middle-school teachers met regularly in seminars over a 2-year period. The purpose of the seminars was to provide the teachers with opportunities for open, reflective discussions of mathematical ideas with peers and mathematics-education scholars. During the seminars, there were many discussions of mathematical and pedagogical considerations, and vignettes from two of these discussions are presented here.

Vignette 1. Midway through the first year, a teacher brought to the seminar group a question about a student's answer to a division problem, and the group discussed the meanings of quotients and remainders. In the dialogue that follows, a teacher (T1) had just told the group about a student who had said that $37 \div 5$ was 7 remainder $\frac{2}{5}$. In the portion of the discussion included here, the teacher struggled to understand, with the researcher-leader's scaffolding, the difference between $7\frac{2}{5}$ and 7 remainder $\frac{2}{5}$:

T1: I was expecting 7 remainder 2, but I knew 7 remainder $\frac{2}{5}$ was OK too, but I didn't know for sure why. It was kind of hard to explain to him [the student] that he had the right answer.

Leader: Are those two the same: 7 remainder 2 and 7 remainder $\frac{2}{5}$? For $35\frac{1}{2} \div 5$ is 7 remainder $\frac{1}{2}$ correct?

T1: Yes.

T2: But that's not the remainder.

T3: But the thought process is right.

Leader: Let's talk about the difference between 7 remainder 2, 7 remainder $\frac{2}{5}$, and $7\frac{2}{5}$ and what they all mean. Could they all be correct or not?

T1: $37 \div 5 = 7\frac{2}{5}$. Wouldn't that be the same as 7 remainder $\frac{2}{5}$?

Leader: Is it? $7\frac{2}{5}$ is a number. It is a quantity. It is the answer. If you say 7 remainder $\frac{2}{5}$, then does it mean the same thing? If I parceled out 5 groups of 7 and had 2 left, do I divide the 2 up and share them? If I do, the answer is $7\frac{2}{5}$. Or do I just put the two aside and not consider them a part of the sharing situation? Then it's 7 remainder 2.

T1: But the real answer, the correct answer would be 7 and $\frac{2}{5}$ of 5 because that would be 2. This is the first time a student came up to me and said I did this. I had to think about it first. It was tempting to say, "You're right. Okay, I'll let you go."

T3: I have to really think about this and what it means, because the book gives the answer *Remainder 2*, and then when we get into a word problem where we need the remainder to be expressed in another way, it is hard for students to understand. The book doesn't give enough examples for you to be able to determine what's the most appropriate way to write the remainder and what does it mean in the context. Thinking about that now, I'm going to approach it a lot differently.

The discussion continued for another few minutes, looking at other examples, before the time was up for the day.

This vignette highlights some of the five forms of mental activity discussed by Carpenter and Lehrer (chapter 2, this volume). The mental activity of reflecting about mathematical experience calls for conscious examination of the role that activity and thought play in learning. The teachers were reflecting on what they were learning and that their reflections went beyond trying to make sense of this task as learners; they were also reflecting on how their students would make sense of the task.

In describing the mental activity of making knowledge one's own in chapter 2, Carpenter and Lehrer recognized the need for learners to take responsibility for their own learning by striving to understand. These teachers were personally invested in this task because the task was generated from a question asked of one of the teachers. The teachers were not simply learning by listening to the leaders but instead were taking responsibility for their own learning by questioning the leaders and each other. The mental activity of making knowledge one's own also means that learners must adopt a stance that knowledge is evolving. This notion does not apply only to children; the researcher–leaders approached all of the interactions with the teachers from this stance. This point of view led the leaders to recognize some months later, while reviewing the seminar transcripts, that the issues raised in Vignette 1 had not been fully resolved by the teachers and that the topic needed to be revisited.

Vignette 2. The following year, the same example shown in Vignette 1 was presented, but expanded as follows:

For 37 ÷ 5, make up a word problem
where the answer is 7;
where the answer is 8;
where the answer is 2;
where the answer is 7;
where the answer is 7.4;
where the answer is 7 remainder 2.

The first part of the discussion excerpted here focused on making a word problem for 37 ÷ 5 where the answer is $7\frac{2}{5}$:

T4: Something with a pie that you're dividing up. How much pie would we eat all together? If you can serve 5 people from one pie and there are 37 people in the class, how much pie will we need?

T5: There are 37 inches of ribbon. We need five bows. How long could each bow be? It's still not a good problem because you wouldn't have a bow that's $7\frac{2}{5}$ inches long. It's not long enough to make a bow.

T3:   If the idea was to get the fullest skirt, and we have 37 yards of material. What's the most material each person could use for a skirt?

Leader: Why is it that the earlier problem situations involving kids aren't working for $7\frac{2}{5}$?

T3:   You can't cut kids in half.

T5:   You can't have $\frac{2}{5}$ of a person.

Later in the seminar, the group discussed problems where the answer would be stated as 7 remainder 2, the most commonly given answer to $37 \div 5$ but the most difficult to interpret within a context. In this portion of the discussion, teachers returned to the problem from the earlier seminar:

Leader: So when is the answer 7 remainder 2?

T5:   It would be like the bus problem, 37 kids and 5 buses—7 remainder 2. How many are left over?

Leader: But then wouldn't the answer be just 2?

T4:   But when you're talking about division, that's the most common answer you'll get—7 remainder 2. You hear that more often, 'cause that's how we taught kids to say it.

T5:   Unless you're using a calculator. Maybe it's not as common now that kids have calculators.

Leader: What's the difference between $7\frac{2}{5}$ and 7 remainder 2? I'll put it in context. We have 37 cookies. We're going to share them among five girls. You could say the answer is 7 remainder 2 or $7\frac{2}{5}$. What would be the difference?

T3:   In the $\frac{2}{5}$, you're going to take what's left over and split it up among all the girls. When you have remainder 2, that means those two you're just going to leave for the teacher.

Leader: So in the case of $7\frac{2}{5}$, tell me what the 7 means.

T5:   In that case, it means that 5 is your thing that you're trying to distribute the 37 into. That's the number of pieces. And you can do that seven times.

Leader: Are those two [in the remainder] being distributed or not?

T5:   They're not being distributed in the first case [7 remainder 2]. Whereas in the other one, they are.

Leader: So in the second case, this 7 and the $\frac{2}{5}$, it sounds like they—

T4:   Everybody gets $7\frac{2}{5}$.

Leader: [T1], do you remember last year when we discussed this? We talked about whether the answer to 37 ÷ 5 could be written as 7 remainder $\frac{2}{5}$.

T1: But $\frac{2}{5}$ is part of the quotient. It's not the remainder. If we say 7 remainder $\frac{2}{5}$, then each person got 7 cookies, and there was $\frac{2}{5}$ of a cookie left. But there are 2 cookies left. Why? What did I say before?

At this point, we could conclude that the teachers understand and can distinguish clearly between $7\frac{2}{5}$, 7 remainder 2, and 7 remainder $\frac{2}{5}$, as answers to 37 ÷ 5. However, when discussing the mental activity of reflecting about mathematical experience, Carpenter and Lehrer pointed out that not all relationships are equally productive, and learning with understanding involves developing relationships that reflect important principles.

What were the important principles in this vignette? To the leaders, there were three. First, the leaders wanted the teachers to grapple with different interpretations of division. Second, the leaders wanted the teachers to consider how the unit was affected during multiplication and division. Third, the leaders wanted the teachers to recognize the effect that providing a context had on the kind of reasoning they, and subsequently their students, were likely to find useful as they worked through these tasks. Carpenter and Lehrer noted in chapter 2 that articulation requires reflection in order to lift out the critical ideas of an activity so that they become objects of thought. The leaders' three principles were critical ideas, and at this point the leaders wanted to support the teachers by making the three principles explicit.

The leaders, therefore, turned the conversation to the interpretations of division. An earlier seminar had focused on meanings of all four operations. For division, two interpretations had been discussed: a partitive, or sharing, interpretation (e.g., 12 candies being shared by 3 children, with the question being the number of candies each child received); and a measurement, or repeated subtraction, interpretation (e.g., 12 candies shared so that each child received 3 candies, with the question being the number of children receiving candies, i.e., How many times can 3 be subtracted from 12?). The new element in the dialogue that follows was the meaning of the remainder in these two types of situations:

Leader: When you think about the interpretations of division, measurement and partitive, which is this? Thirty-seven cookies shared among five?

T4: That's partitive.

T6: Yeah. The other would be 37 cookies, give 5 to each student.

T5: How many students can get 5 cookies?

Leader: Now there really is a remainder 2, isn't there? Can the answer be $7\frac{2}{5}$ now?

T6:   No, because that would mean you have $7\frac{2}{5}$ people.

Leader: Does 7 remainder 2 make some sense now?

T3:   Yes. You know, I really appreciate the insight you have given me on measurement and partitive division. It's something I really didn't think about before. But it's so important

Leader: Suppose we go back to the bows. Let's say they are going to be 5 inches long each, what do the two numbers mean—the remainder 2 and the 7 in that problem?

T5:   The number of bows you make is the 7. And the remainder is how much is excess?

The final segment of this seminar transcript dealt with the referent units for the quotient and the remainder. The group had discussed referent units in other contexts. For example, in $\frac{3}{4} \times \frac{1}{2} = \frac{3}{8}$, the referent for $\frac{3}{4}$ is $\frac{1}{2}$ (we are finding $\frac{3}{4}$ of $\frac{1}{2}$), whereas the referent for the $\frac{1}{2}$ and for the $\frac{3}{8}$ is one whole. The teachers had come to realize that many of the errors made by their students were made because they did not understand referent units:

Leader: So there's an interesting question about the referents here. The remainder and the quotient refer to two different things completely. The 7 refers to the number of bows, the 2 to the number of inches left.

T7:   And $\frac{2}{5}$ could mean something there. You can write $\frac{2}{5}$ or point 4.

T8:   But if you were talking about ribbon, you would say, "And I have 2 inches that I can't use." I don't think you would say, "I can make $7\frac{2}{5}$ bows."

Leader: The point being made is worth repeating. If we have 37 cookies and we're sharing them among five people, we have 7 cookies for each person and 2 cookies left. In both cases the units are cookies. In this case, this is how much each of us get [7], and this [2] is how much is left over. But if we talk about how many 5-inch bows can be made with 37 inches, you end up with seven bows and 2 inches of material left. They don't even refer to the same units of measure anymore. Let's go back to cookies and cookies, giving each person five cookies. It seems that when you're doing a partitive division, then you come out with the same unit of measure, and that's why they can be combined into $7\frac{2}{5}$ or 7.4. But when you're using the measurement interpretation—

T7:   But it can still be combined. You can still have $7\frac{2}{5}$ bows.

T5:   But people don't think like that. When you're using that measurement model, the unit itself is what's most important, so that anything that's leftover is not one of those. Because 5 is what makes it, so what's leftover—you don't even talk about it. I wouldn't say "$\frac{2}{5}$ of a bow" because that's meaningless.

T9:   If this were flour, you could combine parts of cups together, but you can't combine pieces of fabric and have one piece of fabric.

Leader: But you see, this discussion that we're having now can only be had if you're talking about a situation. It can't be had if you're just dividing numbers. And most of the time the kids in school just have numbers—they don't have situations to talk about. So there's really nothing to talk about at all.

T5:   That's true of any computation that you do out of context.

Leader: But it's especially troubling with division because of the remainders. Kids don't have any idea what to do with those.

Discussion.   Teachers come to understand the teaching–learning process by engaging in the same mental activities that are essential for students to learn with understanding. Consider how these seminars encouraged the teachers to engage in the various types of mental activity discussed by Carpenter and Lehrer in chapter 2. They note that although ideas take on meaning from the ways that they relate to other ideas, learning must go beyond relating ideas to existing knowledge by creating or constructing rich, integrated knowledge structures (relationships). Vignettes 1 and 2 portray not only the struggle to construct a pedagogically sound understanding of division with remainders but also show how the teachers began to connect ideas of quotients and remainders with different interpretations of division and to consider the role of referent units in division setting. Carpenter and Lehrer also suggested that applications provide an important context for developing meaning. In Vignette 2, no contexts had been used and interpretation of the remainder appeared difficult, but setting the fraction problems in real-world contexts helped clarify many of the issues raised. Third, the seminars provided an atmosphere in which the teachers could articulate their thinking and reflect on their own learning. The outcome of these mental activities for them was that they took ownership of the mathematics they were responsible for teaching.

Fourth, the process by which learners come to articulate their thinking about an idea (another mental activity) requires that learners have time to consider and reconsider the idea in relation to what they already know about the relationships constructed (through the first mental activity discussed). The normative practice of the seminar leaders of staying with a problem until its many ramifications had been explored and of probing through provocative questions and examples did not pass without notice by the teachers. The success of the discussions and the increased under-standing the teachers felt for the mathematics led them to examine their own questioning strategies and, in effect, gave them permission to stay with a problem for longer periods of time in their own classrooms, even returning to it when it seemed profitable to do so. The teachers claimed that they could now manage and even enjoy these long classroom discus-sions for two reasons: (a) They had begun to listen to their students and to focus on what students understood rather than on what they themselves wanted to teach, and (b) they were no longer afraid of the responses they would get when they asked hard questions.

Both seminars began with seemingly simple questions surrounding the task of dividing 37 by 5. The ensuing discussions show, however, that the surrounding issues are actually quite complex. The mathematics of focus for these seminars was the mathematics of the classroom. This focus allowed the teachers to explore, in depth, the mathematics that they taught and to think about the difficulties their own students had with these concepts. We contend that focusing on either students' thinking or on mathematical concepts alone will not be enough to empower teachers to make mean-ingful instructional changes. Teachers need to experience a meaningful interplay between the two, an interplay that is more difficult to attain as the mathematical concepts become more complex and more interrelated.

IN CONCLUSION

A major assumption has permeated all of the work reported in this book: The goal of mathematics education is that all students learn worthy mathe-matics with understanding that increases throughout schooling. This book provides a set of existence proofs that classrooms that promote under-standing of worthy mathematics can be developed. They are exciting places for observers, more exciting for teachers, and perhaps the most exciting for those fortunate students who are learning mathematics in them.

It is clear that teachers were the main developers of the classrooms. However, the authors as researchers participated with the teachers to construct real classrooms that coped with the variety of problems faced in schools. As we worked with teachers to understand and apply the research-based knowledge we had, we learned as much as if not more than the teachers about the teaching–learning process that enables understanding to occur. And we became convinced that the construction of classrooms that promote understanding is dependent on thoughtful, knowledgeable teachers who have participated in professional development programs that enable the development of their own understanding of mathematics, students' thinking about mathematics, and the interdependence of the two. When this happens, classrooms that promote understanding will proliferate.

And the learning will not stop there. The research base that forms the foundation of teaching and learning with understanding will grow so that *all* students will learn with understanding. Sufficient classrooms that promote understanding could produce a generation of citizens who are not satisfied with procedural knowledge but seek instead to understand how mathematics can help them solve the complex issues they will be facing.

REFERENCE

National Council of Teachers of Mathematics. (1989). *Curriculum and evaluation standards for school mathematics.* Reston, VA: Author.

FOR FURTHER READING

Hiebert, J., Carpenter, T. P., Fennema, E., Fuson, K. C., Wearne, D., Murray, H., Olivier, A., & Human, P. (1997). *Making sense: Teaching and learning mathematics with understanding.* Portsmouth, NH: Heinemann.

Author Index

Subject Index

A

algebra, 133-137, 139-140, 142, 146, 149-150
  classroom examples, 137-139, 140-141, 142-145, 146-148, 150-154
articulation, 22-23, 29, 36-37, 170-171
  in classroom examples, 58-59, 99, 106-107, 124-130
assessment, 159-164
  formal, 161-162, 171-177
  growth over time, 162, 177-180
  informal, 161, 165-171
  role of teacher in, 180-183, 189-190
Authentic Statistics Project (ASP), 109-115, 115-116, 124-125, 130-131
  classroom examples, 116-118, 118-119, 119-122, 125-128, 128-130
  journaling in, 123-124

C

Children's Math Worlds, 39
classroom examples
  algebra, 137-139, 140-141, 142-145, 146-148, 150-154
  fractions, 90-97
  measure, 80-85
  nets, 68-70
  number, 46-50
  ratio, 100-104
  statistics, 116-118, 118-119, 128-130, 199-122
  triangles, 72-79
  wayfinding, 64-67
Cognitively Guided Instruction (CGI), 38-39, 50-52, 57-59, 186

Conceptually Guided Instruction (CBI), 52-53, 57-59
construction (of knowledge), 20-21, 26-27, 37-38, 168
  in classroom examples, 57-58, 98, 105-106, 115-118
content, *see* curriculum
curriculum, 5-7, 187-188
  subject matter, 7-15
  task selection, 9-13
  traditional, 4-5, 133-134, 139-140

D

division (instructional example), 192-197
domain mapping, 9-10
dynamic geometry, 15

E

equity, 33-35, 41-42, 189
  normative practices and, 36-38
  in problem contexts, 35-36
  in program evaluation, 38-39
  in program implementation, 39-41
extension and application (of knowledge), 21-22, 26-27, 165-167
  classroom example, 58, 98, 106, 118-122

F

formal assessment, 161-162, 171-177
fractions (classroom examples), 90-97
functions, 146